IN BED WITH THE
TUDORS

Naked boys striding,
With wanton wenches winking.
Now truly, to my thinking
That is a speculation
And a meet meditation.

– 'Colin Clout' by John Skelton

IN BED WITH THE
TUDORS

The sex lives of a dynasty from Elizabeth of York to Elizabeth I

AMY LICENCE

AMBERLEY

This edition first published 2013.

Amberley Publishing
The Hill, Stroud
Gloucestershire, GL5 4EP

www.amberleybooks.com

British Library Cataloguing in Publication Data.
A catalogue record for this book is available from the British Library.

ISBN 978 1 4456 1475 5

Typesetting and Origination by Amberley Publishing.
Printed in Great Britain.

Contents

Introduction

It is not convenient to be a man when women go into labour.
  – Joseph, from the Coventry Mystery Cycle

To push or not to push? Home or away? Boy or girl?

While giving birth isn't quite that simple, the modern, Western mother has an unprecedented degree of choice when it comes to her experience. Even if the delivery does not go quite to plan, and few do, she retains a measure of confidence and ownership of the event beyond the reach of previous generations. Encouraged to write a detailed 'birth-plan' and opt for an active labour, she can deliver her children in the comfort of her own home, or in birth pools at midwife-led units or warm, safe hospital wards, with her partner by her side. Every stage of a pregnancy is monitored, with carefully written notes and recorded tests; she has the option to hear her unborn child's heartbeat, discover its gender and see it wriggle in 3D. Midwives are only at the end of a telephone, day or night; various forms of pain relief are available on request and, following the delivery, she is encouraged to return home, happily breastfeeding, as soon as possible. Following her maternity leave, she may resume her career, confident that her child will be cared for by well-trained and regulated professionals.

In these aspects, motherhood has changed greatly in the last 500 years. Yet birth is unpredictable. Even now, every woman's experience is different. The duration and circumstances surrounding any new arrival can defy even the most careful planning. Babies rarely appear on their due date and tend to take as much or as little time as they need. Birth plans often get adapted or abandoned; perhaps their value lies more in exercising some advanced control over an unknown quantity. For the first-time mother, the reality can form a surprising contrast with the mental image her planning has inspired. She has this in common with mothers of all eras.

For the Tudor mother, there were far fewer guarantees. Birth frequently proved to be a life-threatening occasion, in which the Church and popular superstition played a significant part. Pain relief was illegal, with one midwife being burned for using opium to assist labours in 1591, while the customs of centuries were being challenged by immense religious and cultural change. A woman expecting a child had little choice but to put her trust in the hands of other women and the remedies that had been passed down by word of mouth through the generations, even when these had been outlawed. As her time approached, she might rub her belly with powdered ants' eggs and tie a piece of wild ox skin about her thigh. She might call out to her favourite saints and sprinkle her bed sheets with holy water, while closing the chamber door upon daylight for several weeks together. Problems arising during the birth may be caused by lurking devils or ignored superstitions; she may have rolled up her mat the wrong way, gazed at the moon or tiptoed through the May dew. As her contractions intensified, she would rely on herbs and the panacea of prayer; interventional surgery was only performed in extreme cases and usually resulted in maternal mortality. Assuming she was one of the lucky ones and her baby was born healthy, it would be washed in wine and rubbed with butter so the harmful air could not enter its pores. She would not emerge from her chamber for a month, after which she would process, veiled, to be purified and then perhaps undertake a pilgrimage to leave offerings of eggs and herbs, or money and jewels, at the shrine of the Virgin Mary. Does this make her experience of birth vastly different from that of women in the twenty-first century? In her time-specific context, yes; birth customs and gynaecological understanding varied greatly in the Tudor era from those of today. Yet, in her reasons for performing these strange rites, little has changed. While much of this may seem like lunacy, the Tudor mother also experienced the hopes and fears of women of all time, regardless of whether they are depending on an epidural or the milk of a red cow to get them through. Facing such life-threatening circumstances, it is no surprise that a successful lying-in would become the cause of female celebration.

No one can escape from the times in which they were born; we are all conditioned by a complex interplay of personal, social, cultural, national and spiritual factors that shape our identities in the times in which we live. While basic human emotions do not change, the ways in which people explain them, the ways they make sense of their immediate and wider experiences, do. Tudor women were born into a world which placed little value on their gender and expected them to conform to a limited range of roles. While some women broke the rules, either through courage, failure or accident, the transgressors of strict sexual and social codes were frequently punished and rarely lauded. Acts of rebellion, self-assertion and individuality were not valued as they have been in subsequent, post-Romantic centuries. Tudor mothers' experiences of marriage, sex, pregnancy and birth were an illustrative function of their world, as are those of modern women. Their life expectancy and consequently their expectations of life, were limited by factors of inequality and health that would be rejected or easily treated today. Common infections could kill and frequently did; gynaecological health was poorly understood and prone to misdiagnosis; doctors were almost exclusively male and expensive. Women could only own property or goods if left it in their own right; marriage meant the immediate transfer of all they owned, including their own person, to their husband. Few were literate, although this was progressing among aristocratic circles, yet a vast oral tradition of maternal wisdom was the average Tudor woman's inheritance. The importance of female communities cannot be underestimated and is reflected in the exclusivity of the birth chamber. While a considerable number lived in a household with at least one servant, apprentice or peripatetic support, the daily routine for most was frequently domestic and gruelling. Friends, relations and neighbours were vital to women of all ranks.

The status of motherhood was high during the sixteenth century. It was most women's ultimate ambition, although this was overdetermined by the dominant male culture. This is partly because the general status of women was lower; becoming a mother topped the list of the most desirable options available, reinforced by religious, cultural and legal doctrine. At all stages, issues of female fertility were rife with paradoxes. The act of birth could be a woman's making or undoing. Delivery could be dangerous but also offer protection. A woman's moment of greatest weakness was also her empowerment, extending to all those closeted within the freedom of the lying-in chamber. Outside the church, virginity was seen as a threat by men collectively and individually; even within, only relatively small numbers of conforming female divines were tolerated. This is by no means to suggest that wives and mothers were necessarily venerated or respected, although in some degrees their lives were easier than their spinster sisters. They fitted more easily into social boxes. Even after decades of female monarchy, the court records of litigious late Elizabethans illustrate the dangers incurred by women living outside the prevailing codes. Most decisively, the Church shaped the rites of passage of a woman's life through its ceremonies and rituals. These marked every stage of her being, from birth to death, offering a range of supports and comforts during the childbearing years. Personal faith, set against the upheavals of the English Reformation, played an important but hitherto neglected part in the story of Tudor childbirth.

Then, as now, the union between a woman and a man was a matter of unquantifiable personal inclination. Raw human emotions have changed little over time: sixteenth-century wives hoped for happy lives and successful pregnancies just as much as their modern counterparts, although they could ultimately exercise less control over this. In Tudor times, aristocratic marriages were usually arranged for dynastic benefit, while those of the middle and lower classes were equally dependent upon financial restraints at the opposite end of the scale. Yet, even without the romantic notion of a companionate marriage, all relationships are shaped by the behaviours and mores of those involved. For a Tudor wife, from the queen down to her scullion, their husband's authority was law. There was little escape from mental or physical cruelty; expectations were that a man would not beat his wife too loudly or too late at night. Divorce was equable with treason; separation and sexual or maternal failure would be blamed on the wife, usually as divine judgement for their immorality. Yet women still broke the rules, frequently and publicly. The lower down the social scale, the less they often had to lose. The higher up they found themselves, the more dangerous their illicit and challenging behaviour could prove. For England's queens, their public role sometimes conflicted with their private inclinations but those who acted on their desires could find retribution to be swift and decisive.

The lives of Henry VIII's wives are already well known, as is his daughter Elizabeth's virgin state. I do not intend to repeat much of their histories already in print. In exploring the maternal and marital experiences of Tudor queens from 1485 through to 1603, I have focused on the specific gynaecological factors of their moment in time, from their sexual experience, fertility and conception, through to the pregnancy and circumstances of their deliveries. That is to say, the conditions of Elizabeth of York's first pregnancy differed from her second, third and subsequent ones, just as they did from those of her predecessors. Her delivery of a daughter is not comparable with that of Catherine of Aragon or Anne Boleyn, yet there are certain parallels, such as in the phantom pregnancies of mother and daughter in the 1510s and 1550s. In some cases this has concurred with existing material yet the wider context of their confinements and their implications can often shed new light. The balance of material is uneven also: Elizabeth of York and Catherine of Aragon were the most regularly pregnant queens, while astonishingly the birth of Edward in 1537 marked the last male royal arrival on English soil until that of Charles II in 1630. Of course other women gave birth during this period and I have drawn on their stories also. The experiences of Henry's childless wives as well as that of his daughters can also shed light on issues of marriage, fertility and inheritance. While my focus is predominantly on the Queens of England, I have juxtaposed these with examples of women from other walks of life, in order to better delineate the experience in its universality. The delivery of a queen in her luxurious chamber can hardly be equated with that of an unmarried servant girl giving birth in a church porch. In spite of the obvious advantages though, England's queens were less free and less able to be maternal than their poorer counterparts. The very intimate and private act of birth was, for them, a State occasion; their bodies were dynastic vessels for reproduction

11

above all and their success or failure was international news. For at least two Tudor queens, childbirth undermined and ultimately destroyed their power while it was the cause of premature death for others. Fortunately times have changed. While twenty-first-century women will recognise much in the stories of Tudor mothers, they will also appreciate the advances in medical, social and cultural factors that have so significantly improved their lot.

1

Elizabeth of York & Arthur
1485–1486

The First Tudor Heir

I tell you, masters, without lett
When the red rose so fair of hew
And young Bessy together mett
It was great joy, I say to you.
A bishopp them married with a ringe,
The two bloods of great renown.
Bessy said 'now may we sing,
Wee two bloods are made all one.'[1]

On 18 January 1486, a wedding was celebrated in London's Westminster Abbey. The bride, not yet twenty, was tall and slender and blonde. Her pink-and-white Plantagenet beauty would become legendary, celebrated in art and sculpture, verse and prose: chroniclers of the present and future would define her by her long flowing golden locks and regular features. The eldest child of notoriously good-looking parents, she would set the standard of beauty for an age. As Elizabeth of York approached the altar, feeling all eyes on her, she may have wondered about the man with whom her future lay: a man she scarcely knew; a man who had spent most of his adult life in exile, technically her enemy, who was about to become her husband. She knew it was no love match. If she was lucky, mutual respect might develop into something deeper. Despite her beauty, Elizabeth's attraction lay in her identity, her family line; she was fully aware of her role as a dynastic tool and this was the most important day of her young life so far. Perhaps she was proud, even triumphant that her family's reputation was being reinstated and their continuing position assured. Perhaps she was nervous, as she headed into a life she understood to be full of difficulties and suffering, beside the privilege of status and wealth; after all, she had witnessed her own mother's tumultuous ride as queen and knew that much depended upon the vagaries of fate and the disposition of her husband. He was a king, yet he was still also a man, whose personal, intimate rule over her would be complete.

Waiting at the altar, the groom was ten years her senior, with pale blue watchful eyes and dark hair crisply curled in the European fashion. Together they made an impressive pair: England's newly anointed king and the daughter of the popular Plantagenet Edward IV, uniting the country after decades of bloody civil war. Only six months before, Henry Tudor had been a nobody, waiting for the tide of fortune to turn in his favour on the battlefield, a thorn in the side of the ruling Yorkists. He was a man stained by the mud, sweat and blood of battle: a man who had gambled and taken the ultimate prize. Now he was Henry VII. History would record him as the progenitor of a remarkable dynasty, a wise and prudent figure who ruthlessly squashed his enemies, bringing a long-lasting peace to the nation; yet all this lay in the future. Elizabeth cannot have known the character, abilities or ambitions of her new husband, nor he hers. They were virtually strangers to each other and the directions of their lives were still to be determined. Nevertheless, their significance could not be underestimated: on this marriage rode the fortunes of their people. Around them blazed hundreds of torches, illuminating the rich tapestries and hopeful faces of the nation's decimated nobility. One contemporary foreign commentator wrote of the match that 'everyone considers [it] advantageous for the kingdom' and 'all things appear[ed] disposed towards peace'.[2] Later chronicles termed it a 'long expected and so much desired marriage'[3] and recalled that harmony 'was thought to discende oute of heaven into England' when these 'two bodyes one heyre might succeed'.[4] Yet hindsight can confer many such poetic turns of phrase. At the time, Henry's reign was in its infancy and Bosworth's truce could still prove fragile. There was no guarantee that the turbulent decades were, in fact, over; no neat historical line was drawn in the sand at Bosworth indicating the end of the Wars of the Roses; Henry's end could prove as swift and bloody as his predecessor's. Yet the new king knew better than to rest on his laurels: soon the first rumours of rebellion would threaten his delicate position and they would not be the last. His own family was small; as an only child he had relied on the support of his stepfather Thomas Stanley, Earl of Derby, as well as the country's disaffected magnates, in order to seize power but such alliances could prove infamously fickle. Henry needed to establish his family line. The rapid production of heirs would be seen by the world as a mirror for the health of his claim to the throne: a son would confirm God's approval of the match and the new Tudor monarchy.

No descriptions survive of the actual wedding but accounts of Henry and Elizabeth's separate coronations offer a taste of the day's finery. From the start, the new regime was characterised by an understanding of the importance of impressing the people with numbers, pageantry and ceremony. Appearances were critical. Royalty should look the part, to elevate them above their subjects and display the divine and earthly power at their disposal. The bride would have looked striking, with her rich clothes, jewellery and golden hair. White wedding gowns were not the Tudor norm: Henry IV's daughter Philippa had worn one back in 1406, for her marriage to Eric of Pomerania, but it was as a favoured colour rather than a tradition. Elizabeth's wardrobe of the late 1480s did contain kirtles and mantles in white cloth of gold of damask, trimmed with powdered ermine, but she was equally likely to have chosen velvet, in rich tawny, blue, purple or crimson. Her garments would have been designed well in advance and worked by hundreds of seamstresses, embroiderers, furriers and jewellers. The choice of fabric was as significant as the style of dress: sumptuary laws dating back to the 1360s had confined the wearing of cloth of gold and purple silk to women of royalty, another important distinction of status at a time when upstarts jostled for power. Elizabeth's wedding dress was an opportunity to reinforce her legitimacy through colour, material, design and decoration; it was not just a pretty dress, its sumptuousness sent a barely coded message. No doubt it would have been studded with precious gems, embroidered with thread of gold, set with intricate lace and brocade, delicate filigree tissue and silk ribbons. For the Tudors, simplicity and elegance did not equate – as ornamentation was a measure of status, the more the better: descriptions of their clothing can make the modern reader wonder just how all these elements were combined in one outfit! The bride's golden hair might have hung loose, as befitted a maiden, or else been caught up in a net dotted with pearls and gold tassels. Perhaps the bridegroom put aside his habitual black velvet jacket, furred with the skins of black lambs, in favour of the purple cloth of gold tissue, shirt of crimson sarcanet (soft silk) and satin doublet worn during his coronation. One unused plan for that event imagined him dressed in the Tudor colours of green and white: 'a doblet of gren or white cloth-of-gold satyn, a long goune of purpur velvet, furred with ermys poudred, open at the sides and puffed with ermyn.' Later during the proceedings, he was to wear a shirt laced with silver and gilt, a velvet belt, hose laced with ribbons, a cap of crimson garnished with gold and a surcoat with gold ribbons at the collar and cuffs.[5] Whatever choices they made on the day, the dazzling appearances of Henry and Elizabeth distinguished them as the personifications of divine majesty and temporal wealth.

The royal pair were married by the ageing Archbishop of Canterbury, Thomas Bourchier. It was an appropriate role for a man whose long, distinguished career had placed him at the very heart of the country's shifting fortunes. Himself a grandson of Edward III, he had initially been a reconciling figure in the wars, before siding firmly with the Yorkists and officiating at the coronations of Elizabeth's parents. More recently, he had crowned Richard III, witnessed a dramatic turn in that ruler's fortunes and anointed his conqueror as England's new king. The wedding ring Bourchier blessed that January was a solid gold band, costing 23s 4d and weighing two-thirds of an ounce, making it a 'hefty' size in comparison with its modern equivalents.[6] It had been ordered in advance, arriving at court at New Year, when preparations for the wedding day were well underway. Several English gold rings in the collection of the Victoria and Albert Museum suggest its appearance and possible decorations: one cast gold band made around 1500, as part of a group of popular medieval poesie rings, was engraved 'God joins us together', followed by the dates and initials of the owner's wedding. Another bore the message 'observe wedlock' on the outside, with the warning '*memento mori*' carved within, while a third was decorated with hearts and floral sprigs around its engraving 'think of me'. It had been traditional for brides to wear a blessed ring since the eleventh century, and by the medieval period custom dictated that it would be worn on the ring finger of the left hand. Popular belief stated that so long as it was worn, the ring would protect against unkindness and discord. If he wore one, Henry's ring may have been similar to the museum's dazzling gold band made around 1450, encrusted with a natural diamond crystal and spinel rubies from Afghanistan or one of the signet rings engraved with religious or heraldic symbols. Other signet rings in the collection are decorated with trees, domestic animals such as tethered dogs and even a cradle, perhaps in anticipation of the union bearing fruit; one impressive fifteenth-century example includes a red spinel gem, carved with a crowned head and engraved 'there is none like him'. As he blessed the rings and heard the couple repeat their vows, Bourchier was fulfilling his final duty to the State: he would die that March at Knole, his Kent home, at the grand old age of eighty.

The couple had something of a chequered history. Still in her teens, Elizabeth's archetypal golden beauty, virtue and lineage made her a focus of popular sympathy, yet her position at Henry's side had by no means been guaranteed. She was the product of a secret, controversial marriage and the quirks of civil war had seen her childhood ricochet between luxury and exile. Her father had married her mother for love; a beautiful widow with two sons, who had refused to become his mistress and so, controversially, became his queen. When Elizabeth arrived, in 1466, conceived a year after the marriage, she was the first of three girls born to the couple in rapid succession. Then, their fortunes turned. The princess's life changed dramatically as dissident nobles captured and dethroned her father, forcing her mother into sanctuary and accusing her grandmother of witchcraft. The unstable Henry VI was reinstated as king and the Yorkist family's future was uncertain. Elizabeth was offered as a significant pawn in the 1470 peace negotiations, her hand offered in marriage to the rebel Earl of Warwick's nephew, but the realm's truce was short-lived. With her father forced to flee to the Netherlands, the little girl accompanied her mother to the safety of Westminster Abbey, where the heavily pregnant queen was delivered of a son, the future unfortunate Edward V.

Only after the bloodshed of Barnet and Tewkesbury in 1471, followed by the murder of Henry VI, had the Yorkist line regained control. Elizabeth was offered again as a marital bargain, at the age of eight, in a betrothal to Prince Charles of France and after that, her position remained relatively secure until 1483. By the age of seventeen, she had grown accustomed to the impersonal nature of national and international politics, aware that she and her siblings were instruments of family advancement and that the personal aspect of her life was always secondary to duty. Then, unexpectedly, everything changed. At only forty-one, the charismatic and capable king's health deteriorated, variously reported to be the result of poison, excess, typhoid or pneumonia. His death in April left his children and his wife's unpopular family vulnerable. Edward was succeeded by his twelve-year-old son, the baby who had been born in Westminster Abbey amid the civil turmoil. The Protectorship of the boy was given to his uncle Richard but the little king and his ten-year-old brother were incarcerated in the Tower of London that summer and never seen again. Following the executions and murders of Elizabeth's other remaining male relatives, Richard III proclaimed his niece illegitimate, fuelling reports of the invalidity of her parent's union and her father's paternity. However, as the Yorkist heir, Elizabeth retained the best claim to the throne and in spite of her reduced status, Richard considered strengthening his title by making her his wife.

It was rumours of this intended marriage that crossed the Channel and spurred Henry, Earl of Richmond, into action. His claim to the throne was tenuous in the least, through the female, illegitimate line, dating back to John of Gaunt, while his father had been the child of Henry V's queen, Catherine of Valois, by her Welsh page. Separated from his mother as a small boy and having spent the last fourteen years in exile, a marriage with his guardian's daughter Maud Herbert and a relatively quiet life had, until recently, seemed more likely. Edward IV offered a significant ransom for the capture of 'the imp', as he called Henry, who after his death, moved to Paris and collected a group of rebels about him. One failed attempt at invasion had already sent him back across the Channel with his tail between his legs and in the summer of 1485, he had been the rank outsider at the Battle of Bosworth, mounting a challenge to the established Yorkist king. Yet things had gone Henry's way that August and his shrewdness and political cunning were already marking him out as a monarch to be reckoned with.

The royal pair may have only met for the first time that autumn. Henry's enforced exile for fourteen years meant any previous meeting would have taken place when Elizabeth was a small child. The match had been suggested by the two mothers, Elizabeth Wydeville and Margaret Beaufort, having both suffered at the hands of Richard III. Despite her declared illegitimacy, Henry was determined to have Elizabeth as his wife, swearing an oath to that effect at Rennes Cathedral on Christmas Day 1483 and acquiring papal dispensations early in 1484 and again in January 1486, just two days before the ceremony. As soon as his reign was established, he summoned his bride to London and established her at Coldharbour, his mother's house on the banks of the Thames. An ancient building originally named La Tour, comprising two linked fortified town houses, it had previously lodged Alice Perrers, mistress of Edward III and more recently, Elizabeth's aunt, Margaret of Burgundy. Repairs made during 1484–5 listed a number of chambers or suites of rooms within its tower, as well as a Great Hall on the river side. It was here that Henry and Elizabeth's first meeting probably took place.

Once the marriage ceremony was concluded, the couple processed the short distance from Westminster Abbey to the Palace. Founded by Edward the Confessor, it was close to, but not within, the City of London, then much smaller than today and centred around the modern 'square mile'. Subsequent kings had extended and enlarged the site; in the twelfth century, the Exchequer and Treasury had been incorporated, combining the king's official residence with the administrative heart of the country. For Elizabeth, it was familiar territory; she had been born there and would have spent a large portion of her childhood in the palace. Until it was destroyed in a fire in 1513, Westminster was the most frequently used and expensive of the Crown's establishments, the only one of Henry's many possessions to be referred to as a 'palace'. The huge Norman Great Hall, the largest in Europe, was often considered too large and impractical for use, with the smaller twelfth-century White Hall being more frequently in use and directly adjoining the king's private chambers. However, it is not impossible that for a royal wedding feast, the vast scale of the former, with its 6-foot-thick walls, may have been considered more suitable: a map of 1520 shows it to have been about four times the size of the White Hall. One surviving plan for Henry's succession describes the ceremonious procession from Abbey to Palace, with the king followed by his bishops and chamberlain, cardinals, lords, Knights of the Bath, nobles, heralds, officers, trumpeters and minstrels. Upon arrival, he retired to his chamber, before 'when he had pleasur sumwhat rested hym, in the same estate, with those nobles, he may retourne in to the said hall, ther royally to be serued as is according to the fest'.[7] In January 1486, Henry and Elizabeth would have processed in state, surrounded by their witnesses, the short distance that took them down towards the river and into the palace, where they paused for a brief respite, perhaps a rest and change of clothes, before entering the Hall for their wedding banquet. Traditionally called a 'wedding breakfast', in pre-Reformation days, this would literally break the fast of the bride and groom: sometimes it referred to the Mass itself and the wine and spices served immediately afterwards. In this Catholic era, no one would receive the sacrament unless they had fasted all day, so the 'break-fast' might equally relate to afternoon or evening.

Every aspect of the celebratory meal would have been sumptuous and splendid. The preparation and service of food was a highly skilled process, employing an army of specialist staff in Westminster's kitchens and creating further opportunities to demonstrate the new regime's power and wealth. Strict protocol on seating and service were followed; the tables set with damask cloth, scattered with flowers and herbs and set with the best cutlery and plate, surrounding the ceremonial silver and symbolic *nef*, the usually ship-shaped vessel carrying salt or spices. Such pieces were intended to mark status; seating positions 'above' the *nef* were infinitely preferable to those below and nobles may have brought their own impressive utensils to reinforce their rank against that of their neighbours. One surviving set of Henry VIII's knives were set with a multitude of precious gems, and drinking vessels were of silver and gold. Carvers, sewers (serving drinks), cupbearers, pantlers (bread bearer), ewerers (linen and hand-washing) and waiters were choreographed by the Master of the Hall, prominently placed to announce their arrival. The food was offered first to the king and queen, after having been tasted to ensure it contained no poison; it can hardly have been more than tepid as it approached the end of its long journey but presentation was almost more important than taste. Like their clothing, the feast was an important signal of their status. The dishes chosen for a wedding table would have combined the best ingredients with colourful and inventive display.

Attached to the late fourteenth-century cookbook the *Forme of Cury*, a feast menu of three courses suggests a list of dishes comparable to that of the 1486 wedding banquet. Among the richest delicacies were larded boar's heads, baked teals, pheasants and curlew, partridge and lark, duck and rabbit, almond and chicken pottage in white wine and saffron, pork and cheese tarts with ground figs and pastry points, stuffed chicken and mawmenny, a pottage of shredded pheasant with fried pine nuts and dates, coloured red with sandalwood. All was washed down with spiced wine sweetened with honey, ginger and saffron, thickened with flour and egg yolk. Each course was followed by a subtlety; a fabulous allegorical creation, sculpted out of marchpane (marzipan) or spun sugar and painted or covered in gold leaf. Subtleties might take the forms of crowned birds or beasts, castles, battles, religious scenes or ships, designed to be showcases for a master artisan's skill and the king's purse. In 1487, the first course alone of Elizabeth's coronation feast comprised wild boar, deer, swan, pheasant, capon, crane, pike, broth, heron, kid, lampreys and rabbit, all heavily spiced, in sauces or gelatin, served with raisins and dates. This was followed by various sweet dishes containing baked cream, fruits, nuts, custard tarts and a subtlety. The first Tudor wedding feast must have been equally sumptuous. The existence of aphrodisiacs and association of culinary and sexual appetite had been long established; chestnuts, pistachios and pine nuts were used as folk remedies to excite the libido and the consumption of meat was considered beneficial for potential parents, likewise phallic-shaped foods like asparagus and those on which sexual puns could be made, like the 'apricock', which arrived in the 1520s. All these delicacies were a mere prelude to the intimate event that would follow: after a long afternoon of feasting and entertainment, husband and wife were ready for bed.

The formal bedding of a newly-wed couple was a matter of ritual and significance at all levels of society: even after a church service had been concluded, a marriage was not considered binding and could still be dissolved, until consummation had taken place. For royalty, the implications for sexual failure went beyond mere embarrassment, with consequences that could spark dynastic wars and political or religious change. With many aristocratic marriages arranged in their participants' infancy, consummation was usually delayed until the onset of physical maturity, considered to be the age of twelve in girls, fourteen in boys. Henry's own mother had delivered him at the age of thirteen but even at the time this was considered too young, as the resulting damage to her fertility proved. Although Henry and Elizabeth were well past this age, it is unlikely either had much sexual experience. Despite the upheavals of her childhood, Elizabeth had been closely guarded during her father's reign; recent theories regarding her amorous intentions towards her uncle Richard, based on a dubiously interpreted letter by seventeenth-century historian George Buck, find little tangible evidence to support a physical relationship or romantic understanding between the two. A royal bride's most powerful bargaining point was her virtue; as the mother of future heirs to the throne, her morals must be beyond reproach. It seems almost unthinkable that Elizabeth's virginity was not intact before her first encounter with Henry. However, for a man approaching thirty, living a secular life, whose regal and marital ambitions had only recently been clarified, abstinence was far less likely. Henry's exile in Brittany was concurrent with his sexual maturation and he would have had little reason to resist casual affairs; culturally, it may even have been expected. However, no reports of such behaviour survive. In the absence of evidence either way, it must remain within the realms of possibility.

Henry and Elizabeth most likely spent their wedding night in Westminster's painted chamber, the Palace's most luxurious apartment containing bed, fireplace and chapel, richly decorated as its name suggests. A 1520 map of London shows a complex of smaller buildings overlooking narrow gardens leading to the river, with a view over to Lambeth Palace and the surrounding marshes. Two visiting fourteenth-century monks recorded that on the chamber's walls 'all the warlike stories of the Bible are painted with wonderful skill' and the bed's canopy contained the famous image of the coronation of Edward the Confessor, attributed to Walter of Durham.[8] This was habitually Henry's chamber, dominated by a four-poster bed that required preparation by ten attendants who would search the straw mattress with daggers to discover any potential dangers, before the ritual laying down of sheets, blankets and coverlets. Some truly sumptuous beds had been created long before then; perhaps that of Joane, Lady Bergavenny, in 1434, with its black and red silk hangings embroidered with silver woodbine, represented the sort of luxury Elizabeth and Henry would have enjoyed.[9] As the ceremonial 'bed of state', the couple may have passed the night here, after which the queen would be established in her own chambers and afterwards visited there by her husband. They would not normally share a bed except for the occasions when intercourse took place. Wherever they slept, Henry and Elizabeth's official marital bedding would have been an important stage of the day's proceedings. The protocol followed on the wedding of Prince Arthur and Catherine of Aragon in 1501 gives some indication of the formalised, public nature of this most intimate aspect of their union. At around eight in the evening, the royal bride was escorted to her chamber by her ladies, undressed and put to bed; the groom followed, dressed only in his shirt, accompanied by his gentlemen, musicians, priests and bishops who pronounced their blessings before wine and spices were served. The void or voidee was a mixture of expensive sweet and sharp spices considered to have beneficial medicinal and digestive effects, as well as sweetening the breath, warming the constitution and engendering strength and courage. Almost a secular alternative to the Mass, it was an integral part of the marriage celebrations and would be intended to fortify bride and groom before their night together. Sometimes, before they left, onlookers required the naked legs of a couple to touch, in order to leave satisfied, as in the case of Princess Mary Rose, whose marriage to Louis XII of France in 1514 was considered consummated when her bare leg touched that of his proxy. Even as late as the seventeenth century, royal newly-weds could expect to be observed embracing and kissing before a group of onlookers. This served as a crude reminder that with the privileges of royalty came the loss of personal identity and autonomy over one's body, the functions of which were of valid interest to the State.

To Elizabeth, in 1486, the room must have seemed initially crowded, overflowing with well-wishers, servants, statesmen and clergymen but eventually, the doors were closed and the couple were left alone. Although the doors were closed upon them, they may not have been free from eavesdroppers. Privacy was a rare luxury, even in the richest palace in the land. Medieval and Tudor architecture determined a degree of physical proximity that meant sex must have been a less sequestered business than it is today; rooms and beds were routinely shared, even among the aristocracy. Returning from Moscow in 1568, Thomas Randolph commented that the Muscovites 'eat together' but 'lie apart', unlike the English, implying a good deal of bed sharing. Servants notoriously accompanied their masters to the bedrooms of wives and mistresses and slept outside the door, on truckle beds on the floor or in antechambers, as in the case of Catherine of Aragon and her twelve-year-old serving boy Juan de Gamarra.[10] Henry V is rumoured to have kept his steward and Chamberlain in the same room while he slept with his wife Catherine of Valois;[11] one hopes her experiences with her second husband, Owen Tudor, were more intimate. Sometimes servants played key roles in the exposure of adultery or the dissolution of an unsuccessful match, as well as performing necessary practical duties. Also, it was an occasion when the monarch was at his most vulnerable and defenceless; given the recent decades of conflict and furtive assassination, a king in bed needed watchful eyes around him. On a practical level, thickly curtained beds afforded amorous couples some privacy while allowing unseen access to those bringing in provisions or building up fires. While it is unlikely that many couples were literally overlooked, brides could expect their dirty linen to be aired quite publicly the next morning: in 1469, the bloodstained bed sheets of Isabella of Castile had been proudly displayed as proof of her lost virginity, while, significantly, those of her impotent half-brother's bride were not. Given the importance of royal consummation and the lengths taken to ensure it had taken place, there may have been eyes and ears at the keyholes in Westminster that January.

However, there is a chance the marriage may already have been consummated. Elizabeth's first child arrived the following September, exactly eight months after the wedding, a time frame which has given rise to much subsequent historical speculation. Assuming Prince Arthur was full-term, this would put his conception date around a month before the ceremony, in mid-December 1485. This was not unusual or impossible; after Bosworth, the couple had undergone a formal betrothal before witnesses and Henry had been zealous in the acquisition of Papal dispensations. Parliament had approved the match on 10 December 1485, suggesting consummation around that time, almost exactly nine months before the birth. A verbal promise of marriage or 'handfasting' could be enough to license physical relations, and Henry's eagerness to secure his bride and father an heir may have led them to share a bed before the ceremony. Within the privacy of his mother's Coldharbour house, this may have been easily achieved. Occasionally desire dictated a rapid consummation: Philip of Burgundy could not wait a week for his marriage to the beautiful Juana of Castile in 1496 and although this may not seem compatible with the supposed cold and careful reputation of Henry, it cannot be ruled out. The young, strong, healthy man of 1485, with years of abstinence and exile behind him, was still a long way from the miserly portrait of his widowhood, which has shaped many later interpretations. Perhaps his intention was to elicit divine blessing, as which, a speedy conception would have been received; perhaps his actions were dictated by sensitivity for his young bride for whom the wedding day and night would represent considerable pressure. Both possibilities are not incompatible. Contemporary belief stressed the necessity of female enjoyment in order for conception to take place. The female body, considered to be a poor shadow or imperfectly formed version of its male counterpart, could only conceive if orgasm took place, during which a female 'seed' was emitted to mix with that of the male. The public pressures of the wedding day may not have created a relaxed environment conducive to female conception; perhaps Henry was being strikingly modern in soliciting his virginal wife's pleasure. Alternatively the little prince may have simply arrived early: Bacon certainly believed that Arthur was born 'in the eighth month' although he was 'strong and able'. In either case, the nineteen-year-old bride must have conceived on the occasion of consummation or else very soon after, her ready fertility providing to king and country encouragement that God had blessed the union.

In the summer of 1486, while Henry rode north in response to rumours of unrest, Elizabeth travelled to Winchester to await her confinement. It was a deliberate choice. As England's ancient capital, the reputed site of the fabled Camelot, it was a romantic bastion of popular culture: William Caxton had printed Thomas Malory's *Le Morte d'Arthur* in 1485, a compilation of well-known fables and stories that had been woven into written and oral traditions since at least the twelfth century. Geoffrey of Monmouth's *History of the Kings of Britain*, embellished by Norman writer Wace, as well as Layamon's *Brut*, established the Arthurian idyll as a golden epoch and formed the basis of most subsequent chronicles for centuries. Edward I had hung a huge round table in the castle's great hall; tapestries bore the arms of the mythical Arthur's ancestors and alchemists repeated Merlin's prediction of the union of a red king and white queen, which had been responsible for the creation of the first Arthur. Queen Elizabeth's own father had genealogical trees drawn up to establish his own connection with the great British hero and Henry's banner at Bosworth had borne the red dragon, Arthur's heraldic device, against a white and green background. In 1486, Winchester was carefully selected as a symbolic location to realign the new dynasty with its Welsh heritage and recreate a context for the iconography of the new regime. Henry wanted to endow his firstborn son, the hope of his fledgling dynasty, with the strength and riches of national myth. Later chroniclers stated that the child was named to 'honour the British race', describing the people 'rejoicing' in reaction to the child's name, which made foreign princes 'tremble and quake' at the choice, which was to them 'terrible and formidable'.[12]

Some doubt has arisen among modern biographers as to the exact location of Arthur's birth, with accounts divided between Winchester Castle and the Prior's lodgings at the nearby Abbey. Built as part of William the Conqueror's system of strongholds across Britain, the castle was expanded in the thirteenth century into a huge flinty edifice flanking two courtyards, of which only the Great Hall remains today. It would seem a logical place for Elizabeth's lying-in but if she had any intentions of delivering her child there, her mind may have been changed by the castle's deteriorating condition. By 1486, it was considered old and draughty: its discomforts belonged in the era of civil warfare, rather than in the urbane, sophisticated, new European court Henry was forging. The royal party probably settled instead at the Prior's House, now renamed the Deanery, at St Swithin's Priory. Strong evidence for this comes from John Stowe's Chronicle, published in 1565, which describes the baby's christening procession: the 'hole chapel met with my lord prynce in the qwens great chamber', from where the child was carried into the church and up to the 'hyghe aultar to St Swithin's shrine', which would have been a prohibitive journey for a newborn, had he arrived in the castle.[13] It is far more likely that they remained in residence there while the Prior's House was made ready. This three-storey stone building, with its arched entrance portico, was used to house distinguished guests separately from the pilgrims lodged in the usual guest house.

Winchester lay on one of the major highways of medieval England, a centre for pilgrimage housing around thirty Benedictine monks in 1500, who kept open house for visitors under the new Prior Thomas Silkested. There, Elizabeth's ladies would have gone about the business of readying a chamber for her lying-in, against a backdrop of monastic business, punctuated by bells and the sound of voices raised in prayer and chant. Far from being austere and chilly, the Priory would have been able to extend their guests a warm welcome. As one of the richest monasteries in the land, St Swithin's would have had no problem catering for their royal guests: Cathedral rolls show the variety of the monks' diet, which, in 1492, included meals of venison, beef, mutton, calves' feet, eggs, dishes of marrow and bread; on fast days they had salt fish, rice, figs and raisins. The rolls are full of details for the provision of 'good' beer, cheese, salt, wine, butter and candles; the gardener was to supply apples in season every two days and flowers for Church festivals. A further entry records the duties of the cellarer to include the upkeep of various pets acquired by the occupants. The curtarian was responsible for providing for visiting bishops and royalty while the porter was to make up the fire in snowy weather.[14] While there was little understanding of the nutritional needs of pregnancy, kings were particularly well placed to satisfy any specific cravings their wives developed: in the fifteenth century, oranges were often given to expectant mothers as a treat, a practice that was so well known that John Paston the younger felt obliged to apologise when requesting some for a woman who was not pregnant. If the Tudor heir was born at the Priory, he and his mother would have been well catered for.

In addition to the provisions offered by the monks of St Swithin's, the king's mother had been anticipating the practicalities of Elizabeth's delivery. As soon as the child had quickened, around Easter of that year, Margaret Beaufort set work on her Ordinances, outlining the protocol and detail of the lying-in chamber. She was impressively thorough, from the number and colour of cushions in the room to the ranks and duties of those women in assistance. Under her formidable direction, the Prior's apartments would have been transformed into a little cell of luxury, furnished to the highest quality with all the necessaries of birth. First, the chamber was hung with heavy Arras tapestries, covering the walls, ceiling and windows. Draughts and fresh air were not considered healthy for the newborn, nor were bright lights, and the efforts of childbirth were reputed to strain a mother's eyesight. Additionally, the secure darkness would protect against the attacks of evil spirits who might threaten mother and child as their lives hung in the balance before the administration of baptismal and churching rites. The tapestries chosen were carefully scrutinised for their subject matter. Provoking or disturbing scenes, including hunts and wild or mythological beasts, were rejected for fear of their startling effects, in favour of scenes of love and romance. A mother looking upon violent scenes might transmit some of her emotional response to her unborn child, irrevocably shaping its features or character. One window alone was left uncovered, so that a woman may have light and look outside if she desired. Next, a huge temporary pallet bed was prepared, where Elizabeth would labour. A giant, 8 feet by 10, it lay in the middle of the room, stuffed with wool and down, covered with crimson satin. The colour was regal but it may also have minimised the inevitable blood stains. Beside it were set two cradles. The first was 5 feet long and beautifully adorned for ceremonial use, embellished with the royal arms and buckles of silver. A smaller cradle of wood, hung with pommels of silver and gilt, with ermine-lined bedding, was reserved for sleep.

When Elizabeth finally entered her lying-in chamber, the room radiated heat and light. Despite the September mildness, candles illuminated the gloom, embroidered hangings kept out the cold, and piles of thick blankets sat waiting, along with fresh chests of linen and double petticoats. The list of material provisions was exhaustive and precise: exact quantities and types were listed, including yards of fine linen from Rheims and Rennes, imported Tartarin silk, fine lawn and wool, fustian pillows stuffed with down, furred panels, head sheets, a canopy of satin, posts to support the canopy, cushions and mantles all in a red and gold colour scheme. Cupboards were stocked with wine, food and spices to revive her during her ordeal, as well as the glittering plate that marked the status of mother and child. Daily supplies would be brought to the chamber door, but Elizabeth would not expect to emerge again for several weeks, probably more. It was a physical and symbolic isolation, where darkness and comfort made the environment for the child's arrival as womb-like and safe as possible. By inference, the richness of the surroundings mirrored the richness and special 'otherness' of the Queen's body: women across the country would prepare their chambers, or not, according to their differing social degrees. At the bottom of the scale, the poor, servants and beggar women would give birth in barns, church porches, at roadsides and in the houses of strangers. They could expect public intervention and debate concerning their bodies, their character, morals and relationships; they might be physically moved across parish boundaries to avoid expense or examined by midwives and civil officers to determine paternity and intention. Childbirth was everyone's business.

No Tudor birth was of greater significance than that of a future heir to the throne. With the dynasty in its infancy, the new regime's survival could turn on Elizabeth's performance in the lying-in chamber: she was literally delivering the future. The outcome of her pregnancy had a significance the Tudors believed was foretold in the stars. In 1490, Henry VII was presented with the translation of a work by thirteenth-century Italian astrologer Guido Bonatti, outlining the influence of the heavenly bodies at the exact moment of a child's birth. The manuscript contains an illustration of a bare-breasted, newly delivered mother, lying in a bed hung with blue drapes and red patterned covers; the ground is depicted like grass and the stars overhead give a sense of the universality of the childbirth experience. The mother is placed at the centre of the world; a metaphor that held more than a degree of reality for England's new queen. No doubt Henry was waiting nearby, briefly relegated to second place. In lodgings around the city, courtiers, doctors, astrologers, astronomers, ambassadors, priests and prophets nervously anticipated the all-important news. A successful delivery for mother and child was paramount; after that, all depended upon the infant's health and strength. Arthur's first few days would be crucial and his survival governed as much by luck as the mixture of superstition and custom that governed medicine at the time. The Tudors did not yet understand the circulation of the blood, let alone foetal development. Medical diagnosis was made in terms of the four humours, with female illnesses addressed by 'balancing' or purging the body: Elizabeth may even have been bled before giving birth, to remove 'bad influences', weakening her considerably at a time when she most needed her strength. Even her women, with all their wisdom and good intentions, perpetuated the myths and ignorance that could contribute to high infant and maternal mortality. At the very least, no one understood the need to wash their hands.

As a symbolic 'womb' for the birth of the dynasty, Elizabeth's little Winchester nucleus was entirely female in character. Closing the doors would exclude all men until after the child's arrival, even the king and male doctors. She would be attended entirely by her 'good sisters' or 'gossips', who took over the usual daily ceremonies of service as well as specific maternity duties. Among the women gathered to perform this office in September 1486 were the two grandmothers, Margaret Beaufort and Elizabeth Wydeville, who had arranged the match, as well as Elizabeth's sisters Anne and Cecily, whose youth would have limited their involvement. Seclusion also preserved the dignity and majesty of the queen in a society that venerated motherhood as the defining factor of a woman's life; Elizabeth was labouring to secure the future of the realm while trying to maintain the decorum becoming to her status. Submission, regality and purity were the watchwords for a queen, an image etched in medieval culture by the pens, laws and expectations of men. The symbolic closing of the chamber doors was a deference to her femininity and status: no one would raise an eyebrow there if she were to succumb to the usual human passions during labour. It would not be fitting for the court to hear her screams of agony or witness her dishevelment: these were for the eyes of her women only. Now all Elizabeth need do was rest and wait.

As the queen's labour began, her gossips would have gathered round to follow certain folkloric rituals. It was customary for mothers to remove all fastenings: rings, buckles, bracelets and laces were thought to mimic a state of strangulation in the body which could be transmitted to the child. Likewise, no one in the chamber would cross their legs, arms or fingers. The labouring woman's abdomen might be rubbed with creams made from a mixture of brandy, distilled marjoram and saffron to aid contractions. Tied around her belly, magic girdles and pieces of paper inscribed with 'charms' offered protection, and belts hung with cowrie shells were thought to bring good luck through their resemblance to, and therefore sympathy with, the vulva. In her hand, a mother might clasp an 'eagle stone' or *aetites*, a larger stone which contained a smaller stone within its hollow centre, rattling when shaken: according to medieval theories, nature left 'signatures' to imply use, by which these were a natural echo of her condition and could alleviate pain and prevent miscarriage. Eagle stones were worn on the arm during pregnancy and transferred to the abdomen when labour began; a variant was St Hildegard of Bingen's twelfth-century remedy of holding a jasper stone during birth. Agnus Dei were also popular religious tokens, for those who could get hold of them; they were wax discs stamped with the image of a lamb and flag, blessed by the Pope and supposedly offering protection from sudden death and the malice of demons. In some places, the skin of a wild ox was tied about a woman's thigh and snakeskin or hartskin belts were worn, the placebo effects of which can only be imagined, in the absence of modern forms of pain relief. Herbs and flowers were used to help lessen the intensity of contractions, including the oils of lilies, almonds and roses, cyclamen, columbine, aquilegia, wild thyme and musk: some must have really helped, such as meadowsweet, which would later be synthesised and called aspirin. Other potions included the more bizarre ants' eggs, powdered eel liver, virgin's hair, ale and red cow's milk. Although it is unlikely Elizabeth's labour was aided by all of these, she would have had access to the most expensive and rare ingredients. Enemas were also given to aid dilation and sometimes 'subfumigation' was used, by channelling herbal vapours into the wombs; women were also given special powders to make them sneeze, as this was thought to help expel the child. Even though some of these sound extreme to the modern reader and may even have given the Tudor woman cause to smile, childbirth could prove a deadly and dangerous event: for a nation heavily steeped in superstition, there was some correlation between these practices and the odds of survival.

Religious comforts were also available to a Catholic queen. From pre-conception devotions and pilgrimages, through all stages of pregnancy and parturition, there were appropriate prayers and saints to petition for intercession. The Church clearly distinguished between the times when a woman was expected to attend church and when to stay away; from maternal repentance as the child quickened, to Mass before labour, baptism by the godparents and, finally, churching. Elizabeth would have taken Communion before entering her chamber, its blessing extending to her unborn child in the eventuality of tragedy. Birth was the most significant and dangerous of all rites of passage, when a woman was susceptible to malign influences as she languished in spiritual limbo, so direct access to the fortifications of faith was essential. Reading the Gospels during the delivery was one well-practised method of ensuring all went smoothly; prayer books and books of hours would have also been used to pass the hours of waiting. A crowded reliquary in the birth chamber would display a range of artefacts such as holy bones and girdles, phials of blood, tears or milk and shards of the true cross, through which Elizabeth might commune with those saints associated with childbirth. During her ordeal, she may well have held the famous Westminster girdle, supposedly made and used by the Virgin Mary,[15] which the next generation of Tudor mothers would favour. Pre-Reformation Catholics believed in the real, comforting presence of saints during labour as well as the power of prayer. Mary, whose cult following in medieval England was profound and ubiquitous, could stand above the complexities of womanly status and identity as a parallel, or objective correlative, of shared experience: through her, all labouring mothers could be brought closer to God in time of danger.

In the long dark hours of labour, Catholicism, pseudo-religious practice and superstition were easily blurred. As Elizabeth hovered between life and death, devoid of any pain relief and uncertain how long her travail would last, she would have sought whatever comforts her ladies could offer. The earliest surviving manuals relating to pregnancy and childbirth were recipe (receipt) books, including the Anglo-Saxon *Lacnunga* or 'Remedies', and the ninth-century Bald's *Leechbook*, containing a number of magic charms or incantations to be invoked against disease, misfortune and attacks by demons, often through the ritualistic repetition of words or actions in patterns of three or nine. One of the charms relates to 'a delayed birth', intended to induce overdue labour, while another assists in the onset of sudden stabbing pains, supposedly caused by the machinations of 'mighty women'. Pagan ritual and Christian rites were mingled in many early medical texts, translating into a variety of practices in the Tudor delivery chamber. The Catholic Church had its own prayers to combat these customs, including one included in a 1425 prayer book, containing an English rubric and Latin prayer composed by St Peter for labouring women. Interestingly though, the Latin was written with feminine endings, indicating that it was intended to be read by a woman, which, in practical terms, could only have been accessed by a tiny literate minority. The benefit of charms and prayers alike lay in their formulaic, repetitive patterns, which could help concentrate the mind and the exercise of some small form of control over a bewildering and helpless experience. The word 'abracadabra', now associated more with stage magic, was a popular part of a repetitive chanting formula. It is not difficult to picture commoners and queens alike incanting verses through gritted teeth as their contractions take hold. One tenth-century charm, from the South of France, written in Occitan, would have been recited by midwives to establish a rhythm in accordance with a woman's contractions and to establish a pattern of regular breathing. Similar English secular and religious lyrics would have been used in many birth chambers around the country, from those of queens downwards. Such traditional rhymes must have been part of an experienced midwife's repertoire:

> A swollen woman
> sat in a swollen road;
> a swollen child
> she held in her lap;
> swollen hands
> and swollen feet,
> swollen flesh
> that will take this blow,
> swollen wood
> and swollen iron
> that will give out this blow.
> The pain goes out
> from bone to flesh,
> from flesh to skin
> from skin to hair
> from hair to grass
> let Mother Earth receive the pain.[16]

No record is made of the midwives in attendance on Elizabeth, although at least one would undoubtedly have been present. They were indispensable as the only females allowed to physically intervene during the process and touch the queen's reproductive organs. It is possible that Elizabeth was attended by her mother's favourite midwife, Marjory Cobbe, who had attended Elizabeth

Wydeville's final confinement only six years before. During the months of her pregnancy, the queen would have been attended by doctors and physicians, such as Walter Lemster, to whom Henry granted £40 a year for life that February. The royal nursery would be presided over by Elizabeth Denton, who, in 1509, received the gift of Coldharbour House for life as a reward for her services. As unlicensed practitioners, midwives would have been chosen according to their moral standing, appearance, experience and reputation; quite probably they already had associations with the family and may have delivered siblings, cousins or friends. The varying reputations of 'wise women' could be determined by factors beyond their control, like maternal health and infant mortality but they were usually older women, past their childbearing years, who had been in attendance at many lyings-in. There was little prenatal care in the modern sense but once they arrived in the birth chamber, they assumed absolute control. As Elizabeth's labour pains intensified, she may have lain on her pallet bed, walked about the room or knelt. A midwife may even have brought or commissioned her own 'groaning chair', allowing her to attend the delivery while another helped the queen brace herself against the pain and pressed down on the top of her womb. Some midwives used rope tourniquets to aid expulsion while others employed massage, warm towels and applied herbal remedies to speed up uterine contractions. A midwife's job was also to remain calm and be cheery and encouraging, in which she would lead the other women in setting the tone of the chamber.

Unsurprisingly, the male-authored accounts do not describe whether Elizabeth's labour was long or difficult; once the heir had safely arrived, such details may have not been considered important. However, it would have made all the difference for the queen. As a first birth, it was an unknown quantity and probably a daunting experience for the young woman, despite the collective wisdom of her gossips. She may well have observed the births of her younger siblings, especially in attendance on her mother through the difficult months of sanctuary, yet observing and participating differ vastly. Considering her youth and relatively quick recovery, she most likely experienced a relatively straightforward delivery once the baby began to crown during the night of 19/20 September.

Finally, in the early hours of the morning, a healthy child arrived. The prophets were proved right: it was a boy. Following a quick examination, the midwife declared him perfect. The little prince's umbilical cord would have been cut and anointed with powdered frankincense or aloe, before he was washed in a mixture of wine, herbs or milk and rubbed with butter or the oil of almonds, roses or nuts to close his pores, so that the air would not harm them. Then he was tightly swaddled, placed in the cradle and given a spoonful of wine and sugar. The eleventh-century Italian female physician Trotula of Salerno recommended a newborn's tongue to be washed with hot water to ensure clear speech or else rubbed with honey to stimulate a healthy appetite. While her baby slept, Elizabeth delivered the placenta. This was achieved through a 'mini-labour' during which her womb was again massaged until the afterbirth arrived. The women would have checked it carefully before disposal, as any remaining fragments could lead to fatal haemorrhaging later. Finally, Elizabeth was briefly washed down with fine linen cloth or clean sponge and allowed to rest. She was not allowed to sleep for a couple of hours after delivery, so her women would have kept her diverted and cheered with their chatter. Her aching body would have been soothed with the best ointments and cures, using well-known herbal and floral remedies to staunch the flow of blood and ease blood-flow and pains; the days following were crucial for her health and recovery. Natural light was not supposed to penetrate the room for at least three days, as birth was considered to strain the eyesight and a typical lying-in period might last a month or more. Eventually, she would be washed and dressed, perhaps transferred to a state bed and formally 'sat up' to receive visitors. Access to the queen's body still followed strict protocol; no one lower than the rank of duchess or countess was permitted to help her rise from her bed or receive her at her chamber door when she would finally emerge.

It seemed that her ordeal was over. However, in the days following the birth, Elizabeth suffered from an ague or fever, so the court remained at Winchester for her recovery and churching. Perhaps from her chamber she was aware of the town's celebrations of bells ringing in all the churches, Masses, bonfires, revelry and the dispatch of messengers across the country bearing the good news.

Elizabeth's own gratitude for her safe delivery would prompt her to found a chapel in Winchester Cathedral, where Arthur was christened, in her absence, a few days after his birth. It was a grand occasion, again dictated by Margaret Beaufort's Ordinances, with the walls draped in rich arras and floors spread with carpets. The silver gilt font from Canterbury Cathedral was borrowed, lined with soft Rennes linen, to protect the child at the moment of baptism, while coals scented with perfume burned and wooden barriers kept back the throng of onlookers. The main roles in the ceremony were taken by Elizabeth's women; her sister Cecily carried Arthur, wrapped in a mantle of crimson cloth of gold furred with ermine. After his baptism, with salt, oil and water, the child was passed to his godmother, Elizabeth's mother, who presented him as an offering at the altar, before he was richly endowed with gifts and the party celebrated with wine and spices. Then, the baby was returned to his mother's chamber to be blessed by his parents.

Early in October, Elizabeth had recovered sufficiently to process to the church in the wake of a large burning taper for her churching ceremony: following this, she was restored to her role of queen and wife, appearing seated ceremonially below the Cloth of Estate. By the end of the month, the court had removed to Greenwich and after the New Year, plans were drawn up for the establishment of Arthur's household at Farnham in Surrey. His household was overseen by a Lady Governess of the nursery, assisted by a dry nurse, wet nurse and various yeomen, grooms and others who saw to the practical running of the house: 1,000 marks were allocated for its expenses. From that point, Elizabeth's contact with her young son would be intermittent – queens could not be incapacitated by breastfeeding or maternity: other women would feed and clothe him, comfort him at night, play with him and nurse him through illness, until he was of an age for his father to start preparing him for his important future. As the dynasty's bodily vessel, Elizabeth's first pregnancy had been a success. Now she had to begin the process again.

2

Elizabeth of York
& the Future Henry VIII
1487–1503

The Family Expands

For first his sweet and lovely Queen
A Joy above the rest
Brought him both Sons and Daughters fair
To make his Kingdom blest.
The Royal Blood that was at Ebb
So increas'd by his Queen,
That England's heir unto this Day
Do flourish fair and green.[1]

Fourteen months after the birth of her son, Elizabeth was crowned as England's queen. It was perhaps a more glorious moment for her than her marriage had been, and just as spectacular. This time however, there was no one else to share the limelight; this above all, was her day. In a sense, it was also her reward for the rapid production of a healthy male heir; not all Tudor consorts were crowned and their status lay firmly in the hands of their royal husbands on whose orders the ceremony took place. It was a November day in 1487 when the royal convoy of barges sailed up the Thames from Greenwich, streaming with colourful silk banners; on one, a huge red Welsh dragon spouted flames of fire into the water as people gathered on the banks to watch. On another sat Elizabeth and her ladies, dressed in all their jewels, furs and finery. It must have been an impressive sight, even for a city that was used to pageantry. Music would have wafted downstream on the autumnal air and into London homes and streets, heralding their soon-to-be queen's approach. She passed that night in state at the

Tower, then set out the following day to travel the short distance to Westminster Abbey, reclining on downy cushions in a litter of cloth of gold of damask, carried by Knights of the Bath. On her head was a circlet of gold set with precious stones – which would later be exchanged for the crown – and her kirtle and mantle of purple velvet were fronted with lace. The previous day's warnings had been heeded; the packed streets, thronging with Londoners in all their finery, were decorated with rich cloths and banners that hung from the houses along her route. As she passed along the special 'ray cloth' of striped wool, leading from her litter into the abbey, the crowd surged up behind to seize pieces of this carpet, which was thought to have magical properties. Their enthusiasm was so great that riots broke out but the great doors were quickly closed upon the rabble outside, allowing the important business of State to proceed. According to tradition, Elizabeth was anointed twice, once on the chest and once on the head before receiving a ring for the fourth finger of her right hand, a gold crown, sceptre and rod of gold. Onlookers were then cleared from Westminster Hall to make way for the guests: Lords, bishops and abbots; barons, knights and nobles, beside London's mayor, alderman, merchants and distinguished citizens, were seated either side of the dais on which Elizabeth would be served her celebratory banquet. No doubt the food was as sumptuous and plentiful as it had been at her wedding. After the feasting, the Garter King of Arms led the heralds and officers in proclaiming her queen and offering her their sincere gratitude and thanks. If any doubts had lingered about Elizabeth's validity as queen, the birth of her son and her splendid coronation reaffirmed the strength of the Tudor dynasty and the royal marriage. As a young, fertile woman, regularly sharing her husband's bed, expectations for an imminent second pregnancy would have been high.

Yet two and a half years would pass before Elizabeth would conceive again. Given the royal couple's ages and regular periods spent together, as well as the rapidity of Arthur's conception, this represents a significant interval. Easily long enough to suggest fertility issues in a modern couple, it may well have given the royal pair and their physicians cause for concern. Yet such situations were not uncommon among European royalty. Isabella of Castile's seven-year interval between her first and second child puzzled the Spanish court and all her physicians, yet she then went on to deliver a son and three more daughters. Catherine de Medici would be married to Henri II of France for a decade before conceiving the first of eleven offspring. Even after the arrival of their healthy son Arthur, the Tudor imperative for heirs was still strong, as a royal family's future strength lay partly in its size. It must be assumed, therefore, that Henry and Elizabeth were still actively trying to conceive during these years. Political threats and strains would have proved an unwelcome distraction, though, which could affect fertility and performance. 1487 had brought difficult challenges, with Yorkist claimant Lambert Simnel threatening to invade and usurp the throne. His coronation as Edward VI in Dublin that May had forced Henry again into battle, defeating his enemies at Stoke. It had been a powerful reminder that one little boy in his nursery at Farnham was not sufficient guarantee of the Tudor lineage, nor protection against the menace of rival claimants. The hereditary succession was as precarious as his young life, prey to all the dangers of infant mortality that were no respecters of rank. In spite of – or perhaps because of – their early trials, the royal family were close. Whenever possible during this troubling summer, Henry and Elizabeth had remained together. As he prepared for battle, the king had summoned his 'dearest wife and dearest mother' to be with him at Kenilworth; among his last acts before leaving to fight were to pay the wages of Arthur's household and to equip his wife's attendants. Although some chroniclers suggested that Henry was cool towards his wife because of her Yorkist origins, there is no evidence to suggest this. They were together again in London for her coronation and celebrated that Christmas at Greenwich. The following year they were at Windsor for Easter, passed the summer at Woodstock, then on to Westminster in the autumn, providing them with plenty of opportunities to conceive a second child. Yet nothing happened.

There is little doubt that if Henry and Elizabeth were under the same roof, they would have at some point, shared a bed. Although they would often have been lodged in different chambers, depending on their residence, a king would customarily visit his wife, sometimes remaining with her all night, sometimes returning to his own bed to sleep. Elizabeth's overall conception pattern shows that their physical relationship was fairly consistent. Tudor wives of all classes were under considerable pressure to acquiesce to their husband's demands for sexual relations, or the 'debt' of marriage: Chaucer's parson's saintly wife 'has the merit of chastity who yields the debt of the body to her husband, yes, though it be contrary to her liking and the desire of her heart'. A wife's inclinations were not considered important. The feigned 'headache' had not yet emerged as a clichéd deterrent and levels of rape, undue force or at least reluctance among wives must have been high. If this was the case, it follows that married women had inconsistent control over their conceptions. Primitive forms of birth control and withdrawal methods were frowned upon at the very least, following the Catholic line that the prevention of pregnancy was sinful. The only arguments for marital abstinence were put forward by some enlightened religious and medical professionals on grounds of health. As early as the twelfth century, clerical voices had been raised in dissent against the dangers of unchecked fertility for women. Peter Cantor, Chanter at Notre Dame, put the case of a woman who had sustained such terrible injuries during repeated childbearing that her doctor advised against another pregnancy, which would certainly endanger her life. The debate focused on where her duty lay, whether she must submit to her insistent husband or refuse him the marital debt and save herself. It is possible that Henry and Elizabeth exercised some limited methods of control over the pace of their reproduction in the wake of Arthur's birth, but this seems unlikely. Although various later sources have implied Elizabeth's health may have been delicate, the successful delivery of one child and her subsequent recovery suggest no impediment to enjoying a full sexual relationship with her husband. As a queen and a woman, it was her marital and national duty to do so. On both religious and cultural levels, Elizabeth would have been considered receptive to her husband's advances from the moment of her churching, in late October 1486, onwards. For the next two and a half years, she would have been hoping to conceive.

Perhaps she succeeded. While the arrival dates of most of Henry and Elizabeth's children are carefully recorded, some controversy surrounds the arrival of a short-lived prince named Edward, with at least one historian[2] suggesting his birth must have occurred towards the beginning of the marriage, in 1487 or 1488, rather than its usual placing, somewhere between 1499 and 1502. Given the intervals of her subsequent conceptions, of ten months after her second child Margaret and then three months after Henry, her third, Elizabeth's fertility appears to have been strong. The lengthening gaps between the births of her subsequent children are consistent with patterns of dwindling conceptions experienced by aristocratic and noble women married comparatively young and producing larger families. Typically, a rapid number of children were born in the years following marriage, before fertility tailed off and accelerated the arrival of the menopause in the mid-thirties. This pattern is illustrated by the conception rates of Jane Dudley, Duchess of Northumberland, who produced her first child at the age of seventeen and her tenth – and final – when she was thirty-six, and Elizabeth de la Pole, Duchess of Suffolk, who bore twelve children between her nineteenth and thirty-fourth years. Prolonged phases of infertility early in marriages did occur and Elizabeth's failure to conceive may have been caused by the strains of political upheaval, illness or other, now irretrievable, health factors in both partners. It is not impossible that during this time she did conceive and miscarried, or delivered a short-lived heir. On balance, though, the expected arrival of a second heir during these years would have incited more comment, even in the event of a failed pregnancy, indicating a later birthdate for Edward. If this is so, the question of Elizabeth's fertility and the royal marriage remains uncertain. Perhaps after five centuries, these elusive answers may simply be those of timing, health and opportunity.

Throughout these early years, Elizabeth must have been alert to any potential indications of conception. Without modern testing methods, Tudor women could only rely on some rather unscientific physical symptoms. Contemporary accounts listed increased appetite, full breasts, tongue colour, dull eyes, swollen veins, vomiting, strange desires and the end of the menstrual cycle among the early signs. Yet these could still be open to misinterpretation, or caused by other illnesses, especially in an age of poor nutrition and inexplicable illness. A mother still may not have been certain she was expecting until she felt a stretching or quickening within her swelling belly, between four and five months in. During the 1480s, there were few written records for mothers to turn to, even if they had been able to read. *Hali Meidenhad*, a thirteenth-century alliterative prose homily based on the Psalms, graphically warned young girls against the unappealing physical changes pregnancy could bring: the face would grow thinner and shadowed, dizziness would make the head ache cruelly, the womb bulged like a water-skin, stitches developed in the side, discomfort in the bowels, painful backache, heaviness in the limbs and the dragging weight of the breasts. Once a woman was known to be pregnant, there was no lack of dietary advice for her to follow to ensure the birth of a healthy child. Bald's tenth-century *Leechbook*, full of ancient remedies, charms and recipes, had been much recycled and reused by the Tudor era. It recommended pregnant women should not eat anything salty or sweet, nor eat pork or fatty foods or drink beer, nor the flesh of any other 'animal that could beget', or else the child would be humpbacked. Fruit and vegetables were best avoided but wine and ale were far safer to drink than milk or water. Only a very bland diet appears acceptable, although expectant mothers were at least exempt from the fasts that punctuated the Catholic year.

Tudor medicine lacked any detailed or thorough understanding of the workings of the female body or reliable diagnostic tools. Misdiagnosis must have been common. It could lead to the prescription of cures for similar conditions before pregnancy was suspected. A woman experiencing nausea or giddiness in her first trimester might be prescribed powders made from the stones found in a swallow's belly, or the liver of a kite. She might be encouraged to drink 'fine leaved grass' for thirty-three days or the juice of cowslip for nine, or a month's worth of rennet from a hare, or to eat the boiled heart of a stork. Another experiencing swelling in her body or legs might be advised to take elderberries boiled in ale with sparrow's grease; another with stomach pains could be prescribed to make up a little bag filled with wormwood, egremony, spearmint, vinegar, rosewater and a dead chaffinch and lay it on her stomach. The effects of these can only be imagined. Pregnant women needed to be careful from whom they sought advice. Complaints were made against physicians and midwives who prescribed potions and powders that did expectant mothers more harm than good, or caused death. London midwife Cecilia Pople's fumigations in 1598 ended in the premature death of Dorothy Gatersby of Aldersgate and, although she promised to cease practice, the following year she gave pills and purgatives to a Mrs Kennyck in exchange for the payment of a feather-bed cover.[3] Elizabeth could at least rely on the advice of the best physicians in the land, even if their knowledge was imperfect.

Henry and Elizabeth spent Christmas 1488 at Sheen, their fourteenth-century manor house in Richmond. Surrounded by friends and family, the old moated royal lodgings allowed them some privacy from the rest of the court and there must have been much feasting and pageantry. Elizabeth loved music and 'disguisings', the allegorical interludes peopled by saints and dragons, virtues and vices, set to the accompaniment of fiddles and drums. When it came to providing for his family's entertainment, the king spent regularly. Payments recorded by his treasurer John Heron for the court's indoor entertainments a few years later included players, fools, minstrels, musicians, tumblers, card and dice games. By the following Easter, they were resident at Hertford, at which time Elizabeth may have begun to suspect that she was pregnant. At once, she would have made some small changes to her daily routine. A woman was believed to nourish her child with her blood and shape it with her imagination, so once her body had started to display the physical symptoms, all manner of rituals, superstitions and precautions were considered necessary for the growth and delivery of a healthy foetus. To the medieval mind, evil influences were ever-present, waiting to pounce on those who forgot themselves: ritual and observation were essential precautions for personal protection and salvation. The performance of certain actions could be mirrored in 'sympathy' by the unborn child so activities that involved winding or grinding could cause the child to strangulate in the womb and mats must be rolled a certain way to prevent twisting injuries. The noise of guns and bells was to be avoided, as were exuberant dogs who might jump up and cause deformity; the sight of hares might engender a hare lip, a snake would give the baby green eyes and woe betide those who tiptoed through the May dew, as they would certainly miscarry. A mother looking at the moon would produce a lunatic or sleepwalker; ill or deformed people could imprint their maladies; certain places must be avoided for danger and rituals followed to prevent birthmarks. Such marks were considered the sign of a werewolf, as were stubby fingers and excessive body hair. Expectant mothers were not to run, leap or rise up suddenly, nor should they lift heavy burdens or lace too tightly. They should beware extremes of temperature and emotion and sleep as much as they could. Shocks, certain foods, extreme emotions and lasciviousness could all be communicated to an unborn child. Conceiving around the end of February, Elizabeth must have been increasingly aware of her condition by the Feast of St George, 23 April, when Henry made gifts to her including cloth of black velvet, russet cloth and squirrel fur as well as cloth of white blanket, canaber cloth, cords, beds of down and feather, carpet, London thread, crochettes, tappet hooks, hammers of iron and sheets of Holland cloth to furnish her bed. Perhaps these last items were prompted by solicitousness for her comfort, given her delicate state.

At the end of October 1489, Elizabeth went into confinement at Westminster, after hearing Mass and taking a ceremonial meal of spices and sweet wine. The queen's main chamber, with its attendant chapel and views across the river, would have been prepared in advance, with the late summer months seeing a flurry of activity as carpenters, furnishers, painters and fitters of all kinds set to work. It is unclear exactly how the day of admittance was decided; possibly a combination of Elizabeth's increasing size, the onset of practice contractions and the predictions of her women and doctors. It may have been calculated well in advance, according to the child's quickening or else determined on the day by the expectant mother's health. With no accurate means of anticipating due dates, and mistakes frequently made, confinement could be as short as seven days, or stretch for up to six weeks or more until 'late' babies made their arrival. In the autumn of 1489, Elizabeth probably played a part in the decision-making process, along with her mother-in-law, as the court machinery was set in motion for the big changes ahead; after all, this was an important State occasion. The witnesses, led by her Chamberlain, prayed for her safe delivery, as she and her women entered the inner chamber, hung with blue arras embroidered with gold fleurs-de-lys. Her bed and separate birthing pallet were hung with canopy of gold and velvet with many colours, 'garnished' with the symbolic red roses of Lancaster. To one side stood an altar, 'well furnished' with relics, on which Elizabeth would rely to assist her labour, while a cupboard 'well and richly garnished' held other necessaries for the coming weeks. Attending her were Margaret Beaufort and her own mother, Elizabeth Wydeville, temporarily leaving her religious seclusion in Bermondsey Abbey. During this confinement, the strict rules of attendance were briefly suspended to allow her mother's visiting cousin, Francois de Luxembourg, and a group of French Ambassadors to visit her. It must have been a welcome break from the long month of waiting.

After almost a month in confinement, Elizabeth was delivered of a daughter at about nine in the evening of 28 November. The birth of a girl was not always as welcome as that of a boy: it went unrecorded by the London Grey Friars chronicler who did note the arrivals of princes Arthur and Henry, yet girls had their dynastic uses, forging foreign alliances through marriage treaties. There is no reason to suspect that the little princess's arrival was treated with anything less than delight by her parents, considering the existence of a healthy heir and the ability of her mother to go on and bear more sons. The christening was held at Westminster, on 30 November, again using the traditional silver font from Canterbury Cathedral. The Marchioness of Berkeley carried the child from the queen's chamber at the front of a procession bearing 120 torches, followed by Elizabeth's sister Anne holding the lace christening robe. She was lowered into the font and baptised Margaret, after her paternal grandmother. The party partook of spices and wine, trumpets sounded and the child was carried back to her mother. The court would remain at Westminster for Christmas but an outbreak of measles delayed Elizabeth's churching until 27 December, when it was held in private. As the illness had claimed several victims among her ladies, this was a wise decision considering Elizabeth's vulnerable post-partum condition. By Candlemas, in early February, she was well enough to celebrate the purification of the Virgin Mary by watching a play in the White Hall. Seven months later she was pregnant again.

By now Elizabeth knew what to expect in the delivery chamber. *Hali Meidenhad* described the birth process in graphic terms: that 'cruel, distressing anguish, that fierce and stabbing pain, that incessant misery that torments upon torment, that wailing outcry ... fear of death, shame added to that suffering by old wives ... whose help is necessary to you, however indecent it may be'.[4] Such advice was designed to help prevent unwanted and illegitimate pregnancies but more practical advice was on hand for those who were well beyond this stage. Early sixteenth-century birth manuals instructed midwives not to encourage the mother to push before such time as the child was ready to be born, before which 'all labour is in vaine, labour as much as yee list': if all the mother's energy was spent too early, it could become a 'perilous case' indeed. She was to walk up and down until the 'matrice' or womb ruptured, after which she could rest and keep warm. If the waters did not break naturally, it was up to the midwife to rupture them with her fingernail or, terrifyingly, shears or a sharp knife. To strengthen her, a woman might then take a little sustenance in the form of an egg, with butter and bread, wine and water. Babies were delivered in all positions; standing, lying, kneeling, squatting, although many manuals advised the traditional lying flat on the back, braced on the bed with the feet against a log of wood, the better to push against. A pillow might be placed under her back and hips, to prevent them sinking down into the mattress, while a long 'swathe' of fabric under her body allowed her to be raised a little by her women on either side, if necessary. Those present in the room with her had to be careful about their positions too: sitting with crossed legs, arms or fingers was thought to contribute towards a difficult birth. As she prepared to deliver, the midwife would stroke and massage the womb to encourage the child's passage, while continually anointing her genitals with butter or grease until the head began to crown. Traditionally with queens, only the leading woman would be allowed such intimate physical contact: strict protocol dictated even the most unappealing of tasks.

This was the stage when, in the extremities of pain, women made oaths of allegiance and promises to undertake pilgrimage and dedicate their children to God. The realities of medieval and Tudor childbirth were learned through experience, passed down through generations of female oral traditions; Elizabeth's mother and mother-in-law would have been invaluable to her during her confinements. Few descriptions of childbirth have survived in public or private texts. Hardly any pre-Reformation letters and diaries detail the event from a female perspective and published accounts tend to be either literary or medical. It might be assumed that those involved were too busy to prioritise writing the process down, even if they had been able to. The rare female memoirs that survive have usually been preserved by families, particularly when portraying husbands and heirs in a positive light, some of whom edited diaries and memoirs in order to suppress critical voices: Pepys would not have been unique in tearing his wife's writings to pieces before her eyes for his unpleasant portrayal.[5] Medical advice manuals were largely produced for a small, predominantly male readership. Midwives, either formal or informal, would have had little access to them; their collective body of information belonged firmly in the oral tradition, transmitted through inheritance and the female support networks that had their basis in domestic relations. By the time of her third pregnancy, Elizabeth and her women knew what they were doing.

The future Henry VIII was born at Greenwich, in the old manor house of Placentia, begun by Humphrey, Duke of Gloucester, and developed by Henry VI and Edward IV. As such, it was a smaller and less significant royal property, more of a country retreat than the symbolic locations chosen for the arrival of Arthur and Margaret. Within a few years, all that remained of Henry's birthplace would be completely demolished to make way for a grand new programme of building in the Burgundian style. Its positioning may have afforded the heavily pregnant queen a greater degree of privacy and quiet than she would have found at Westminster; apparently it was her favourite house. Assuming the physicians' calculations had been correct, Elizabeth would have taken to her chamber early in June, to await the birth at the end of that month. The usual mechanism of preparations would have ensured all was ready for her enclosure in her chamber, from the yards of cloth and hangings about her bed, to the tapestries on the walls, cradles, pallet bed, all in the richest colours and fabrics, as well as the indispensable reliquary. It was her first summer confinement; perhaps in the heat she requested that the one uncovered window might be left open, so she could look out down to the river and watch the distant craft sailing past in the long days of waiting. Finally, on 28 June 1491, the ordeal came to an end; she was delivered of a sturdy, golden-haired son.

A child's safe arrival triggered the next phase in the frenzy of activity of the birth chamber. While Elizabeth lay back and rested, exhausted after her ordeal, the focus of her attendants shifted to the child, to secure its safety and establish the all-important gender and state of health. Superstition continued to govern this element of the procedure. While some gossips remained to comfort and congratulate the mother, it was the midwife's next job to cut the umbilical cord; a task of immense significance, as a child's navel was believed to hold the key to future fertility: if it was wrinkled, the mother would bear more babies, if smooth, her child-bearing days were over. The cord also had magical qualities of protection: some people carried a dried piece of it around as a charm to fend off witches, which was a very real fear for pregnant and labouring mothers, illustrated by a case of July 1582, when the Kent assizes found Elizabeth Johnson, a spinster of Kemsing, not guilty of having bewitched one Elizabeth Fremlynge so that she gave birth to a stillborn child. The caul and placenta were removed from the child and left to dry, thought to bring great fortune and an indicator of baby's future health, although as superstition became increasingly frowned upon, midwives were directed to bury them. As usual, the child's navel was dusted with powder of aloe and frankincense to speed recovery, while the midwife examined the new arrival carefully, checking his breathing and wiping his ears, eyes and nostrils. Cases of jaundice were treated with tree bark boiled in barley water or clarified whey. Then the little prince was washed gently in any of a number of substances; wine, milk, mallow, rue, sweet butter, myrrh, linseed and barley water, or rubbed with oil of acorns – supposedly another preventative measure against the perils of death before baptism – before being swaddled and laid in the cradle. Alternative methods of care included swathing them in roses ground up with salt to absorb moisture from their limbs and the mouth and gums cleansed with a finger dipped in honey. As she looked on the face of her sleeping newborn baby,

Elizabeth cannot have predicted what the future would hold for him. As a second son, Prince Henry was the necessary 'spare heir', significant as a safeguard but not expected to rule. His arrival was celebrated but few records were made of the event. His birth was a comparatively quiet business: it is symbolic that Margaret Beaufort only briefly mentioned his arrival in her Book of Hours, writing over a correction, while his elder brother and sister's exact time of arrival had been noted. He was baptised in the nearby church of the Friars Observant, which had been decorated for the purpose with tapestries, cypress linen, cloth of gold and damask, around a temporary wooden stage on which stood the Canterbury silver font. Wrapped in a mantle of cloth of gold trimmed with ermine, he was anointed and blessed by Richard Fox, the Bishop of Exeter. Soon, this tiny prince would be sent away to join his sister at her Eltham nursery where he would be brought up among women and quickly learned to 'rule the roost'.

Between 1491 and 1501, Elizabeth bore four, possibly five, more children. She conceived again only three months after the birth of Henry and went into confinement shortly before his first birthday. While awaiting the delivery, she was brought news of the death of her own mother Elizabeth Wydeville, who for the first time had declined to assist her during labour. When a second daughter arrived on 2 July 1492, the queen named her Elizabeth. The little girl was the first of the royal children to die in infancy, taken by an 'atrophy' or wasting disease at the age of three, and was buried in Westminster Abbey. Regular, unpredictable infant mortality was a sad fact of Tudor deliveries and was no respecter of rank; in many families, rates of survival could be as low as 50 per cent, although some families suffered fewer losses. Those dying at birth or within a week were known as 'chrisom children', still wearing the white baptismal cloth, while those surviving the dangerous first months could still be prey to all manner of dangers. It is impossible to know, across time, exactly what factors contributed to specific deaths but undeniably traumatic deliveries, illness, poor hygiene, malnutrition, cot death, accidents and imperfect understanding of childcare were contributing factors. In spite of their grief, Henry and Elizabeth knew their daughter had been in receipt of the best available care. In addition, Elizabeth was three months pregnant.

again. Princess Mary was born at Richmond on 18 March 1496.

Elizabeth's childbearing record and advancing age, by the standards of the time, may have affected her fertility. She did not conceive again for over two years. Perhaps the pilgrimage to Walsingham she undertook in the summer of 1497 was related to conception; it had certainly been a difficult period with the presence of the pretender Perkin Warbeck at court and the great fire that had razed Sheen Palace to the ground that Christmas. Payments made by Henry to Elizabeth's physician Master Lewis and her surgeon Robert Taylor in 1498 may have been related to a pregnancy or birth: certainly by May that year, she had fallen pregnant again. At the relatively advanced age, in Tudor terms, of thirty-three, she went into confinement for the sixth time at Greenwich in February 1499. Although this pregnancy went to term and the little prince Edmund was apparently healthy, something had caused concern in those attending the queen. The Spanish ambassador reported that there had been 'much fear for her life' but in the end, the delivery proved straightforward. Perhaps she had experienced a more difficult pregnancy or her age and general health provoked doubts: she had just passed her thirtieth birthday when she delivered Mary back in 1496 and those three extra years may have been considered significant. Possibly these fears combined with political and dynastic dangers: her confinement coincided with the culmination of years of threat from pretender to the throne Perkin Warbeck. In the event, however, the delivery proved comparatively easy and another male heir was welcomed and celebrated. Sadly though, the little prince died at fifteen months and was buried at Westminster: perhaps he was weak or underweight from the start, or Elizabeth's unrecorded complications during the pregnancy gave grounds for concern at the time. Alternatively he may have fallen prey to any one of the infantile illnesses of the age, unpredictable and often untreatable with contemporary medicine. His death may have coincided with the conception of the mysterious Edward, putting this child's delivery date somewhere in the summer of 1501; alternatively he predated his brother in birth and death, arriving in 1497 or 1498. Perhaps the very closeness of these pregnancies lay behind the concerns for the queen's health.

In late 1501, Elizabeth witnessed the arrival of the Spanish infanta Catherine of Aragon, whose marriage with Prince Arthur, just turned fifteen, had been planned since their early years. The queen's eldest son had grown into a tall, slender, serious young man, much in the mould of his father; contemporary portraits show him thin-faced and delicate-looking with a certain tenderness about the eyes and mouth. His bride was to be the beautiful, auburn-haired daughter of King Ferdinand of Aragon and Isabella of Castile, an extraordinary pair of joint rulers renowned for their warlike nature and ruthless, separate control of their individual territories. Catherine had arrived that October in Plymouth after an apparently smooth and uneventful crossing: they were married almost six weeks later. London turned out in its finery to watch the event. According to the chronicler Hall, the bride was conducted to St Paul's through streets decked with beautiful pageants, wise devises and prudent speeches, with ballads and instruments making 'heauenly noyes'. The city officials lined up to welcome her, dressed in 'costly apparel both of goldsmythes work and embraudery, ryche iewelles, massy cheynes' upon horses with glittering trappings, hung with gold spangles and bells. She was led into the church by the already charismatic ten-year-old Henry, Prince of Wales. A 6-foot wooden platform had been erected inside, covered in fine red worsted, making a sort of stage above the heads of the crowd. Here, Elizabeth and Henry watched as their son was married, both bride and groom dressed – unusually – all in white and being 'both lusty and amorous'. This was followed by a four-course feast in the Bishop's Palace, using plates from four cupboards, with dancing and 'costly disguising', before the formal bedding ceremony of the couple at Baynard's Castle, much unchanged since Elizabeth's day, for what was to become the most controversial wedding night in Tudor history.

One issue would later come to dominate Catherine of Aragon's life. The question of what the two teenagers did in bed over the course of the next four and a half months would irrevocably determine the course of British history and the development of the Church of England. It is, by now, a familiar question; perhaps the overriding question of the dynasty, dividing man and wife, parents and children, monarch and subject, and continuing to divide historical interpretation to the present day. So, during their short-lived marriage, did Catherine and Arthur sleep together? Did they consummate their union in the full sense, or was it, as Catherine was to later insist, a slow, cautious, innocent connection between two children who had no reason not to believe they had time on their sides? Did their failure to connect on their wedding night preclude any subsequent relations? Catherine later claimed they shared a bed on seven occasions but that full consummation had not taken place. Her waiting women and Arthur's gentlemen were divided on the issue; some even suggested that the force of their sexual passion had weakened the frail young man, paralleling the accusations levelled at the death of Catherine's brother Juan and his supposedly 'over-passionate' wife Margaret, in 1497. Their ceremonial bedding was public enough, with Arthur cheered along by his fellows, with dancing, pleasure and mirth, as well as trumpets sounding, as their friends witnessed the young groom climb into bed beside his wife and receive the blessing of a priest, that they should be protected from 'phantasies and illusions of devils'. After that, only Arthur and Catherine knew exactly what had passed between them. Hall's chronicle would later insist that 'this lusty prince and his beautiful bride were brought and joined together in one bed naked and there did that act, which to the performance and full consummation of matrimony was most requisite and expedient' but he was three at the time of the wedding and writing in the early 1540s, when it was expedient to believe in the union's success. Later, when the matter became of national importance, the expressions and testimonies of servants would become crucial and the events of that November night and following morning would be analysed and debated. In the autumn of 1501, however, there was no foreshadowing of the immense consequences of the teenager's courtship, and the series of jousts, pageants and feasts continued unabated. The king and queen watched their newly wedded son and his bride enjoying tournaments on the newly sanded tilt yard by the river and lavish Burgundian-style disguisings in Westminster Hall. Ironically, one of these pageants included eight 'goodly' knights overcoming the resistance of eight 'goodly and fresh' ladies, who yielded to the forces of love. The subtext for Arthur and Catherine couldn't have been clearer.

However, tragedy awaited the newly-weds. Barely six months later, terrible news reached Elizabeth and Henry in London. After the wedding ceremonies, the young couple had departed for Ludlow, where they had settled into the imposing defensive borders castle. The location was remote and the weather extreme, exacerbating the damp and dirt: a local outbreak of the sweating sickness took hold in the late spring, a painful disease that would dispatch most sufferers within days. Both Arthur and Catherine fell ill. While she survived, he succumbed on 2 April 1502 and the sixteen-year-old Spaniard became a widow after only four and a half months of marriage. The sweat may have been to blame, or else the tuberculosis assumed by nineteenth-century historians. The official record of his funeral related that a long-term disease may have been the underlying cause: 'a pitiful disease and sickness' of 'deadly corruption did utterly vanquish and overcome the (healthy) blood'. It is possible that this was testicular tuberculosis, which can cause increased libido but dampen performance, which may provide answers to the lingering questions of Arthur's marriage and death. The London messengers were afraid to break the news to the king, delaying until the following morning. Devastated by their loss, the king and queen consoled each other as best they could, with Elizabeth telling Henry they still had a 'fair, goodly' son and were young enough to have more children. This was no idle promise. Within weeks, she had conceived again.

The fears that had surfaced during Elizabeth's previous pregnancy were ominous for the advent of her final child in the winter of 1503. That July at Woodstock, she had been unwell and in September her apothecary was paid for delivering 'certain stuff' for the use of the queen. The fact that she had conceived so quickly after consoling Henry with the idea of a new child, suggests she was still fertile but that the couple may have previously decided to limit their family due to her ill health. As she prepared for her confinement, two nurses visited her in November, the start of her final trimester, which may have been routine but may equally have indicated that something was amiss. On the fourteenth, a Mistress Harcourt saw her at Westminster and twelve days later she was attended by a French woman at Baynard's Castle. New bedding and curtains were ordered, accounts for the delivery of bed linen were settled and the girdle of Our Lady of Westminster was delivered mid-December. Right up until the end, Elizabeth was on the move. At the end of January, she travelled from Richmond to the Tower of London where she gave birth to a daughter a week later. This was in itself unusual: previous retirements to her chamber had occurred three or more weeks before labour began, allowing for misdiagnosis, preparation and the long hours of 'travail'. Elizabeth had barely settled herself into her Tower lodgings before she was seized by violent contractions and she gave birth to a daughter, Catherine, on Candlemas day, 2 February 1503. Perhaps the child was born prematurely or else the date had been miscalculated: contemporaries recorded that she had intended to lie-in at Richmond and was delivered 'suddenly', which must have been a surprise after her previous pregnancies. Soon after the birth it became apparent that Elizabeth was seriously ill; possibly puerperal fever had set in or heavy bleeding; perhaps she had sustained an injury during the delivery. A messenger was sent into Kent to try and locate a Dr Aylsworth or Hallysworth but nine days later the queen was dead.

Most Tudor mothers did not die during childbirth. Surprisingly, the odds of survival were fairly good, providing there were no complications. Roger Schofield[6] estimates the likelihood of maternal mortality at 1 per cent per pregnancy and between 6 and 7 per cent across a woman's childbearing years, giving them a similar chance of dying of non-birth-related causes. Another case study, of sixteenth-century Aldgate, suggests the figure was more like 2.35 per cent,[7] as crowded and insanitary as urban areas undoubtedly were. Then, as now, complications arose that were met with varying degrees of response according to the skill and experience of the age. Difficult deliveries and breech births, without preventative action being taken, could lead to maternal and infant death. One 1513 work contained images of sixteen unnatural birth presentations and advice to the midwife to oil her hands, apply butter to the cervix and try to turn the baby, using all her 'diligence and pain'. If this state continued, brute force was needed to expel a reluctant foetus. There were no forceps during this time, being invented by the Chamberlain family in the late Elizabethan period but not made public until over a century later. One or two famous contemporary cases of Caesareans were carried out in Europe but these were not used in England and certainly not on a live mother; maternal death inevitably ensued and live children were cut from dead mothers using damaging metal hooks. In the event of failure, religious help was sought. One miracle of St Thomas of Canterbury recorded how an infant arrived arm first; the midwives pushed it back, hoping the child would turn, whereupon it began to swell. The normal procedure would be to then cut off the arm in order to save the mother but prayers were offered and saintly intervention supposedly resulted in a successful birth. In many cases though, practical interference, contemporary wisdom and prayer were not enough. The more babies a mother bore, the greater her risk of death and resulting illness, with the increased physical toll on her body and advancing age. For some, birth complications made their very first pregnancy fatal while others bore in excess of ten children and survived into comparative old age. Significantly more women did die young though, of illnesses resulting from delivery, poor hygiene and contemporary lack of anatomical understanding. Pregnant Elizabethan women in particular, had their portraits painted in case their forthcoming confinement was to end in tragedy.

The interval between Elizabeth's delivery and death suggests the birth itself was a success but that a subsequent fever took hold or internal damage later caused a haemorrhage. Status, wealth, provision, duty, love, attention and experience were still not sufficient to save the queen's life; it proved that bearing a child involved as great a risk for royalty as for her female subjects. In addition to the dynastic importance of Elizabeth's life, the intimate association of Catholic ritual, prayer and famous relics during her confinements transcended the bodily event of her deliveries, advocating a personal relationship with the saints. Clasping the holy girdle, with her chest of relics and the Canterbury font on hand to christen England's heir, it must have seemed to those around that higher authorities were blessing and witnessing the union and its offspring. It was also significant for the superstitious Tudors that she had given birth at Candlemas, the day of the

Virgin's purification, suggestive of the queen's eternal rebirth and spotless purity. Elizabeth was the metaphoric and literal mother of the nation, bearer of heirs: in popular memory, she would be elevated to a saintly maternal figure, devoted to her religion and her family.

The semi-deification of Elizabeth began at once, with the wail of church bells across the nation and the iconography of her funeral. Colour and light were carefully deployed to intensify her saintly sacrifice. Dramatic white banners were lain across the corners of her coffin, signifying the manner of her death, while the main body of it was draped with black velvet surmounted by a cross of white cloth of gold: two sets of thirty-seven virgins in white linen and Tudor wreaths of white and green lined her route to Westminster, carrying lighted candles, and the torchbearers wore white woollen hooded gowns. More than a thousand lights burned on the hearse and the vaults and cross of the cathedral were draped in black and lit by 273 large tapers. The coffin was spectacularly topped by a wax effigy of the queen, dressed in robes of estate, her hair loose under a rich crown, a sceptre in her hand and fingers adorned with fine rings. Icons of the Virgin at shrines across the country hardly deviated from this description. Before burial, the effigy, with its crown and rich robes, was removed and stored in secrecy at the shrine of Edward the Confessor; so this lifelike, regal image of the queen was absorbed into a collection of holy relics and icons, interchangeable with the symbolic objects that assisted her during childbirth. Part of the effigy still exists in the museum at Westminster Abbey, its face, neck and chest painted white, its features regular and serene, unsmiling but beneficent. Elizabeth's adult life had been devoted to producing the future heirs of the Tudor dynasty. Her children would reign in England, Scotland and France yet she had paid the ultimate price for serving her king and country. *The Monument of Matrons*, published during the reign of Elizabeth's namesake and granddaughter, included a prayer for a mother who had not survived childbirth, thanking God for delivering 'this woman our sister, out of the woeful miseries of this sinful world'.[8]

A seventeenth-century ballad recorded Elizabeth's loss and Henry's inconsolable grief:

The Queen that fair and Princely Dame
That mother meek and mild
To add more Number to her Joy
Again grew big with Child:

All which brought comfort to the King
Against which careful Hour
He lodg'd his dear kind hearted Queen
In London's stately Tower.

That Tower that was so fatal once
To Princes of Degree
Proved fatal to this noble Queen
For therein died She.

In child-bed lost she her sweet Life;
Her life esteemed so dear
Which had been England's loving Queen
Full many a happy year.

The King herewith possess'd with Grief
Spent many Months in Moan
And daily sigh'd and said that he
Like her could find out none:

Nor none could he in Fancy chuse,
To make his Wedded Wife
Wherefore a Widower would remain,
The Remnant of his Life.[9]

The anonymous seventeenth-century pamphleteer was only partly correct. There is no doubt that in the spring of 1503 Henry VII was prostrate with grief. He contained his sorrow long enough to organise his wife's funeral before withdrawing from the public eye. It was not contemporary practice for husbands and wives to be present at their spouse's interment. The loss of Arthur, compounded by the deaths of Elizabeth and their newborn daughter, represented a terrible blow for a still relatively young man. However, within two months, the State Papers of Spain record that he was already entering into negotiations to find another wife. Rapid remarriage was not uncommon at the time, even when unions had been affectionate and companionate; and particularly when they had not been. Parish records list burials followed only a few months later by remarriage among Henry's subjects. A king needed a consort and a court needed a female head. His contemporaries would not have thought of him as callous; husbands often found new wives with what seems like indecent haste to the twenty-first-century eye but this should come as no surprise: for Tudor men and women, marriage was a safeguard against sin in the eyes of the Church, a comfort and support as well as demarcating social standing and advancement. The romantic notion of a lifelong union was rare and many marriages were contracted between widows and widowers: it was more a realistic reflection of the fragility and brevity of life and the need for comfort. Initially, Henry's immediate family and fellow monarchs would have been sympathetic. Then, they heard his choice of bride.

As early as April 1503, news had reached Spain of a projected match between the king and his widowed daughter-in-law Catherine of Aragon. Arthur's early death had left her in a difficult situation politically and financially, but more awkward still were the wranglings between the two countries over the long-overdue payment of her dowry. There had already been talk of a match between Catherine and Prince Henry, the new heir, when he came of age. The thought of the seventeen-year-old girl being wedded to her forty-six-year-old father-in-law appalled Catherine's mother, Isabella of Castile, who described it as 'a very evil thing; one never before seen ... which offends the ears' and urged Henry to send her daughter home. But did Henry really intend to marry his son's teenage widow? The lines of diplomatic communication were notoriously unreliable and subject to rumour and misinterpretation; the supposed match may have had more to do with Henry's hopes to extract the protracted Spanish dowry or answer the difficult questions of provision for Catherine than actual desire or intention. Being obliged to maintain Catherine's household and wait until the twelve-year-old future Henry VIII came of an age to allow them to wed may have seemed too protracted and restrictive for the king.

Marriage to Catherine would have solved his immediate problem while opening up further potential foreign alliances for his son.

Her mother did not see it that way. Resolute and warlike, Isabella could not easily be put off. Instead, she offered her niece, Queen Joan of Naples, as a more suitable candidate. Born in 1479, Joan had been married to her own nephew and widowed young, at seventeen in 1496: her comparative youth and family connections made her a suitable match for Henry and she was still young enough to have borne him more children. With only one son remaining out of four, he had learned the imperative of having the proverbial 'spare heir'. By October 1504, Spanish ambassador de Puebla wrote to report that he had spoken at length to the king about the match, who had expressed great 'pleasure' at the thought of it and was questioning him as to the lady's beauty and personal attributes. The following June, he sent ambassadors to Naples, whose detailed report back gives a good indication of the physical attributes Henry required in a new bride. In response to a series of his questions, the king learned that she was aged around twenty-seven, her 'unpainted' face was 'amiable, round and fat', cheerful and demure, her skin clear and complexion fair and clean. Her teeth were fair and clean, with lips 'somewhat rounded' and hair that appeared brown under her headdress. It was difficult to discern her exact height as she wore slippers and her figure was hidden under a great mantle. Her arms were round and 'not very small', hands 'somewhat full and soft', fingers fair and small, of a 'meetly' length and breadth, her neck 'comely and not-misshapen'; there was no discernible hair on her lips and her breasts were 'great and full and trussed somewhat high'. She was recorded to be a good 'feeder', eating meat twice a day and drinking cinnamon water and hippocras wine. These descriptions were apparently pleasing to Henry on a personal level, as by that July, rumours had reached Spain of a potential marriage treaty.[10]

However, by March 1506, Henry was entering into negotiations for the hand of another woman. The Archduchess Margaret of Savoy was recently widowed and very rich. It would have been a powerful union for England, although the use of a rival may have been intended to hurry the Spaniards into an alliance. Political and financial obstacles may also have been to blame. Born in 1480,

Margaret was named after her step-grandmother Margaret of York, sister to Edward IV and Richard III; she was also the sister of Philip 'the Handsome' of Austria, the brother-in-law of Catherine of Aragon through his marriage to her sister Juana, and had been briefly married to Catherine's brother Juan. After his death she delivered a stillborn child, and a second, short-lived marriage had been childless, after which she had vowed to remain single and was known at the Savoyard court as 'lady of mourning'. Luckily or unluckily for Henry, Margaret refused him and he returned to consider another Hapsburg alliance.

By 1506, Catherine of Aragon's sister Juana had attracted the nickname 'the mad'. She was beautiful but considered deeply unstable. Her almost obsessive love for her husband Philip the Handsome was complicated by his infidelity and coldness: her maladies were more likely attributable to depression and neuroses. She was imprisoned and manipulated by him, suffered continual attempts to undermine her and eventually lived apart from him. Juana and Philip had been forced by bad weather to land on the English coast in 1505, where they had been royally entertained by Henry VII and reunited with Catherine. Philip's sudden death in September 1506, of typhoid fever, put Juana back on the marriage market, although potential suitors may have been put off by her refusal to let him be buried and have his body removed from her presence. At this time though, she was five months pregnant with her sixth child. Unsurprisingly, these negotiations also came to nothing.

Henry VII did not remarry. It is difficult to know, at this distance, just how sincere his marital attempts were; whether they were driven by personal factors or simply another facet of the complicated game of European politics, or both. It would be misleadingly anachronistic to separate these motives and see his attempts at wooing as anything less than his royal duty. If he was looking for comfort, he might have found a willing wife closer to home, among his own nobility; dynastically, the pool of available women failed to provide him with a successful candidate. Perhaps it was the very geographical and political distance between him and these potential brides that made them attractive; the king was the ultimate prize in the delicate game of foreign alliances and to commit himself may have risked alienating other potential unions. He was spoilt for choice, so long as his marriage remained theoretical. There is no doubt about the genuine grief he exhibited at the loss of his wife, retreating 'to a solitary place to pass his sorrow' and seeing no one except 'those appointed'. Ill health increasingly plagued him during the last years of his life, as he resigned himself to his losses. His heir was the now teenage future Henry VIII, already a charismatic and confident boy, who would soon need a wife of his own.

3

Catherine of Aragon & Henry, Prince of Wales
1501–1510

Widowhood & Fertility

O men, how ill do you bestow your time, and paines! Alas, wee women die not, but are tormented even to death: for those that are accounted the most expert and skilful among you, take not that care of us which they should; you fill whole Libraries with your writings … making little or no mention … of our cruel and insupportable torments.[1]

The death of Elizabeth of York deprived the young widowed Catherine of an important ally and benefactor. It was primarily the queen who had liaised by letter with Isabella of Castile to orchestrate the marriage with Arthur and oversee many of the arrangements. More importantly, she was a sympathetic maternal figure whose experience would have been invaluable to Catherine in her future role as wife and mother. Shortly before her death, she had sent her daughter-in-law books, and arranged her transport to court, where she could recover from illness in comparative luxury, rather than remaining in Ludlow, with its bad weather, ill vapours and bad memories. From 1503 onwards, her status uncertain, Catherine existed in a sort of social and marital limbo, dependent on the king's scant support and effectively reduced to penury. Between the ages of sixteen and twenty-three, she struggled to feed herself and her own household: the magnificent feasts of her wedding celebrations in the autumn of 1501 were consigned to memory. Yet throughout this time, she continued to hope that Henry would announce her betrothal to his younger son, and that once he came of age, she would again be a bride and, ultimately, a queen. Marriages among royalty and the aristocracy were commonly made in the mid- to late teens, to maximise the child-bearing years. For Catherine, the peak of her fertility coincided with uncertainty and dearth.

Then as now, a woman's ability to conceive was influenced by her access to good-quality food, her activity levels and her sexual availability. A teenage girl needed to attain a certain body weight for the onset of the menarche, or 'flowers' and subsequent regularity of her cycle. Having already reached the age of puberty before her marriage to Arthur, Catherine had clearly been menstruating but the effects of her poverty could have caused the complete or temporary cessation of her periods. Hypothalamic amenorrhoea can be triggered by stress, anorexia or bulimia: in terms of diet, the availability of protein and fat in Catherine's diet and the regularity of meals would have been a significant factor. A lack of vegetables may have led to the condition Chlorosis, an iron deficiency that is often cause for concern during pregnancy. As a devout Catholic, she fasted regularly, further affecting her body's menstrual cycle, yet understandably, her strict devotions may have represented the only facet of her life over which she could exercise any control. Modern responses to her condition might encompass psychosomatic illness and hypochondria, exacerbated by malnourishment, although the devotional aspect of her life makes diagnosis more complex. The pattern of the ensuing six years of poverty and ill health, coinciding with her most fertile period, may have had a lasting impact on her reproductive abilities. Contemporary medicine was of little assistance.

Tudor understanding – or misunderstanding – of the body united a strange blend of Christian theology, Greek and Roman ideas, astrology, astronomy and superstition. Physical health was still connected with personal morality, so an ill body was considered the product of an ill mind or behaviour, which, coupled with the belief that misfortune and disease were visitations of God, frequently made diagnosis more a matter of character and reputation than science. Illness was considered to be divine judgement, for which error a sufferer would search their past behaviour and make amends. The body was considered to be comprised of four humours: blood (air), phlegm (water), black bile (earth) and yellow bile (fire), each with their own degrees of heat and moisture. These would determine an individual's temperament and prescribe a certain diet and set of medicines. Illness could be caused by an imbalance of one or more elements, diagnosed through urinology and treated by bleeding, purges and balanced with the opposing element. Therefore, a hot and dry complaint would be prescribed foods that were considered cold and wet and vice versa. This also lent itself to bodily types, determining certain characteristics and needs; the hot and moist sanguine characters were red-cheeked and corpulent and supposed to be amorous, happy and irresponsible; their opposite cold and dry melancholics were thin and sallow, introspective and sentimental. Overall, four basic character types dominated, reducing all patients to a simple, formulaic diagnosis. The connection between mind and body would not be understood for centuries.

In August 1504, Catherine was recorded as suffering from an 'ague and derangement of the stomach', which lasted three days and left her with a bad cold and cough. 'Ague' was an unspecific, catch-all term for fever, which could encompass a number of illnesses from flu to malaria onwards; the symptoms included alternating temperature, sweating and shivering. Born in mid-December, making her a Sagittarius, Catherine would have been considered warm, dry and choleric in temperament and would have been treated by herbs and foods that were considered cold and wet. Recovering enough to travel from Westminster to Greenwich in late summer, Catherine fell ill again, this time more seriously than before, experiencing daily swings between 'cold and heat', lacking appetite, her complexion changing 'entirely', plunging her women into despair. Her physicians had confidence in her recovery, though, purging her twice and attempting twice to bleed her, 'but no blood came'. The subtext of this was sexual. Bloodletting was one contemporary means of treating menstrual problems: undischarged blood was supposed to pool in the body and required release through some other outlet. It was not considered different to other forms of bodily bleeding, like a man suffering a nose bleed, all to rid the body of excess fluid. To the early Tudor surgeons, bleeding from a vein was the same as menstrual bleeding. Physicians had little faith in, or understanding of, nature's ability to efficiently design the female body: it was considered an imperfect representation of the male form and the monthly cycle was understood to be its method of shedding unnecessary, accumulated blood, without which the womb would become overrun with fluid and could 'choke' or 'suffocate'. Trotula of Salerno wrote that a woman who failed to menstruate as the result of fasting should eat good food and drink to 'give her good blood'. Bleeding a patient was the most common way to treat this condition, to prevent consumption by body heat and the development of 'mannish' characteristics. Among many beliefs regarding the female cycle was that the failure to menstruate made a woman dangerously 'masculine' and prone to many forms of madness and fits. Other remedies included hot baths, pessaries placed in the vagina or, for married women, intercourse.

Menstrual blood was also feared by men and formed part of a wider misogynistic suspicion of women's bodies and minds. One belief claimed that it could damage the penis on contact, or that men might unsuspectingly consume it in love potions! It had the power to turn new wine sour, make fruit fall from trees, kill beehives, give dogs rabies and make crops turn barren. A child in a cradle could be poisoned by the gaze of an old, premenopausal woman, whose accumulation of blood would lead to poisonous vapours being given off by her eyes! It was considered an essential but corrupting force; children conceived during periods were supposed to be red haired and 'puny'. Menstruating women carried round nutmegs and nosegays to conceal any arising odours, as the corrosive power of the female reproductive fluids, transmittable through smell, constituted a real fear at the time. To stem a heavy flow, women were advised to take the hair from a particular animal's head and bind it to a 'green' or young tree; another 'proven' remedy advocated burning a toad in a pot and wearing the powder in a pouch around the waist. If this failed, recipes using comfrey, nettle and blackberry, alongside the repetition of 'magical' numerical formulae, were suggested. Female sexuality and bodily functions of all sorts formed a dangerous taboo, loaded with superstitious significance. As one of a number of mysterious maternal excretions, including placentas, umbilical cords and birth cauls, the supposed 'magical' properties of female blood were treated with suspicion by those excluded from the birth chamber. Catherine's inability to produce sufficient blood for her physicians may have given cause for concern over her future reproductive abilities, while not necessarily being understood to be a function of her poor diet and religious habits. She insisted that further attempts be made at bleeding, yet the doctors preferred to purge her instead, giving her herbal remedies designed to cleanse her internally that could bring on vomiting, diarrhoea and other violent reactions.

Catherine's erratic menstruation was not uncommon at the time. The regularity with which women's commonplace books contain recipes to 'bring on a woman's courses', or cure amenorrhoea, suggest this must have been a common problem. It was also, probably, a euphemism for abortion, including herbs to stimulate contraction and the expulsion of blood: the herb rue, drunk in the evening, was supposed to be particularly effective, as were savin and mixtures of wine and hyssop. Shepherd's purse, St John's wort, Bishop's weed and wallflower were all suggested and could be found growing wild, according to one medieval Herbarium. Some texts were explicit, stating that wallflower mixed in honey and wine, applied to the vagina, 'takes the foetus from the womb'; more euphemistically, pennyroyal could 'bring foorth dead fruit'. A 1476 medical text included recipes for inducing menstruation with a blend of soda, figs, garlic seed, myrrh and lily ointment, or else pulped cucumber flesh mixed in milk. These could be drunk or inserted into the vagina on pessaries of soft wool.[2] Others suggested dates, hazelnuts and saffron. Fine lines demarcated their administration: it was safe to drink rue in the evening but lethal in the morning. While it was illegal to induce abortion or interfere in any way with the growth or delivery of a healthy child, such remedies protected the user by expressing their dual purpose and warning against misuse. In addition, the interchangeability of treatments for amenorrhoea and abortive methods, indicate the danger many unsuspecting women were exposed to, often at the expense of their reproductive health and sometimes resulting in death. One medieval herbal stated it was written 'so every man, woman and child' could 'be their own physician in times of need'; and possibly their own executioner too. Abortion could also be procured through massage and, as advised by Avicenna of Persia, by prolonged baths, drugs, fasting, intercourse and increased respiratory effort which deprived a foetus of air. One potion to abort a child included goat's milk and gum resin, while suppositories to achieve the same effect were made up of black olive oil, larkspur, rosemary, marjoram and laurel seeds. Needless to say, all forms of abortion were considered acts of murder at the time and contrary to the law of God; if it could be proven, a woman might face the same death sentence as one who committed infanticide. In many cases it would be very difficult to prove that deliberate termination rather than miscarriage had taken place, but when courts were presented with seemingly incontrovertible evidence, they ruled harshly. In 1503, pregnant spinster Joan Wynspere of Nottinghamshire drank various poisoned and dangerous draughts which killed herself and her child, yet this did not prevent a court of finding her guilty of murder.

London records of late sixteenth-century medical practitioners cite examples of 'wise women' and practitioners called to account for their activities. In many cases, the boundaries between prenatal care and the procuration of abortion appear to have been broached. A midwife named Christina admitted administering dangerous combinations of rhubarb and laurel to patients in 1598 and an Anna Baker was accused by another woman of giving fumigations and purgatives in 1589. Jane Rogers of Tower Hill, a confessed midwife, was reported in 1600 for having charged 11s to administer unction, nine potions and two purgations while Alice Minsterley was warned about her purges in 1585, 1597 and 1602, with the threat of imprisonment. In 1602, Susanna Gloriana, a French woman residing in London, was accused by a Jane Pickman of administering a successful purge of syrup of hyssop and roses to a Mary Brett, before killing her with a 'herbal bath'. Gloriana confessed but was shown leniency for being poor, pregnant and breastfeeding a child: her husband paid £20 as a bond to ensure she would cease practice. At the same time, Rose Griffin of Fetter Lane was practising as a midwife, issuing purges and lozenges made from antimony, sarsaparilla and senna, which had weakened many women: she would confess and be imprisoned in 1607. Cecilia Poplar of Aldgate had prescribed purges and fumigation for one Dorothy Gatersby, resulting in her patient's death: she was also known to have used this treatment on two other women, who were then still living.[3] The secret, feminine nature of childbirth and reproductive health could be a double-edged sword: while creating authentic oral traditions of experience and wisdom, it also appeared to license quackery and bad practices, so long as they were conducted by women. By the 1550s, physicians were advocating that, after the first trimester, women should not be bled or take pills or take pills or purges without the 'counsel of an expert'. Definitions of what constituted expertise were still likely to differ, though.

Catherine's reduced circumstances were again causing concern in March 1505. She wrote to Henry VII complaining of the 'misery' in which she lived, which should 'reflect dishonour on his character' and explaining that she had not wasted money on luxuries, rather, that she had been forced to borrow in order to eat.[4] Writing to her father in April the following year, her situation had not improved: Henry would give her no money for food, which caused her the 'greatest anguish' as her household were 'ready to ask alms and herself all but naked'. Dramatically, she concluded with a plea for a Spanish confessor, as she had 'been for six months near death'.[5] That October she suffered further attacks of fever and by the spring of 1507, she was writing even more explicitly, that she was driven to sell her gold and silver as her household were 'obliged to live in rags'. She reported to the ambassador de Puebla that she had 'suffered martyrdom' and begged to be released from her 'humiliating position' as soon as possible.[6] At the same time though, her health seemed to improve a little. Continually plagued by illness since her transference from sunny Spain to England's damp climate, her former recoveries were described more as 'appearances than ... reality', as she had now begun to regain her 'natural healthy colour'. However, the constant embarrassment and difficulties of her penury were weighing heavily on her spirits; these 'moral afflictions' were 'beyond the reach of the physician'. She wrote again to Henry and as always, her pleas put the needs of her women first, now reduced to five in number, who had not received the smallest sum of money since their arrival in 1501.[7]

By 1509, a full seven years after she had been widowed, Catherine's financial situation was still desperate. She had sold her household goods and, after appealing directly again to the king, was rebuffed with a complete denial of his obligation to support her and that her current food allowance was only given as alms. Between the ages of sixteen and twenty-three, Catherine cannot have afforded to furnish her table in a way that befitted her status or facilitated her fertility. Through her most fertile years, privation, ill health and religious fasts contributed towards an erratic menstrual cycle and probably left her underweight and undernourished.

Catherine's contemporaries may have perceived another reason for her frequent illnesses. Physicians believed sex was essential for good health and that abstinence could lead to illness and even sterility: the multitude of ailments suffered by 'green' maidens could only be cured by marriage, whose 'cold, damp' wombs craved the complementary 'hot, dry' male seed. Seventeenth-century writers described symptoms ranging from hysterical fits and sores suffered by their virginal patients, to the 'strangulation' of the womb, which could fill the brain with a dark smoke and cause melancholy, madness and even prompt suicide.[8] One writer described the descent of a bride-to-be into terrible 'mother-fits', five or six times a day, at the thwarting of her proposed marriage:[9] as the century progressed, these symptoms could prove even more dangerous when mistaken as signs of demonic possession. Herbal remedies included ingredients such as coral, aloe, myrrh, rhubarb, nutmeg, amber, cloves, cinnamon, aniseed and wormwood. Inevitably, female body shape was linked with sexual appetite: larger, ruddy women were full of moisture which dampened their lust while lean and post-menstrual women were filled with perpetual desire. However, all women were insatiable by nature, as they had been designed for breeding: it was their strength and their greatest flaw in the patriarchal world. Men could not do without them, yet denigrated and feared them for their perceived weaknesses and the temptations they offered, warning each other not to be 'milked' by lascivious women.[10] Once again, balance was advocated. Excessive desire could corrupt women, so their lust should be controlled by hard work, religious devotion, meditation and fasting. The ideal was a modest but regular pattern of sexual relations within marriage. And for Catherine, that ideal was looking increasingly unlikely.

On the death of a prince or king, it was customary to wait several months to determine whether or not his widow was pregnant, with the resulting implications for the line of succession. In 1502, Henry VII had delayed appointing his second son as Prince of Wales, possibly to safeguard against the possibility that Catherine might be carrying an heir to Arthur's title. Again, Catherine had experience of such a situation, as her brother's widow was found to have conceived shortly before his death, as would her sister Juana, married to Philip the Handsome. However, such hopes would imply that consummation had taken place, so if Catherine's later assertions of virginity are to be believed, she must have known there was little chance of any pregnancy. In the meantime, her parents wrote urging the formalisation of her betrothal to the young Prince Henry, then a boy of eleven. That June, Ferdinand, Isabella and Henry VII pledged to do their utmost to achieve a papal dispensation for the match, which was necessary as the couple were related in the first degree of affinity and Catherine's marriage to Arthur was 'solemnised according to the rites of the Catholic Church, and afterwards consummated'.[11] This appears to belie the letter sent to Spain by Catherine's chief gentlewoman Doña Elvira, who wrote of the bride's quiet disappointment and her continued virginal state, yet to smooth the way for a new union of such familial proximity, a thorough dispensation was needed to cover every eventuality. Isabella followed this with a statement clarifying her belief: 'although they were wedded, Prince Arthur and the Princess Katharine never consummated the marriage. It is well known in England that the Princess is still a virgin … but … it has seemed to be more prudent to provide for the case as though the marriage had been consummated.'[12] That December, Pope Julius II issued a dispensation for the marriage to go ahead, even in the case of consummation. Finally, it looked as if the young widow's future was in hand. A treaty was signed asserting that the wedding would go ahead once the prince had come of age. However, those arranging the match had failed to take account of one important factor: the bridegroom.

In June 1505, the fourteen-year-old Prince Henry made a declaration before the Bishop of Winchester, repudiating the betrothal. Explaining that he had been contracted in marriage 'during his minority', he now asserted himself, as being 'near the age of puberty', to denounce the match as 'null and void'. Whether this was an act of personal defiance, or part of his father's attempts to secure an alternative foreign match or attain the long-awaited dowry, is unsure; certainly it coincided with the one of the princess's worst periods of privation and illness. For Catherine, her future was cast into doubt again, as she approached her twentieth birthday without any indication of soon becoming the queen, wife and mother she had been raised to expect. Delay and uncertainty shadowed the following years. The death of her mother Isabella in 1504 and her father's remarriage and fathering of a son, in addition to further wrangling about her dowry and the complications arising from her sister's widowhood, drew the process out further. In March 1507, Ferdinand wrote in sympathy with her 'miserable and trying life', although his tone very quickly changed after encouragement from Henry VII and his next letter spoke of the anticipated happiness of the union; that 'ere long, she would be comfortable with her husband in her house'. Further negotiations regarding the payment of her dowry proved inconclusive; her sister Juana was unable to release the necessary money and Ferdinand continued to propose that Catherine return home if Henry found their current terms unsatisfactory. Through 1508, the marriage was again being discussed as a certainty, yet Henry was still delaying in order to consider a marriage for his son to Eleanor of Austria. Time, however, was not on his side. The following February, ill health meant he was unable to complete his habitual journey to commemorate his wife at Westminster although he did give alms to a woman who lay in child bed, on the sixth anniversary of Elizabeth's death. At the end of February, aware of his deteriorating condition, he retired to Richmond Palace and shut himself away in his private chambers. Few people were allowed access and he died that April, possibly of tuberculosis. When the news reached Catherine, she must have been exhilarated and terrified at the possibilities the next reign might offer her.

Less than three months later, the pauper princess was a married woman, heading to her coronation. The wheel of fortune had carried her from the penury and dependence of her widowhood, up to the centre of the dazzling new court and the role she had been born to fulfil. Now, eight years after arriving in the country, its crown would finally be placed upon her head. That Saturday in late June was bright and clear: all London turned out to see the procession and pageantry of their new king and queen, dazzled by the display of precious gems and magnificent fabrics, as well as the youth and beauty of their new rulers. The colouring of Catherine's train emphasised her newly reinstated regality and purity. She wore white embroidered satin and her long auburn hair fell loose to her waist from beneath the coronet set with oriental stones. Two white palfreys dressed in white cloth of gold bore the covered litter, in which she sat, through the London streets hung with tapestries and cloth of gold, from the Tower to Westminster Palace. Her retinue rode similar beasts, attired in gold, cloth of silver, tinsel and velvet; scarlet and red cloth, silk, green and white cloth and other clothing 'necessaries' to equip 160 of the king's officials alone had cost over £4,700. The loyal waiting women, who had served the princess through her years of penury, rode in a splendid chariot and wore the regal cloth of gold, anticipating the feasting and jousting that would fill the long hours of the midsummer night. Ahead of Catherine rode her husband of two weeks, her former brother-in-law, Henry VIII. The ten-year-old boy who had given her away in marriage to Arthur had grown into an impressive young man. Tall, strong and handsome, he was only days short of his eighteenth birthday and the chroniclers vied to outdo each other in the expression of his qualities. The 6-foot 2-inch king had inherited the auburn colouring of his Plantagenet forebears; he was clean shaven and wore his hair cut short and straight in the French style. Thomas More described the 'fiery power' of his eyes and 'twin roses' of his cheeks.[13] For their journey, he wore a cloak of crimson velvet, furred with ermine, a jacket of raised gold, embroidered with diamonds, rubies, emerald, pearls and other rich stones. His horse was dressed in damask gold and all the gentlemen of his retinue wore scarlet or crimson velvet. The following day, they were crowned together in Westminster Abbey and the last of

Catherine's long-cherished ambitions came true. It seemed that fortune had finally rewarded her patience.

The pair had been quietly married at Greenwich less than two weeks before, on 11 June. The palace had undergone significant change since Henry's birth there, as his father had undertaken a huge programme of rebuilding, between 1498 and 1504, resulting in a red-brick Burgundian-style complex around three great courtyards. The service itself was conducted in one of the queen's closets, possibly in the chapel royal: such closets were screened off from the body of the chapel to allow for privacy. What happened on their wedding day remains shrouded in secrecy. No record remains of the ceremonial proceedings, clothing or celebrations and certainly no formal, public bedding. With one exception, Henry was to be notoriously discreet about the arrangements of all his marriages. Only their words survive for posterity, prearranged a week in advance. Archbishop of Canterbury William Warham asked the king whether he would 'fulfil the treaty of marriage concluded by your father ... and the parents of the Princess of Wales ... and, as the Pope has dispensed with this marriage, to take the Princess who is here present for your lawful wife?'[14] Henry replied that he would. The contrast with Catherine's first wedding, eight years before, could hardly have been more pronounced and perhaps this was Henry's point. He wanted to distance himself from the medieval protocol and practices of his father. Days before the match, already at Greenwich, Catherine had officially renounced her dowry of 200,000 crowns in favour of Henry, drawing a line under the political and financial struggles of the past few years.

Various theories have been put forward to explain the sudden, secret marriage. Henry may have been fulfilling his dying father's last wish, as he wrote to Margaret of Savoy, by maintaining the union with Spain or additionally, preventing her leaving the country with such a large sum of money, although she had hardly benefited from it. In July, Henry explained to Cardinal Sixtus de Ruvere that the 'high virtues' of the princess had influenced his decision and Catherine's coronation had caused 'incredible demonstrations of joy and enthusiasm'; to Ferdinand, he wrote that 'if he were still free he would choose her in preference to all others'. Writing with hindsight, chronicler Edward Hall contradicts this and rewrites earlier events, suggesting the young king was wrongly urged to it by his counsellors, without true knowledge of the 'word of God' and that there were 'murmurings' against the marriage from the start. In fact, Henry's true motives were probably less than mercenary. The new king was a romantic at heart. His notions of chivalry and romance may have been stirred by the plight of the impoverished yet beautiful young infanta whom his father had treated so badly: just like his renouncement of his father's hated tax collectors Empson and Dudley, this may have been a belated moment of filial rebellion. Also, the match was convenient: the amorous new king wanted a wife and a suitable Spanish princess was on hand. Many indicators suggest he genuinely desired Catherine. The Pope had issued his dispensation and there were precedents of remarriage in families: two of Catherine's sisters, Isabella and Maria, had, in turn, been married to the same man; the second match was flourishing and had produced many children. There was no reason to suspect the new royal pair would be less than fruitful.

The wedding night would have been spent in the five-storey royal apartment block, overlooking the surrounding gardens, orchards and river. The recent improvements of 1502–04 had been designed by Elizabeth of York, who had been very fond of the palace, and included new walls, gardens, gallery, kitchen and tower, as well as fresh painting. Catherine would have been lodged in the queen's chambers that formed an 'L' shape, at right angles to Henry's, which sat parallel to the Thames. Provision for her household indicated that thirty-three women were employed in her service, comprising countesses, baronesses, knights' wives and gentlewomen, including an Elizabeth Boleyn, Henry's future mother-in-law, to advise and prepare her in her new role. A select few would have carefully dressed her and assisted her into bed to await her new husband, although the ceremonial aspects of her 1501 bedding; the music and voidee and blessing of the sheets with holy water may have been lacking. Leaving Catherine in the marital bed, her ladies tactfully withdrew. If, as she asserted with such conviction in later life, she had retained her virginity despite her union with Arthur, Catherine must have finally anticipated becoming a wife in the full sense, as her lusty young husband entered the chamber. The cloistered nature of the young king's upbringing meant it was unlikely that Henry had had the opportunity for any sort of sexual experience, yet it appears that the marriage was consummated quickly and fully. Whatever was lacking in experience was made up in enthusiasm; by later accounts, their physical relationship was a consistent success through the early years of their marriage. There was no recorded public display of bloodstained sheets the following morning, although this barbaric custom was becoming less practised and was not in keeping with the privacy and quietness of the ceremony. In spite of her years of penury, Catherine's youth was a significant factor in her fertility and by the time of her coronation on Midsummer's Day, the new queen may have already fallen pregnant.

The young couple were delighted that Catherine had conceived so promptly after the marriage. She had fulfilled the promise of her heraldic device, the Spanish pomegranate, an ancient image of abundance found in many Renaissance images of the Virgin and child. The couple's obvious fecundity appeared to validate the royal union and, by extension, the Tudor dynasty: there was no reason to doubt that the family would continue to expand, following the example of the previous generation. Elizabeth of York had come from a prolific family and Catherine's siblings had proved themselves fertile. The pregnancy was announced in November 1509, five months after the marriage, around the time of her quickening. Henry eagerly ordered preparations for the cradle and nursery. Her father Ferdinand, who had lost three stillborn children and a daughter in childbirth, urged her to take especial care as it was her first; she should avoid all physical activity, as even writing could tire her. But all progressed well; the child moved in her womb, her dresses were unlaced and preparations were begun for the lying-in at Greenwich. Orders were given for a birthing or 'groaning' chair and a copper gilt bowl to receive the blood and placenta; the silver font was to be sent from Canterbury Cathedral; sheets, cushions and linen arrived by the cartload along with a predictable host of prophets, apothecaries and astrologers. In mid-January the royal couple arrived, amid much pomp and excitement, to await the delivery that March. However, at seven months, Catherine experienced 'only a little pain in her knee', before going into labour, according to her confessor Fray Diego.

Other accounts list that she suffered such 'agonising pains' that she vowed to donate her headdress to the Spanish shrine of St Peter the martyr. On 31 January, she was delivered of a stillborn girl. That was when the confusion began.

In spite of the miscarriage, the queen's belly remained swollen, convincing her advisers that she had been expecting twins and was still carrying one remaining, viable foetus. Such a scenario was not impossible but seemed increasingly unlikely after the reappearance of Catherine's intermittent periods. The swelling was probably the result of some infection or pseudocyesis, a phantom pregnancy, yet the couple's gynaecological naivety and desire for an heir afforded them hope. Whatever Catherine's personal doubts may have been, optimism and professional misdiagnosis helped convince the queen that she was, in fact, entering the final trimester of a pregnancy. Henry's medical advisers at the time included a William Adderston and the 'sage docteur' John Chaunte, as well as an Anne Luke, who had nursed him in his infancy and may have been standing by to assist with the new arrival; earlier she had been awarded an annuity of £20 a year for life and was clearly a valued servant, so her advice would have been trusted. Catherine's last public appearance was Shrove Tuesday; at the end of February the court moved to Greenwich and preparations were made for equipping the royal nursery. Henry ordered red cloth and ribbon, linen and Holland cloth to dress the Canterbury font for the child's baptism, and the whole court ritual of confinement went into motion, according to Margaret Beaufort's Ordinances. The royal cradle of estate was relined with crimson cloth of gold and the pommels repainted to incorporate the queen's coat of arms.

Catherine went into confinement in the first half of March, in a formal procession that ended in the voidee of wine and spices, prayers and blessings. The doors closed. Weeks passed. The ladies waited. Perhaps they tried certain remedies to bring on her long overdue labour: a woman in her ninth month might resort to drinking mixtures made from leek, ale and wine, rue and savin or she may pace up and down her chamber, in the hope that the motion would set off her contractions. For Catherine, nothing worked. When no child appeared and her bloated stomach began to deflate, the couple were deeply embarrassed and initially kept their failure a secret. It was a personal and political humiliation; the king's councillors were 'vexed' and the news had to be delicately put to the nation and foreign ambassadors. Catherine's ladies were blamed for misleading her, but worse, rumours began to circulate about her ability to bear children. Spanish Ambassador Luis Caroz believed her failure to conceive had been caused by irregular menstruation and advised the queen to change her diet. Catherine's chancellor Fray Diego claimed that only the king, two Spanish women, and her physician knew about it but as the weeks passed, the facts could not be denied: eventually she wrote to her father in May, stating she had just miscarried. Catherine was so embarrassed that she did not re-emerge into court life until the end of that month, at least ten weeks since her confinement.

Catherine's letter to her father indicates her sexual naivety. Its details were only recently made known, as Spanish archivists hid them from Victorian researchers, keen to preserve the queen's image. Some modern historians have interpreted this as a straightforward act of deception on her part, while others have seen it as proof of her extreme innocence. To suggest she planned the whole process, deceived the court, kingdom and her husband is probably to accredit her with a sophistication and Machiavellianism far beyond her years and experience, also it denies the serious embarrassment she felt as a result of the mistake becoming known, to the extent that she removed herself from the public eye for an additional month. At worst, Catherine told her father a lie by omission, when she only confessed to her miscarriage four months after the event: 'because it was considered here an ill omen'.[15] It may seem incredible to a reader in the modern age that such basic mistakes could occur, but to a sexually inexperienced Tudor couple, desirous of a child, the workings and anatomy of the female body could give rise to misunderstanding. The subjective and imprecise nature of gynaecological understanding meant that doctors, physicians and midwives, often in conflict and unregulated, could join with astrologers, prophets and astronomers to diagnose and predict exactly what a royal couple wanted to hear. It was an easy matter to tell a king he was expecting a son; less easy to inform him he was mistaken. Even if some had suspected the truth, it would have been a brave doctor who would have dared contradict the couple.

Given the difficulties of diagnosis, many other such mistakes must have been regularly made. By 1612, a French royal doctor wrote that there was nothing so ridiculous as to assure a woman she was with child when her stomach was actually bloated with water or wind, but this advice came a century too late for Catherine. In the light of what happened with her first pregnancy, Henry's personal interest in medicine and the degree of controversy that already surrounded the female secrecy of the birth chamber, it is unsurprising that the king took steps to regulate the industry, resulting in the establishment of the all-male Royal College of Physicians in 1518. Female specialists would remain unregulated for another fifty years.

No doubt Catherine would have had a number of knowledgeable, high-ranking women at her bedside, yet they would not necessarily have practised as midwives. The word derives from an Anglo-Saxon term meaning 'with-woman', like the Latin *obstetrix*, literally, a 'woman who stood before'. Historically, the reception of midwives and medical women has varied, with some societies and civilisations welcoming their abilities and supporting their practice, while others treated them with suspicion. Notable among the success stories are the second-century Greco-Roman Aspasia, whose foreign status allowed her a degree of freedom; the eleventh-century Trotula of Salerno, author of a gynaecological text, *De Mulierum Passionibus*; Cecilia of Oxford, Surgeon to Philippa, wife of Edward III; and Jacobina Felice, an Italian Jewess practising in Paris in the 1320s. Even in the most tolerant climates, medical women were often considered suspect; Felice won her right to continue working after the testimonials of leading noblemen overturned objections by the Paris Faculty of Medicine, who had previously denied her a license. Hyginus' *Fables*, transcribed in 1535, told of an Athenian woman named Agnodice who practised medicine disguised as a man, until jealous competitors accused her of seducing her patients, whereupon she disclosed her secret. She was condemned to death for her law-breaking but was saved by the testimonials of women she had assisted, bringing about a change in the law.[16] Whatever era they practised in, certain qualities were desirable in a woman attending a birth. Frenchman Jacques Guillemeau's 1612 'Happy Delivery of Women' stated that a midwife should be of middle age, not too young or old, not diseased or deformed, neat in appearance with little hands and nails cut short; she must not wear rings or bracelets when at work. In manner, she should be cheerful, strong, merry, 'painfull' (taking pains) and accustomed to labour, well able to spend two or three nights watching with an expectant woman. Her qualities must include patience, politeness and gentleness: she should respect nature and work with it and not be proud, nor a blabber and should not report anything she may see or hear in the birth chamber, excepting in the case of sexual and moral transgressions. This was particularly important in the case of queens and the royal succession.

The role of the midwife was complex and emotive. Women had little choice but to put their trust in such assistants, literally putting their lives in their hands. Trusted midwives were clearly prized and received recompense for their efforts, like the woman who successfully delivered a son at Longleat House in 1560, who received 40s for her trouble. Others were recommended by word of mouth, tending to members of the same family and their friends. Their reputations quickly spread. William Howard of Reigate wrote to Sir William More in 1576, regretting that the midwife who had attended his wife and baby son could not be spared for his daughter-in-law, as she was required by Lady Sidney, who was soon to visit. Oral social networks could be used to denounce careless practitioners, like the Mrs Buckland who a John Genifer claimed, in 1601, was not fit to bring a dog to bed, much less a woman. Equally, the midwife could be a figure of moral dread to an unmarried mother, playing an increasingly central role in court paternity examinations and the report of illegitimate births such as the 1573 labour of Agnes Hollway in Canterbury, which was reported to the ecclesiastical court, and the 1578 bastardy case of Sussex midwife Denise Clarke. Labouring mothers were considered vulnerable to supernatural influences as they lay hovering on the margin of life and death and in Catholic eyes, midwives were uniquely placed to exploit this. Clergymen worried about the use charms and old practices associated with witchcraft, magic and Pagan rites, suspecting them of making extra money by supplying witches with the spoils of the birth for their cauldrons; the caul, placenta and umbilical cord, even body parts, like Shakespeare's 'finger of birth-strangled babe', delivered in a ditch. Cauls were thought to prevent death by drowning so were particularly sought after by sailors. Controversial or inept as some midwives were, not to ask for help could lead a woman into far worse trouble; concealing a pregnancy was against the law and in the event of infant death, a woman could be left vulnerable. In May 1583, Parnell Richarde, a servant from Frinton, was found guilty of delivering a female child alone, which died through her negligence in not asking for the assistance of women. Worse still were attempted deals with midwives, struck by desperate women such as Agnes Bowker in January 1569, whose dead child was bizarrely substituted for a skinned cat with collusion from her midwife. In later centuries, the presence of bystanders in the delivery room was considered essential to prevent the smuggling in of a baby during the phantom, faked or failed pregnancy of untrusted royalty.

Catherine was lucky in that she need not concern herself with practical arrangements. She knew her every need would be catered for in the lying-in chamber. In many cases, though, the role would be determined by area and chance. Not all women had the luxury of choice, especially those in the lowest orders, such as servants or vagrants. Often the office would be performed by whichever females were to hand, especially in the delivery of the poor or those far from home. Some developed a particular reputation and were repeatedly called for; on other occasions, dependent on circumstance, delivery was assisted by the best available alternative. It might have been a neighbour, friend, relative or local woman who had experience in the field; in some cases, though, the resulting debt to the community could be a factor. In October 1593, a woman making 'casual passage' through the 'very poor' Essex parish of Ardleigh had lodged there for two nights, during which time she gave birth. Out of charity, the residents assisted her 'who otherwise with her child might have utterly perished' but then found themselves supporting both, unwilling for the baby to be 'severed from the sucking brestes'.[17] A similar story occurred in the village a decade later, when the village acted to prevent responsibility falling on its shoulders again. Three 'rogue' women with pedlar's packs stayed for two days and nights in an unlicensed alehouse. Perhaps they had been selling wares to pilgrims or travelling between key towns and religious sites to ply their trade. When one of them went into labour late one evening, they were thrown out into the street and looked about for a house to rent so that the child might be born there safely. The constables intervened, carrying the three in a cart to the house of an honest farmer in the next parish of St Botolph, within the district of Colchester. However, the farmer refused to take them in, asking by what warrant the constables brought them, and the constables refused to return them to Ardleigh, so the women were dumped at his door in the pouring rain. Out of pity he let them lie in his barn that night, where the labouring woman delivered her child. They remained in the barn for seven or eight days and then disappeared, abandoning the baby in the nearby parish of Langham. Despite the efforts of the constables, the Justices ruled that the parish of Ardleigh should support the infant until the mother could be located.[18] The prospect for women giving birth in poverty was grim.

Midwives were a frequent, obvious scapegoat for medical men although some of their criticism was clearly deserved. Early midwifery was not regulated; the job description did not imply training, qualifications or social acceptance. The fourteenth-century John of Mirfield complained of 'worthless and presumptuous women who usurp this profession to themselves and abuse it; who, possessing neither natural ability nor professional knowledge, make the greatest possible mistakes and very often kill their patients'. The authors of Tudor and Stuart pamphlets were rarely friends of the profession; a 1632 ballad described a 'constant wife of Sussex', whose midwife suggested she substitute the baby girl she had just delivered for a male child, to save her husband's shame, while another pamphlet told the story of a murdering midwife, whose secret was betrayed by the apparitions of her victims which rose to haunt her house: 'desiring midwives to take heed, how they dispose their bastard-breed.'[19] Other seventeenth-century broadsheets presented midwives as 'the worst of Women-kind' who murdered 'sweet infants from their mother's womb'[20] and others guilty of various barbarous acts of cruelty; to fan the flames even more, some were based on true tales of baby-farmers, lured into the profession in anticipation of easy financial gain. Other scare stories had them tightly swaddling newborns to conceal birth defects as well as drinking and neglecting their charges, often at the cost of their lives. While there were cases of abuse, the successful and popular midwives were scarcely lauded in any comparable way. While popular pamphlets and songs would have been passed on by word of mouth, actual medical texts would have had little circulation among those women practising their own brand of medicine.

Midwives were also excluded from the profession through illiteracy. The intimate details of their private lives rarely went recorded: their stories emerge at points of conflict and social transgression or as edited marginalia in the lives of husbands, fathers and sons. Although female education among the upper classes spread with mid-century reforms to faith, the poor survival of texts such as letters and diaries is a sign of the low general priority given to women's literacy. David Cressy has estimated that in 1500, only 1 per cent of women could sign their names, rising to 5 per cent in 1558 and 8 per cent in 1600.[21] In some cases, a few literate women may have read male-authored medical texts owned by their husbands, fathers and brothers. London accounts list some female medical practitioners as the wives of licensed doctors. If such works were available to them, through legitimate means or not, the information they found may well have been at odds with the experiences of the female community.

Possibly the most influential birth manual of the century was produced by a German doctor, Eucharius Rosslin, in 1513. His *Rose Garden for Pregnant Women and Midwives* addressed a contemporary gap in the market, drawing on his own observations and common sense, to become the standard midwifery text. Rosslin was an apothecary in Freiburg, attending to royalty and the nobility but also overseeing practices in the town, which dismayed him in their carelessness and poor standards, resulting in unnecessarily high infant and maternal mortality. He incorporated classical writings, emphasised the importance of the male in reproduction and urged midwives to be patient and gentle, threatening that God would call them to account. His manual was significant for its descriptions of the use of the birthing stool, covered with cloths for comfort, and the emphasis on positive thinking, the 'sweet words' to give the mother 'hope of a good speedie deliverance'. The first English edition was translated by Thomas Raynalde as *The Birth of Mankynde* and dedicated to the short-lived Catherine Howard, fifth wife of Henry VIII, in 1540. An anonymous treaty named *The Knowing of Woman's Kind in Childing* was already extant and clearly aimed at a male audience, while a third important manual, *The Expert Midwife*, by Swiss Jacob Rueff, appeared in 1554, in Latin and German, building on much of Rosslin's work. While an English edition was not available until 1637, it would have been accessible to a learned elite and summarised much existing practice. This publication has been identified as marking a transitional period between the confinement of female remedies to the domestic sphere and the development of gynaecology as an increasingly masculine discipline. Rueff addressed different parts of his manuscript to men and women separately, indicating that women were expected to be the ones involved in the birth process while men were excluded from touching the female genitalia and must rely instead upon surgical instruments.[22] The full and detailed *Happie Delivery of Women* by Jacques Guillemeau would be published in London, in English, in 1612, marking a further shift away from the herbal and superstitious towards the theoretical and physiological. At the time of Catherine of Aragon's pregnancy confusion, however, none of this material was yet accessible to those advising her.

By the end of May 1510, as she emerged to face the shame of her mistake, Catherine was genuinely pregnant again. She must have conceived during her period of confinement or very soon after. According to the Catholic practice of churching, sexual relations between husband and wife should not be resumed until she had emerged from her chamber and been purified; of course, the confusion over her pregnancy invalidated this and the pair may have attempted conception in response to the failed appearance of any child. Equally, there may have been a second reason for Catherine's eagerness to invite Henry back into her bedroom: it appeared that, less than a year after her wedding, she had a rival for his affections. Distressingly for her, while she had been closeted at

Greenwich awaiting the child that did not come, Henry's attention had strayed to the younger sister of the Duke of Buckingham, the married Anne Hastings. The affair had been conducted under the pretence that the wooing was on behalf of Henry's Groom of the Stool, William Compton: from 1519, he certainly lived in an adulterous union with her and probably did procure women for Henry to visit at Compton's home in Thames Street. Between them, Buckingham and Hastings removed the king's paramour from court but the incident sparked the first argument between Henry and Catherine. The queen may have first heard of the incident when an angry Henry ordered her to dismiss Elizabeth Fitzwalter, Anne's sister, one of her favourite waiting women, who had first raised the alarm. Although Henry considered it was little more than a timely dalliance, Catherine was wounded by the quarrel and the breach was visible to the whole court. Yet the queen held the trump card. She was pregnant again.

Catherine was still deeply embarrassed and ashamed by her previous experience. No doubt she approached the possibility of pregnancy with caution this time, waiting until she was certain before making any sort of announcement. In the meantime, she rested and relinquished unnecessary journeys and risks; that summer she stayed in the relative peace and safety of Eltham Palace and did not accompany Henry on his annual progress. Chastened by recent memories, the couple took especial care with Catherine's welfare, ordering the best available food and medical advice. Constipation was a recognised side effect of pregnancy and expectant mothers were advised to eat spinach mixed with butter. If this failed, they might use 'suppositors' made of honey and egg yolk, or Venice soap; the last eventuality was the prescription of a 'decoction' of senna leaves by a medical practitioner. She would have tried not to exert herself at all, taken lots of rest and avoided the extremes of thought and emotion as dictated by custom. The precautions proved successful. Her second confinement took place at Richmond in December 1510, where the court had moved that autumn. A suite of rooms were prepared on the first floor, overlooking the gardens and river. Following a special Communion service to prepare her for the process, she was led in ceremony through the palace to the specially prepared quarters on the first floor, staffed only by women. Again, the chambers were hung with rich tapestries, lined with carpets and scattered with cushions: no expense was spared for her comfort: an 8-foot by 8-foot bed dominated the room, dressed in rich material lined with fur. She also had a simpler pallet stuffed with wool and down, encased in Brussels cloth. Her linen had been prepared long in advance; fine robes and petticoats, cloaks and necessaries to keep her warm and comfortable, as well as clothing, swaddling bands, pads and blankets for the child. A cradle of estate, large enough to hold a full-grown man, sat beside a smaller crib, showing the contrast between ceremony and the practicalities of sleep. The traditional single window was left uncovered, allowing for the view south over a walled garden, down to the Thames. A wet nurse was on hand, as were other experienced women and the future godparents, while the gentlemen of Henry's chapel prayed constantly for her success and recovery. Her ladies may have rubbed her belly with powders made of cumin seeds, date stones, dried saffron and white amber to soothe her pains. One religious ritual that may have appealed to Catherine was the laying on her belly of a cross, which may have given her a point of focus to calm her and channel the pain. This time, her hopes and preparations were well founded. In the early hours of the morning of New Year's Day, 1511, Catherine was delivered of a son, whom they named Henry. The little boy would have been washed gently in a mixture of wine and herbs, swaddled and laid in the cradle, while Catherine began the slow period of recovery. She had done her duty. England had its prince.

When the news was proclaimed, London went into celebration. Days of public rejoicing and partying followed, with bells ringing, wine flowing, cannon at the Tower booming and bonfires burning in the streets. Catherine lay-in for at least three weeks as custom dictated, and therefore did not attend the elaborate christening four days later, when the processional route to the chapel of the Observant Friars was newly gravelled, strewn with rushes and hung with arras. The child was wrapped warmly and carried in procession under a canopy with great ceremony to be anointed at the font. Expensive gifts were given to Elizabeth Poyntz, the wet nurse, and the French king Louis XII, the child's godfather, rewarded the midwife handsomely. Very quickly, the little prince was established as a separate being from his mother. His own large household contained a daily carver, sewer, usher, gentlemen of the chamber, chaplains, waiters, grooms, men of the counting house, bakehouse, pantry, buttery, cellar, kitchen hands, almoners and clerks: forty-four men were named in the inventory of his household, not including nurses, four cradle rockers and women, overseen by Elizabeth Denton. Yeomen oversaw the meals of his wet nurse, testing each dish for poison, lest it be passed on to the child through her milk. Magnificent jousts, pageants, feasts and tournaments followed, on 12–13 February at Westminster. A special gallery was built for Catherine and her ladies to watch the proceedings; she was clearly up by then, churched, and had recovered enough to travel up from Richmond. No expense was spared; only the Field of Cloth of Gold would exceed it as a celebration during Henry's reign. Elaborate pageants were played out before Catherine in the tilt yard, as she sat in rich furs beside burning braziers to keep out the February cold. Henry famously took the role of Sir Loyal Heart, wearing his wife's initials embroidered everywhere. The day ended with feasting in the White Hall at Westminster, followed by music, dancing and celebrations. Yet the king had not forgotten to whom he owed his happiness. In contrast to the court festivities, Henry undertook a pilgrimage to Walsingham to give thanks to the Virgin Mary for the safe arrival of their son: finally God had favoured his marriage.

4

Catherine of Aragon
& Mary
1511–1518

Saints, Pilgrimage & Infant Mortality

*Kind virgin of virgins, holy mother of God, be present
on behalf of thy devoted handmaidens their earnest prayers
to the Son, thou art the benign assister of women in travail.*[1]

Soon after the arrival of Prince Henry, the king went on pilgrimage
to the Shrine of Our Lady at Walsingham. As devout Catholics,
Catherine and Henry, in common with the majority of their
subjects, believed in the healing and protective power of saintly
intervention; donations, prayers, offerings and visits to their shrine
were one way the Tudors might seek to influence their health,
wealth and destinies. Walsingham was by far the most popular of
many locations associated with fertility, pregnancy and childbirth,
and formed the centre of the East Anglian cult of the Virgin Mary. It
had been founded in 1061 by Richeldis de Faverches, widow of the
Lord of the Manor of Walsingham, following three visions which
had taken her, in spirit, to Nazareth and the house of Mary, at the
time of her visitation by the angel Gabriel. The Norfolk chapel had
apparently been miraculously constructed, while Richeldis kept a
vigil of prayer and came to be known as the English Nazareth.
In 1150, a priory was constructed beside it and royal patronage
increased its popularity to the extent that the value of the jewels
and offerings before the shrine was so great by 1346 that it needed
to be locked overnight. Walsingham was a favourite destination
for Henry VIII in the first decades of his reign; after around 1520,
he would stay at nearby Barsham Manor and walk the 2-mile
journey to the shrine barefoot before dedicating some rich token

of his esteem: a jewel, money, or once, a gold circlet for the neck of the statue of Mary. Henry's devotion to the cult was profound, in spite of the lengths he would later go to destroy its trappings; during these early years, he frequently visited shrines dedicated to her across the country, leaving notable offerings at our Lady in the Tower at Coventry in 1511, Ipswich in 1522, Prinknash in 1535 and Lincoln as late as 1541. With Catherine convalescing back in London, Henry rode enthusiastically to give thanks to God and 'all the heavenly saints', for blessing them with a son and heir.

The saints, especially Mary and others associated with childbirth, would have formed a significant element of a Catholic queen's lying-in. Elizabeth of York's chamber had contained a magnificent reliquary and among Catherine's possessions were talismen and icons, from which she must have drawn strength during her labours. Included in a later list of artefacts that accompanied her on her travels were pictures of the Virgin Mary and her mother, St Anne; an ivory diptych depicting Mary and the infant Christ, and an image of a queen petitioning Our Lady and St Elizabeth, who had supposedly given birth to John the Baptist after her menopause.[2] The stories of saints' lives, or hagiographies, would have been accessible on some level, written or oral, in many Tudor communities and women of all classes would offer their prayers, promises and undertake pilgrimages for a range of fertility, gynaecological and childbearing issues. Given the regular Catholic observation of saints' days and instances of popular customs and literature on the topic, it is possible that most women carried some sort of mental list of which saint went with which ailment, or else they knew a woman who did. *The Golden Legend*, a compilation of saints' Lives by a thirteenth-century archbishop of Genoa, was translated into English by William Caxton in 1483 and reissued at least seven times before 1538, but a robust oral tradition would have kept such stories in circulation among the illiterate. The saints were not distant in pre-Reformation days; they were very real, active companions to daily life, influencing ritual and custom as well as determining fortunes for good or ill, rather like the fairy godmothers of children's literature. The private, personal intimacy between supplicant and saint made them as relevant and real to everyday trials as conversations with friends and family. The image or icon of the saint gave them the necessary human face and their relics and associated locations were also charged with divine qualities: they were imbued with life and could transmit it to the sick and suffering. Nor did Mary have the monopoly on cures; there were hundreds of saints with whom the supplicant could establish direct communication, on almost every aspect of life, transcending temporal, class and physical boundaries. The fourteenth-century St Bride had brought a child back to life; Saint Anne, the mother of Mary, could intercede for infertile women and St Margaret of Antioch assisted those who were pregnant and labouring; her name was the most frequently mentioned in women's wills in Norwich from the fourteenth century up to the Reformation and, at the height of her fame, over 200 churches nationally bore her dedication. St Clare could help heal the eyes, St Agatha soothed sore breasts, St Felicitas could ensure an unborn child was male, while the aptly named St Uncumber could rid a woman of an unwanted husband in exchange for a gift of oats. St Catherine's chapel at Abbotsbury in Dorset attracted women requesting a husband and on St Agnes' Eve young women would ask the saint to show them their future spouses in a dream. Communication with the saints was one way of levelling social inequality, as was the intermingling of travellers on pilgrimage.

By the advent of Henry VIII, the shrines dotted across the country, particularly those dedicated to the Virgin Mary, were particularly favoured by women at crucial stages of their reproductive lives. In 1443, Margaret Paston undertook a pilgrimage to Walsingham to supplicate Our Lady for a cure for her husband's illness; during the pain of labour, Margaret of Hamilton vowed to visit Canterbury and give thanks for a safe delivery; the barren wife of William of Lincoln travelled to Canterbury and afterwards was fruitful, while one infertile woman supposedly gave birth to a piece of 'dead flesh' which turned into a child after prayers were offered to Our Lady. Across Europe, relics of Mary's clothing, hair, milk, slippers, wedding ring and even nail clippings could be viewed. At a shrine in Thetford, it was reported that the Virgin had revived a deceased child and according to Benedict of Peterborough, St Thomas of Canterbury could transmute water into milk. Nor was pilgrimage a one-off; it formed a regular part of Catholic life. Even as late as 1538, 500 or 600 pilgrims a day visited the shrine of St Asaph in Flintshire, and the shrine to Our Lady at King's Lynn was so popular that a double staircase had to be installed to deal with the vast numbers of visitors. No doubt sufferers made repeat visits in the hope of easing pain; the panacea of the pilgrimage process may well have brought psychological and, consequently, real physical relief. Some shrines were known for curative specialisms, usually determined by the saint to whom they were dedicated: two thirds of the visitors to that of Godric of Finchale near Durham and St Frideswide in Oxford were female. Promising health and wholesomeness in uncertain times, pilgrimage, with all its attendant psychological stages, lay at the heart of English devotional culture.

Pilgrimage was particularly important for women. It empowered them in a world where they could exercise little or no control over their fertility and were exposed to the very real possibility of death in childbirth. The devotional but active nature of pilgrimage – planning, often lengthy travel and absence from home – could be a comfort for those under pressure to conceive as well as a distraction from their suffering. Motivation could be found at all stages of the reproductive cycle: conception, safe pregnancy, quickening, delivery, avoidance of pain, to grow a healthy child, to expel a dead foetus, for milk supply, help with post-partum pain and a speedy recovery. Women experiencing deep joy following conception or delivery must have knelt to give thanks alongside those suffering the pains of loss and infertility. Particular centres catered to this ever-growing market, like the 1180 shrine to St Frideswide of Oxford, where women were cured of headaches and sleeplessness, as well as sexual ailments. Further afield, Rachel's tomb on the road to Bethlehem was a regular stopping point for those asking for assistance in marriage, pregnancy and birth: as was often the case, ritualised physical contact was particularly important, with women adorning the tomb with red string, which was then worn as a fertility aid. Important shrines were the holding places of the holy relics loaned out to royal and aristocratic women in childbirth: the girdle used by Catherine of Aragon from Westminster was one of an army of holy items: Bath Abbey, Rievaulx, Newburg, York, Kelham, Haltemprise, Basedale,

Bromholm and Thetford were among other places boasting girdles as well as combs, garments, images and ampullae of water or blood and bone fragments. Mary's milk and part of her churching candle were venerated at Shelford, and Kaldham housed the finger of St Stephen, which labouring women liked to hold. In Burton-on-Trent, women leaned on the staff of St Modwena; at Grace Dieu Monialium, part of the tunic of St Francis was loaned out, as was the shirt of St Thomas at Derby. Badges brought back as souvenirs from the Marian shrines would have been used as charms against pain and suffering of all varieties and lent or bequeathed to daughters, sisters and friends in labour. Wax discs or Agnus Dei, badges and crosses could be clasped in the hand, while ribbons were tied about the wrist, thigh or waist of a labouring woman. The souvenirs of recent and long-remembered journeys must have been present in many bedchambers to comfort the labouring, dying, unhappy and unwell. Pilgrims did not just bring home souvenirs: they left offerings too. Displays of wealth were considered directly proportional to degrees of devotion, although humble offerings might realistically represent the same percentage of income as more ostentatious gifts; while poor women might leave valuable eggs, medicinal herbs and milk, noble and aristocratic ladies could endow shrines with riches, such as the jewels and twenty-pound crown of gold bequeathed by Isabel Beauchamp to Our Lady of Caversham in 1439. It must be significant that many of the traditional herbs offered before the Virgin, including bunches of periwinkle, verbena and thyme to be blessed and kept throughout the year, also found their way into potions and balms for aiding reproduction and birth.

As Henry approached the shrine at Walsingham, he was entering a dazzling world. Only a year later, in 1512, the visiting Dutch humanist Erasmus described it as surrounded on all sides with gold, silver and gems, shining brilliantly. For the majority of the visitors, it must have been an intense, incomparable experience, with sculpture, painted glass and colourful altar pieces besides all the usual theatre and paraphernalia of an internationally renowned shrine. Somewhere among it all were the prized phials of what was claimed to be the Virgin's milk. Mary's statue was draped in fine silk set with precious stones, with a lace veil edged in pearls, gold and silver. The additional theatricality of blazing lights must have exaggerated the spectacle and associated these earthly offerings with metaphors of divine light and the revelation and salvation it promised. The piles of attendant jewels, gold and rich fabrics were a contemporary shorthand for spiritual wealth, a reassurance of the long-standing history and authenticity of this form of worship, as well as an indication of the saints' rates of success as healers. A saint with many offerings suggested a high success rate. One contemporary description of the tomb of St Thomas in Canterbury Cathedral gives some idea of just how dazzling the experience must have been as the culmination of weeks, or even months, on the road. The ritual of approach, supplication and departure was a carefully controlled piece of theatre; behind an altar at the top of steps, a wooden canopy could be raised and lowered to reveal a stone plinth, through the open archway of which was revealed a tantalising but brief glimpse of St Thomas' reliquary. This was a casket covered in gold plate, studded with gems, covered with gifts given by visiting kings, past and present. Describing it in 1512, Erasmus wrote, 'the last valuable portion was of gold but every part glistened, shone and sparkled with rare and very large jewels, some of them larger than a goose's egg.'[3] Shrines themselves were a complex multi-sensory display of light, sound, statues, glass, wall painting, prayers, music, water, incense, procession and crowds. Many pilgrims approached on hands and knees, while silver bells tinkled, incense wafted and the prior indicated the precious gifts with a white wand. Surrounding taverns and inns would have resounded with the tales of successful interventions, like one Canterbury woman who spent a day and night in labour after the arm of her foetus swelled and would not be expelled despite all the midwives' efforts; eventually the child turned and was born normally, through the intervention of St Thomas. Stories like this engendered hope in the pilgrims; everyone believed their own miracle was possible. For Henry and Catherine, God had given his seal of approval to their marriage and the new reign: all their hopes were centred on the tiny boy that lay at Richmond.

Then tragedy struck and the child died. He was only two months old. At the end of February, provision was made for his burial, with lengths of black cloth for gowns and banners, wax candles and torches ordered for the solemn procession at Westminster. The grief of the new parents was intense, to the extent that well-wishers and mourners were advised not to offer condolences, for risk of stimulating their pain afresh. The divine blessing briefly extended to their union and the dynasty had been cruelly snatched away; the question they could not avoid was whether they somehow displeased God. Chronicler Edward Hall described the queen's reaction as a 'natural woman' who made 'muche lamentation', while Henry tried his best to comfort her with the notion that it was God's will: according to Catholic doctrine, excessive grief was a criticism of the divine plan and would anger God further. Loss did not drive Henry and Catherine apart; it united them in their desire for another child and by the September of that year, rumours were circulating court that another heir was expected. This was probably a false alarm, brought on by the queen's amenorrhoea or wishful thinking, reinforcing contemporary uncertainties of conception and the workings of the female body. It is unlikely that Catherine would have resorted to one of the popular superstitions or customs for a woman who had borne a dead child. Custom suggested she take some earth from its grave, wrap it in black cloth and sell it to a merchant, after which her fertility would be restored and future children protected. The queen's method of choice would have been prayer and religious ritual. In the end, though, two more years would pass before another child was successfully conceived.

Catherine became pregnant again in the spring of 1513. It was an eventful year, with Henry fighting in France, leaving her, as regent, to deal with the Scottish invasion that would culminate in the Battle of Flodden Field. After the victory celebrations were over, she travelled to Walsingham to pray for a safe delivery, although ironically, this journey in addition to the strain of her regency overtired her and on 17 September, she delivered a son prematurely. Both the Venetian Di Favri and Imperial Ambassadors recorded that the little boy was born alive but died soon after birth. The event clearly took the couple by surprise as Henry was still in France; it is unlikely he would have planned to be away during the confinement; he arrived back in England that October to receive the bad news. Yet their meeting was so 'loving' that everyone witnessing it 'rejoiced': the couple did not abandon hope and within about six months, the queen had conceived again. By June 1514, her expanding belly left no room for doubt. She was observed by the Venetian envoy that August 'pregnant clad in ash coloured satin with chains and jewels and on her head a cap of gold'. They must have hoped and prayed that finally, this fourth child would be strong.

The failure of three pregnancies so far was not untypical for the time but it was an indicator that something might be wrong. It has been suggested in recent years that Catherine's disastrous gynaecological history might be due to her infection with syphilis,[4] with Henry exhibiting what could be interpreted as the secondary signs of the disease in rashes, sores and mood swings, but there is no evidence of Catherine suffering any other symptoms. The case for Henry's infection is equally inconclusive and encompasses none of the contemporary mercury cures, while he did regularly concoct his own remedies for various illnesses of his 'member'. None of the ingredients he frequently used or was prescribed correspond to contemporary cures. In comparison, the French king Francis I regularly undertook such treatments and his status as a sufferer is incontrovertible. Another attempt to explain the miscarriages has been to assign the queen a rhesus negative blood type, which reacted with that of her foetuses, causing expulsion. However, this usually happens in the first trimester of pregnancy and does not account for the many babies she carried to term. Further theories, posed by historian Robert Hutchinson, include the presence in water and food of Listeriosis, a form of bacterial infection which can trigger miscarriage and stillbirth, meningitis and pneumonia in newborn babies; additionally, Henry's sperm cells may have carried an imbalance of DNA material, prompting miscarriage to occur.[5] It is not impossible that a form of extreme anorexia may have been to blame, caused by Catherine's religious fasting, erratic eating and frequent illnesses, especially during the crucial years of her young womanhood, which adversely affected her fertility. Fasting was considered 'medicine to soul and body. It preserves the body from disease, the soul from sin'. This may have been an early form of anorexia nervosa, a method of exercising some sort of personal control in an otherwise chaotic and unpredictable existence, although interpreting Tudor actions according to modern medical definitions and psychological understanding is always fraught with problems. Most recently, suggestions have been made that Henry and his elder sister Margaret may have suffered from untreated diabetes type two, or else that Henry was Kell positive and many have suffered from McLeod syndrome: this would mean he had inherited mutations in his X chromosome. Some or none of these theories may have been true. Despite the ability of modern medicine to offer plausible theories for their losses, the couple may have simply been unfortunate in their high rate of infant mortality; they were not the only family to suffer such personal tragedy.

Infant mortality rates during the Tudor period were highest among newborns, varyingly estimated at around one in five. A considerable number must have suffered life-threatening illnesses during their mothers' long and difficult labours or the subsequent incompetence of those responsible for their arrival. Difficult presentments could result in midwives hacking away at portions of a child's anatomy, assuming it had proceeded far enough to be visible. Before the advent of forceps, difficult deliveries could be aided by hooks attached to an infant's skull, which inevitably proved fatal. If a child was born alive, the first few hours were critical, when poor understanding of hygiene and obstetrics could lead to infection and injury, beside all the other birth complications that modern medicine can more readily handle. As far back as 1277, the Synod of Triers ruled that midwives should baptise any protruding part of any child which appeared unlikely to survive until the arrival of a priest. In their absence, a woman of good character might perform the office, providing another essential role for the birth room gossips. Sadly, a regular feature of many parish registers is the simultaneous recording of an infant's birth and death when circumstances necessitated christening by the midwife at home, shortly before death occurred. This would involve at least being blessed with the sign of the cross or sprinkled with salt, while some placed a coin in baby's cradle or in its hand, practices that were disapproved of after the Reformation. Catherine and Henry's tragic losses were not unique: Henry's own sister, Margaret, wife of King James IV of Scotland, had a similar pattern of loss in her first marriage, with only one child out of six surviving past the age of two. Statistics derived from Tudor parishes indicate the high levels of mortality suffered throughout the kingdom at the time.

The examination of a typical decade in the parish of St Mary the Virgin, Chelmsford, Essex, can highlight the regularity and numbers of childhood deaths. In 1540, forty-nine babies were born and sixteen children died under the age of one, giving a mortality rate of one in four. For the next four years the pattern continued, with child mortality ranging between eleven and thirty-two cases annually: on average, over 80 per cent of all infant deaths happened before the first birthday. The following year was an *annus horribilis* for the city: 1545 saw foreign wars, terrible weather, crop failure and famine. Mortality rates for the entire parish rose dramatically and over sixty children were recorded as dying, a fifth being under the age of one. The second half of the decade saw the death rate fall, fluctuating between nine and twenty-two cases annually, with relatively higher rates of survival for newborns. The historical misnomer of detached, aloof Tudor parents, hardened to the loss of their children, has been rightly questioned in recent years. There is no doubt of the sincere and lasting grief suffered by Henry VII and Elizabeth, Henry VIII and Catherine over the losses of their first-born sons. The case of Thomas and Agnes Parkinson of Bedale, married in 1508, whose only child was stillborn, illustrates the depth of feeling suffered at the loss of a child. The infant was buried nearby in a field but a raven uncovered the grave, filling them with such grief that they parted and lived celibate lives, with Thomas becoming a hermit until the Dissolution, after which he wandered the countryside.[6] In reality, Tudor parents must have been prepared for the possibility of losing a child in a way that is entirely preventable in the modern developed world.

One family in Burnham, Essex, was typical of those suffering very high rates of infant mortality. Agnes Saffold was already married to John, a mariner, when parish records began in 1559; their first registered child was Margery, baptised in July 1560 and buried at the age of four. Less than two years after that birth, Agnes was pregnant again with Elizabeth, born in January 1563, who appears to have survived beyond her youth. A year later she conceived for a third time with Sybil, who lived from September 1565 until December 1567; Richard was born in that October and John followed in January 1570. Martha, born in April 1572, did not survive but within five months Agnes was expecting her seventh child, who also died soon after birth; her eighth was conceived three months later and born in September 1574. Anne followed in June 1576 but lived for five months by which time Agnes' fertility must have been ebbing: she did not conceive again for over four years, giving birth in June 1581 to twins, who both died at the age of two. In a rare marriage that united both partners for almost forty years, Agnes Saffold bore at least eleven children, of whom only four reached maturity.[7] The tragedies of infant mortality could strike any Tudor family, regardless of rank or wealth. Maternal health, infection, disease, malnutrition, medical misunderstanding and the still inexplicable Sudden Infant Death syndrome could all be to blame: little wonder that in the Tudor era, such events were considered to be misfortunes visited by God. Among the royal family, though, the implications for this went far beyond the personal.

While the royal couple's relationship remained close through 1514, England's bond with Catherine's native Spain was souring. Instead, Henry turned to France, rearranging the marriage of his younger sister Mary to favour this alliance; the eighteen-year-old was now to become the wife of the aged Louis XII instead of Catherine's nephew Charles. Mary's beauty was legendary; her middle name Rose was intended to echo her perfection, not just her lineage: a lock of her golden hair survives in the museum at Bury St Edmunds. Among her trousseau of extravagant dresses, Mary took with her to France a selection of silver gilt images of St Thomas, St Catherine and other saints, possibly in the anticipation of childbirth. Her marriage was to prove glorious but short-lived: the fifty-two-year-old Louis showered her with gifts and doted on her in and out of the bedroom yet would die within weeks, leaving her a teenage widow. In the meantime, Catherine was pregnant for a fourth time and Louis was also to act as godfather to the unborn child, if it proved to be a boy. On 4 October, furniture for her chambers and materials for her bed were ordered, including an amount of blue 'saye' and a cradle covered with scarlet, 'for the use of our nursery, God willing'. During the later stages of her pregnancy, it is not impossible that Henry's attentions wandered again: sex during this time was considered potentially dangerous to the foetus and given their record of losses, it is unlikely that the king and queen were sleeping together. Mary's attendant Jane Popincourt has been suggested as one candidate for his attentions: refused by Louis XII on account of her immoral character and later rewarded £100 by Henry, she might have been one of a number of willing court ladies with whom he sought solace while excluded from his wife's bed. His more significant paramour Elizabeth Blount was prominent in the Greenwich court celebrations that Christmas, so his well-known relations with her may have already begun.

Caught between her warring husband and father, possibly distressed by rumours of Henry's affair, the queen was in emotional turmoil when she was delivered of a short-lived son. The suggestion, on the Spanish side, that she had aborted through grief implies she had not yet reached the stage of confinement and the child was premature. Historians have variously dated this occurrence at some point between November 1514 and February 1515 but a letter from Wolsey to Louis XII on 14 November which stated that the queen 'looks to lie in shortly'[8] must date the event to the earlier part of this period, and Di Favri confirmed in a letter home that December that the queen had been delivered of a stillborn eighth-month son, to the grief of the whole court.[9] Chroniclers Stowe and Holinshed claimed it had died soon after delivery, while Peter Martyr related the event at the end of December. References in several modern works of popular history to the birth of a short-lived son the following February scarcely allow for a rapidly conceived foetus to develop sufficiently in order to determine gender. Claims that Catherine miscarried on Candlemas day itself, 2 February 1515, can be cast into doubt by her presence at a play performed at court at Westminster on that night. The confusion arises from a letter in Catherine's own hand to her father, in October 1515, where she writes that she gave birth to a child 'after Candlemas', which may either be a mistake, a deliberate miscalculation or else she was delivered of another embryo barely weeks old, which, given the difficulties of diagnosis, she can hardly have been aware she was carrying. Assuming the letter is correctly dated, translated and authenticated, it would not have been the first time Catherine had 'massaged' the timings of her gynaecological history when communicating with her father. Ferdinand had been suffering ill health for some time and had himself suffered the bereavements of children lost at birth or soon after. Perhaps Catherine again waited for the best moment to break her news. Whatever the truth behind the letter, the latest loss must have been heartbreaking for the queen, reaching her thirtieth birthday, with all four of her pregnancies failing to produce an heir. However, she was still fertile and although her menstruation could be erratic, proved herself able to conceive again. Rumours of a pregnancy resulting in miscarriage that June can be discounted as unfounded; every time Catherine was ill or indisposed, someone at court suspected she had conceived. To the couple's relief, she actually fell pregnant again six months later, in May 1515, cautiously becoming aware of the changes in her body, giving way to certainty in late summer. Rumours circulated the court but understandably, her condition was not made public knowledge until October or November. Henry and Catherine must have been praying that this time, things would be different.

A song dedicated to Henry in 1516, now held in the British Library, reflects his desire for the birth of a healthy son. A double canon or round for four voices, prepared by a Flemish merchant, it includes six compositions written in a circle around a central image of a red rose. An inscription reads, 'hail, root, bringing forth stems of different colours from your shoot, among which one stands out, from whose top there gleams a scarlet rose, where peace and justice stand enclosed and harmonious.' That one stem, topped by the scarlet rose, represented the daughter that arrived in mid-February. Catherine had taken to her chambers at Greenwich, unaware of the death of her father Ferdinand at the end of January; the news was kept from her for fear of provoking another premature or still birth, possibly a sensible precaution given her recent history. The usual preparations were made and had by now become a familiar pattern. As she approached her time for delivery, the queen must have felt a mixture of experience and justifiable apprehension. No doubt she would have prayed fervently and turned to her devotional objects to sustain her through the coming ordeal. Birth room charms, prayers and songs combined folklore, Pagan beliefs and Christianity; older texts such as the *Leechbook* and *Lacnunga* fused these traditions, with some even including simultaneous appeals to Christ and Woden.[10] One of the earliest surviving charms was intended to be said over a grave, to prevent the mother losing the child:

> This is my remedy for hateful slow birth,
> This is my remedy for heavy difficult birth,
> This is my remedy for hateful imperfect birth.[11]

Another charm against miscarriage should be said as the woman stepped over the reclining form of her husband:

> Up I go, over thee I step
> with a living child, not with a dying one
> with a full-time one, not with a doomed one.[12]

A 1526 English translation of the Sarum Missal included a prayer beginning:

> Kind virgin of virgins, holy mother of God, be present on behalf of thy devoted handmaidens their earnest prayers to the Son, thou art the benign assister of women in travail.[13]

Before the prayer book was rewritten in 1549, early Tudor Church liturgies followed the form of the medieval Sarum rite, in which a Mass for expectant mothers was included. The optimum times for attending Mass were on a child's quickening and shortly before delivery; this was actively encouraged with parish priests sending labouring women to receive Communion or else administering it in their chambers. Thomas Bentley's 1582 *The Monument of Matrons* included two sections of thanksgiving prayers '… to be said of women with child, and in childbed and after their delivery' and 'thanksgivings for women after deliverance of child'. The recitation of prayers and charms empowered a labouring woman and her gossips with the belief that they took part of the responsibility for healing upon themselves. Active chanting provided a rhythm for contractions and untied those involved.

The use of repetition, alliteration and Latin gave them a mystic feel, an 'otherness', and allowed some authority of the masculine Church to enter the female birthing chamber. It helped extend religious blessing to a mother at a time when she was considered in danger from supernatural influences. One prayer included by Bentley stressed the expectation of joy an heir would bring:

> A woman, when she travaileth, hath sorrow, for her hour has come; but when she is delivered of the child, she thinketh no more of the anguish, for joy that man is born onto the world. I beseech thee therefore, in the dangerous time of my travail, grant me speedie delivery and joyful holding of my child.[14]

Finally, Catherine was to have 'joyful holding' of her child, although that child would be a girl, rather than the long-hoped-for boy. The court spent Christmas 1515 at Eltham, watching comedies and pageants, dancing and feasting in the impressive great hall. Changes already made to the palace by Henry VII included the addition of tiled floors and glass windows; the royal lodgings stood in a separate donjon, giving them a degree of privacy. It was here that Catherine retired soon after the New Year celebrations to await the arrival of her child. Once again, she would have used her holy relics: images, icons and the girdle of the Virgin as well as the usual material and medicinal comforts available to a queen. A Doctor Vittoria was afterwards rewarded for having assisted at the birth, which proved difficult: was this the first example of a hands-on male midwife, or was his support given at a distance? Tantalisingly, the records do not specify and only the Spanish papers record that in October, Henry requested the presence of physician and 'most distinguished doctor', Hernando Lopez, who may have advised the queen during her pregnancy. Male advice may have been in favour of a more active labour. An early seventeenth-century childbirth manual written by Jacques Guillemeau, surgeon to Henri VI of France, advised that until the final push, the queen was better off walking about, to alleviate the boredom of a long travail, only taking to her bed at the end. She should lie flat on her back with a pillow under her hips, on a little pallet bed with a block of wood at the feet, against which she could push. To keep up her strength, she could take some broth or the yolk of an egg with some butter, or a sort of spiced alcoholic porridge, while her hands should be held by friends, so that she might 'clinch' them. The midwife should encourage her to hold in her breath and strain downwards 'as though she woulde go to the stoole', while the womb laboured to deliver its burden.[15] Whether Catherine's women were as explicit as this is uncertain. She had no family to stand by her at such a time; her sister-in-law Mary, now returned to England as Duchess of Suffolk, was herself heavily pregnant and would give birth the following month. In her absence, Catherine's most trusted ladies-in-waiting must have again performed the necessary offices.

At four in the morning of 18 February, Catherine produced her only surviving child, a daughter named Mary. She would have been wrapped in blankets at once, especially at that time of year and brought close to the fire, with her eyes covered so as not to expose her to sudden light. Her tiny body would be anointed and dried, then she would have been given a little wine and sugar, only the 'bigness of a pease' (a pea) and a drop of treacle: winter babies were given treacle while summer arrivals had cordial water.[16] The little girl was christened the following Wednesday: the court gate to the church door was hung with rich cloth of arras, the path gravelled and strewn afresh with rushes. At the church door, she met her godparents and received her name, before the procession headed inside to a church hung with needlework garnished with precious stones and pearls. Important members of the nobility carried the basin, taper, salt and chrism as Mary was born under a canopy to the font. Everyone must have been wondering whether this child would survive, but the little girl seemed healthy and the days turned into weeks and months. At last, Henry and Catherine could enjoy being parents.

As her newborn baby slept, Catherine lay back and began the process of recovery. For the surviving mother, it was essential that the placenta and lochia be delivered quickly, requiring a second 'labour'. Retention of these cells could lead to severe complication and the size of the placenta could be a factor. In 1607, a doctor, Edward Ayre, used a potion of rhubarb, beaver's stones and oil of juniper to assist its delivery, as had an old woman named Christiania, practising medicine in London in 1598.[17] In cases of excess bleeding, cold compresses and ergot were administered and powders of aloe and frankincense applied to abdomen. French queens were given a special drink of wine, sweet almonds and syrup of maidenhair in order to soothe the throat – which had been strained by groaning during labour – and to bring on the purges, helping the delivery of the afterbirth. Another recipe included oil of Hypericum, rose oil and St John's wort, bound with two eggs and applied to the thighs and legs with linen cloths or flax. A woman might be wrapped in the fleece of a newly shorn sheep to comfort and warm those parts which had been stretched. Difficult and protracted labours could leave even an experienced woman like Catherine vulnerable: vaginal tears incurred during delivery would most likely have been left to mend naturally and therefore left open to infection, although this process would have been aided by the woman remaining in bed for her month. Survival and healing would have depended on the degree of tearing. Wounds that penetrated through muscle into the tissue, today classed as second and third degree tears, could prove fatal through loss of blood and infection. Puerperal fever, caused by bacteria spread on unwashed hands, peritonitis and septicaemia could build up over hours or days unnoticed. Contemporary remedies made a variety of suggestions, including the use of quartz crystals, among other ingredients.

To staunch bleeding:
Take powder of corroll [coral] mixed with gum Arabicke, putt this into water of Planten and drink itt colde, this will stop the bledinge at any time, at any place within the body or without.

For an open wound that will not leave akinge:
Egremony, stampe itt small and temper itt with leaf, till itt bewell moysted, then lay itt to the wound and itt shall cease akinge within a while. So will bugill and honny doe the same.[18]

Catherine, however, was recovering well, unlike her sister-in-law in Scotland. Reports had travelled south of the plight of Henry's elder sister Margaret, whose remarriage following the death of James IV had alienated the pro-French party, who replaced her as regent of her young son, the future James V. Fleeing Scotland, heavily pregnant, she had taken refuge at Harbottle Castle, under Henry's protection. Back in October 1515, she had been delivered of a premature daughter and four months later still lay 'grievously ill', suffering terrible pain in her right thigh, 'the great joint, the seat of sciatica', so that the doctors could do little to help: she urged Henry to send his physician north to tend her, in the belief that she would get well again if the pain would lessen. Her long confinement had 'destroyed her appetite' so that she could barely stomach the recommended invalid's diet: 'almond milk, broth, pottage, boiled or roast meat and jellies'.[19] To compound her grief, while lying ill, she had learned of the death of her younger son by James, the twenty-month-old Alexander. On her recovery, she would travel south and seek refuge in London. Hearing of her terrible news, Catherine must have been doubly thankful for the arrival of her healthy daughter.

The little princess was two years old when her mother conceived for the final time. There were rumours of a pregnancy the following year but it was the spring of 1518 before Catherine suspected she was carrying another child: Henry confided the secret news to Wolsey that April. The dreaded sweating sickness had broken out in London so the royal couple stayed away from the capital, moving between country houses with a scaled-down court. Even that July, when she spent a day hunting, the pregnancy was not 'ensured' but only considered a 'likelihood', although this must have been around the time of her quickening if the baby was to have been full term that December. In July she was already showing, giving them 'great hope and likelihood' and orders were given for purple tissue to drape her bed and a crimson cloth of estate for the cradle. Venetian Ambassador Guistinian wrote to the Pope late in October that the queen was near her delivery, which was anxiously awaited, and prayed that she may have a son, so 'that the King may be at liberty to embark in any great undertaking'.[20] Without a male heir, any potential injury or accident Henry might suffer could cast the succession into turmoil. However, that November at Greenwich, a girl was born, again in the eighth month, as Guistinian claimed, to the 'vexation' of many, as the nation had 'looked for a prince'. It was a final blow for Catherine; at almost thirty-three, her gynaecological history had taken its toll on her fertility and her menopause was only six years away. The couple continued to sleep together, in the hopes of a healthy son following young Mary but as time passed, it became increasingly obvious that the queen would not conceive again and her fortieth birthday inched closer. The age gap between the couple had never been more pronounced. Still in his early thirties, Henry's prospects of an heir were less bleak. Shortly before Catherine's last daughter was born and died, one of her maids of honour had become pregnant with his child. If Catherine could not provide him with a son to inherit his throne, he began to hope that another woman could.

5

Elizabeth Blount
& Mary Boleyn
1518–1526

Illegitimate Royals

While life or breath is in my brest,
My sovereign lord I shall love best.[1]

The above lines, rumoured to have been composed by Elizabeth Blount during her relationship with Henry VIII, point to an affair typical of the values of his early court. Entrenched in a world of pageantry and chivalric ritual, the king would have revelled in the poem's description of him as the 'chieftan of a warrior' who had proved himself 'with spear and sword at the barryoure' as 'hardy with the hardyest'. As king and lover, Henry was paradoxically the master and servant; the object of infatuation as well as the humble suitor of the European courtly love tradition. If the song is genuine, Elizabeth may have been a witness at one of the spectacular jousts staged during the early years of Henry's reign, such as the one described by the Venetian Ambassador's secretary in July 1517, at which time the affair had already been underway for several years. Sixty knights took part: forty wore cloth of gold, while a further twenty were dressed in white velvet and cloth of silver, their horses adorned with silver chain-work and ringing bells. The king and his gentlemen wore silver; he and the Duke of Suffolk tilted eight courses, 'shivering' their lances to the 'great applause' of the spectators. Two tents were erected for the spectators; one of cloth of gold and the other of silk, seating 50,000 people. The event lasted four hours and was punctuated by daring feats of horsemanship, after which, predictably, the king and Suffolk were awarded the honours. A magnificent feast followed, where Henry sat between Catherine and his sister Mary, flanked by Wolsey and the 'handsomest ladies' the court could offer.[2] There is little doubt that Elizabeth Blount would have been classed in this category.

Elizabeth, or Bessie, Blount had arrived at Henry's court as early as March 1512; a golden-haired, blue-eyed, lively, merry girl of twelve or fourteen. It was not long before she attracted attention with her ability to dance and compose songs, which were seen as the acme of accomplishments. Henry's attention would not be held by a pretty face alone; romantically, he required a match for those chivalric skills so central to his early identity as (ironically) 'Sir *Loyal* Heart'. In 1513, the young woman's abilities had ensured her admittance among Catherine's ladies, a privileged and sought-after position for which there was much competition among her contemporaries. Composition, song and dance, sewing, reading and even gambling were all enjoyed in the royal apartments, as well as religious studies and observances. Catherine's household was not so sombre that she and her maids did not enjoy the regular feasting, dances, jousts, pageants and games of the early Tudor court but the queen prided herself on setting a high moral tone and the industrious occupation of her women. When Catherine's back was turned, however, the flirtatious and incestuous hot-house of the Tudor court encouraged love affairs and secret liaisons to flourish. Male courtiers would have been aware of the arrival of a new, pretty face. Although Bessie may have had family recommendations and already been turning heads, noble birth and good looks alone were not enough to guarantee such attention. Her early success indicates that she must have been an exceptional young woman. By the following Christmas, the king would have certainly been aware of her at Greenwich, dressed for a pageant in blue velvet, gold cap and mask as she played the role of a woman of Savoy, in need of his rescue. As she danced in the candlelight, graceful and accomplished, with her typically English good looks, she would have appeared a perfect physical match for the handsome athletic twenty-three-year-old king. Even the nine-year age gap would not have been considered a barrier. It was not unheard of for young girls to be married, like Margaret Beaufort, or even, to become sexually active, as with Catherine Howard; the usual age of female consent was given as fourteen, and twelve for boys.

With the five-year gap between Henry and Catherine appearing to widen each year, there were plenty of beautiful young ladies to divert him during the queen's pregnancies. At Christmas 1514, as she recovered from losing her fourth child, Catherine enjoyed the entertainment so much that she ordered a repeat performance in her private chambers, where Bessie was partnered by the king. By this point they may have already become lovers.

Born around 1500, Bessie Blount was probably the eldest surviving daughter of John Blount and Catherine Pershall of Kinlet, Shropshire. Their marriage was arranged as children: the earliest possible date for consummation was 1495, when John may have attained his fourteenth year, although Catherine was probably younger: it is certain that she bore her first child while still in her teens, perhaps as early as 1498, which has been suggested as Bessie's earliest possible birthdate. An early biographer and descendant referred to her as the second daughter, suggesting the loss of an earlier child: subsequent sons were to die in infancy in 1501 and 1503. The worn names on the family tomb[3] indicate that the second daughter may have been named Anne, while that of the first is considerably longer: in all probability, Bessie was the couple's first-born girl. With no surviving portrait, the image carved on the Blount tomb depicts a conventional, demure-looking young woman dressed in the fashion of the day, her features barely distinguishable from those of her sisters; a funeral brass possibly portraying her is equally impersonal. She was born at Kinlet Hall, although the family soon moved into the nearby manor of Bewdley, Worcestershire. This placed them within easy distance of Ludlow, where several members of her family were to hold prominent positions in the short-lived household of Prince Arthur and Catherine of Aragon. Barely out of their teens, the young married Blounts were regular visitors to the home of the royal couple. In 1502, Arthur's body rested for the night in the chapel at Bewdley on its way to burial, while the funeral procession was lodged in the manor house. It is not impossible that, ten years later, these connections helped place Bessie in the new queen's service. Catherine can hardly have imagined that the small blonde child she recalled would pose any threat to her own position.

Bessie was not the first lady-in-waiting to have found her way into the king's bed. Ironically, Catherine's household, with its high moral tone, provided a pool of beautiful, accomplished young women to tempt her husband. With sex during pregnancy considered potentially harmful to an unborn foetus and able to curdle milk in the breasts, Henry's justification for seeking out other affairs during his queen's unavailability, was, conveniently, her own good health and that of her child. In a typical double standard of the era, a man would not necessarily be expected to abstain from sexual activity during the months of his wife's pregnancy and confinement. While conducting himself with discretion, Henry found it was not always possible to keep his amours secret in the closed world of the Tudor court. As early as 1510, when Catherine was sexually unavailable, his dalliance with Anne, the Duke of Buckingham's sister, was the cause of the couple's first argument. With all indicators suggesting Henry had little opportunity to pursue women during his father's lifetime and was satisfied with Catherine during the first year of their union, Lady Anne Stafford was probably his first mistress. Certainly she received the third-most-expensive gift he gave at New Year 1513, either in reward for her services or as recompense for having to leave court when the affair was discovered. A mysterious French woman, Etiennette la Baume, identified from a single surviving letter, may have entertained him while absent from the marital bed during his campaigns of 1513–14, while the notorious Jane Popincourt, lover of the Duc de Longueville, may have been his companion while she was apart from the Duc in England until 1516. Other sources name Elizabeth Bryan – Lady Carew – as a possible early mistress, after she and Bessie were linked in a letter by Charles Brandon to Henry as the recipients of letters and tokens; she also received gifts of jewels from the king.[4] Henry's affairs may have been facilitated by his close friend Sir William Compton procuring women for the king at his private London home, yet none of these posed a real threat to the queen. Most appear to have been casual short-term liaisons. Before Bessie bore Henry a son in 1519, little real evidence, including the absence of previous illegitimate children, exists for any significant mistresses.

During this time, Henry was a devout, traditional Catholic. The strict civil and pre-Reformation line on adultery and illegitimacy couldn't have been clearer: fornication (sex outside marriage or purely for pleasure) was against religious teaching. Intercourse within marriage was acceptable only for the procreation of children and the penalties for transgression were harsh and public. Children born out of wedlock could be baptised and even legitimised by subsequent marriage vows but the social stigma of bastardy and the legal implications could not be so easily shaken off. Couples engaged in fornication or adultery could receive severe corporal punishment and fines: marriage was the ultimate goal for any respectable Tudor woman, even though poverty, age and the dynastically arranged unions of the nobility might make this impossible. Royals did sometimes marry for love: following her short-lived union to the aged Louis XII, Princess Mary incurred her brother's wrath by secretly wedding Charles Brandon, while Henry himself would choose four of his queens for their personal charms. Brandon had four wives and fathered at least three illegitimate children, while Thomas Wolsey's mistress Joan Larke bore him a son and daughter. At the intense, highly charged Tudor court, illicit physical attraction was inevitable. Young women coveted positions in Catherine of Aragon's retinue in order to find a suitable husband, but often entertained themselves with love affairs in the interim. When temptation occurred, especially among unmarried courtiers, the 'correct' religious or moral choices were either abstinence and avoidance or submission. Of course, in practice, many gave in to temptation. The obvious exception to this was an affair with a king, the honour and financial advantage of which could outweigh any adverse social stigma; to bear a king's child could be the making of a woman and her family. And, in terms of adultery, even with noble-born women whose dynastic imperative should have dictated their purity, Henry clearly managed to square his actions with his conscience.

The majority of the Tudor aristocracy had arranged marriages in their mid- to late teens; these were primarily for political, dynastic and financial advancement; romantic love and sexual satisfaction were often sought elsewhere. Sometimes they were hard, if not impossible, to come by. Double standards allowed men to conduct relations with prostitutes or lower-class women, who were considered more sexually gratifying, while women were expected to be above reproach. Same-sex unions and masturbation were possibly even more abhorrent than adultery, in Catholic eyes, with the wasteful spilling of seed in any context considered an abomination. Anal sex was made punishable by death for homosexual and heterosexual couples in 1533, encompassing all 'unnatural' acts 'against the Will of man and God', including bestiality: Walter, Baron Hungerford was the first to suffer death for this, in 1540. The influential twelfth-century St Hildegard of Bingen wrote that 'men who touch their own genital organ and emit their semen seriously imperil their souls' and 'perverse adulterers change their virile strength into perverse weakness'; instead she counselled 'when a person feels himself disturbed by bodily stimulation let him run to the refuge of continence and seize the shield of chastity and thus defend himself from uncleanness'.[5] A more practical but probably no less successful method included placing cooked lettuce leaves on the overactive member. The fourth-century William of Pagula wrote to parish priests that 'if someone has knowingly and wilfully emitted the seed of coitus in any other way than naturally with his wife, he sins gravely'.[6] This was setting a high standard for communities where privacy and space were luxuries and many multiple households contained large numbers of young people sharing each other's company day and night.

The reality of sexual relations and the family unit was far more complex; with the largest proportion of young people remaining single until their late twenties, the frustrations of a decade of sexual maturity needed an outlet. It is no surprise that informal arrangements and misunderstandings arose; temporary alliances were entered into in good faith and broken when the couple moved on or found alternative partners. A verbal promise of marriage or 'handfasting' could be enough to license physical relations, as proved the downfall of Catherine Howard, Henry VIII's fifth queen. Less than two years after her marriage, it was discovered that she had enjoyed two lovers in her youth, which she had omitted to mention to her new husband. With one, she had exchanged promises, gifts and spent many nights together in a shared dormitory as husband and wife. Catherine might still have kept her head at this point but unfortunately for her, the revelations led to the uncovering of her later adulterous affair. Handfasting could even override later marriages in church, even if consummation had not taken place, as Henry attempted to prove in the case of Anne Boleyn's pre-contract to Henry Percy, and successfully established to extract himself from an unwanted union with Anne of Cleves. Promises could be made any time or any place: bedrooms, kitchens and fields witnessed secret agreements: it wasn't until 1563 that the Council of Trent declared a marriage was void if not celebrated in front of a priest, although English law did not catch up until the eighteenth century. Henry was discreet about the arrangements for his marriages, often to the extent that they were made public by hints and suggestions before his councillors were officially informed. His extramarital affairs were shrouded in even greater secrecy.

It is not clear when Henry's relationship with Bessie Blount began. Besides the reference to them dancing at Christmas 1514, the only certain point in the union is the birth of their son Henry Fitzroy in the summer of 1519, putting a conception date around late September or early October. His elevation to the peerage in June 1525, probably coinciding with his sixth birthday, supports a June birthday. It is possible that they were involved for the entire duration of the intervening time or that Bessie was an intermittent distraction, to whose bed Henry returned while Catherine was pregnant and unavailable. Whatever the truth of their relations, they were indisputably sleeping together shortly before Catherine's final miscarriage, while the court was at Westminster. In early October, at Wolsey's home, York Place, Bessie was again listed as a dancer in the company of Mary Tudor, Queen of France, to celebrate the signing of a treaty for the marriage of the two-year-old Princess Mary and the dauphin. After a 'sumptuous supper' in a hall decorated by huge vases of gold and silver, a 'mummery' of masked dancers in the 'richest and most sumptuous array' was performed, before the company were served confectioneries and delicacies, gambled at dice and danced again until midnight.[7] It would prove to be Bessie's last public appearance with the king; she was about to conceive or was in the early stages of pregnancy and would soon be sent away from court for the sake of discretion.

While Catherine's confinements had been organised along the lines of Margaret Beaufort's spectacular and thorough Ordinances, Bessie was not royalty. She could not be treated in the same way but her position as royal mistress made the significance and conditions of her lying-in unique; she was sufficiently important to be well provided for and honoured, while her adulterous union and the child's illegitimacy ensured everything must be handled with discretion. To deal with this, Henry handed the arrangements over to his trusted and competent minister Thomas Wolsey, whose own mistress had borne him two illegitimate offspring and whose prudence has ensured few details of Henry Fitzroy's birth survive. Bessie was sent to the Augustinian Priory of St Laurence, Blackmore, near Chelmsford in Essex. There, she awaited her lying-in in the moated medieval residence of Prior Thomas Goodwyn, who had held the position since 1513. It was a location notorious for being used by Henry to conduct illicit liaisons and attracted the name 'Jericho', possibly after a nearby river, although little if any evidence beyond rumour survives for any other encounters he may have had there. It may have been the site of his meetings with Bessie and it allowed him to remain close that summer, as he spent part of it staying at the nearby magnificent Palace of Newhall, later renamed Beaulieu. The house still stands and is in use as a Catholic School: the king would have been lodged there in considerable comfort, in one of the twenty-nine great beds, with the use of one of four wooden-floored bathing rooms. From there, he could have ridden the short distance to visit his pregnant mistress, under the cover of hunting or riding. Alternatively he may have stayed at the thirteenth-century Havering Palace, a royal residence of queens for centuries, now demolished. During her confinement, Bessie would have certainly been made comfortable and her experience would not have been too far removed from that of other aristocratic women except in one key area. It had to be discreet.

For a Tudor gentlewoman, one key element of pregnancy was the setting in motion of a supportive female network by spreading her news and gathering together the group of gossips that would be her support during the coming months. Rare surviving letters include the advice, warnings and good wishes of family and friends, through to discussions concerning linen, midwives and medicines: their committal to paper suggests distance between the sender and recipient, so they must give just a brief indication of the oral exchanges that must have taken place on a regular basis during the months of pregnancy. In 1572, Lady Audrey Aleyn wrote to her brother concerning provision for his wife's lying in, discussing wet nursing, christening and attempting to predict gender through astrology: 'I could make you somewhat affeard of a gyrle, for that Femynine signes rule much this yere.'[8] Lady Sidney's sister wrote to her when she was pregnant abroad, wishing God would send her a 'goodly boy': she had confided her fears concerning foreign wet nurses to her other sister, Lady Herbert, who offered the services of a most quiet and careful English nurse, who could be shipped over in time. Anne Newdigate received written good wishes from her kinswoman Lady Elizabeth Grey while suffering illness in pregnancy, while some women sent gifts along with their letters; Anne Bacon thanked her mother Mistress Dutton for sending a generous amount of linen 'towards my lying downe'.[9] However, not even privilege could guarantee the birth experience a mother had hoped for. When in 1575, the daughter-in-law of the Earl of Shrewsbury went into labour in his house, no women were available to attend and the child was delivered by a single midwife and baptised by Shrewsbury and two of his children. While men were barred from the labouring chamber, wives did not necessarily want them to be far away, offering emotional and material support: heavily pregnant Elizabeth Anthony wrote to her husband that his long absence 'hath bread shuch discontent in my mind that I canot be reed of it. You knowe that my time of payne and sorowe is nere and I am unproved of loging and other thinges nedfull'. Sabine Johnson asked her husband to make 'all sped home' from Calais, which she would find a great comfort.[10] No records survive of the women who supported Bessie during her confinement, particularly whether her mother Catherine travelled from Shropshire, although her three sisters were too young to have been involved and probably kept at a remove from the situation. The geographical distance from her family home may have been representative of the new social gulf that had opened between them and their eldest daughter.

As an aristocratic woman's delivery approached, the questions of location became more urgent, depending upon wealth and status, with preparations including the gathering of linen, the making of baby clothes and provision for the care of older children. Although her circumstances were unusual, Bessie was typical in not giving birth at home. It was common for married women to seek out more suitable spaces, perhaps in the home of a neighbour or that of their parents, especially if they were not a home-owner or other circumstances made their usual dwelling place impractical. It would be interesting but probably impossible to know the predicaments of women who chose to give birth under the roofs of their mothers rather than their husbands. Some wives were clearly neglected: when pleading to separate from her husband, Elizabeth Kynaston explained how she had attempted to 'engage and please' him as much as she could, 'to serve and respect him as she always conceived it was her duty to do'[11] but he had denied her the midwife of her choice, resulting in a difficult, long labour; likewise Sir Richard Greville overturned his wife's birth room wishes, causing marital ruptions.[12] In 1566, pregnant Judith Pollard was locked out of her house on a cold January night, her husband refusing to readmit her, so she was taken in by her neighbour Margaret Jones. Anne Wilson's husband refused to provide for her, so that she would have perished but for the charity of neighbours: other pregnant wives were beaten, kicked and attacked.[13] When a woman's virtue was called into question, threatening the line of inheritance, male reactions to pregnancy could be extreme. One case of 1537 saw an Elizabeth Burgh, of Langley Lodge, appealing to Thomas Cromwell for help after her child's premature delivery cast doubt in the minds of her family about its conception. She had given birth while staying with a 'gentleman and his wife', Burgh's kinsmen, who had written to assure her husband that 'he might have no cause of jealousy against her, seeing that the child, by the proportions of his body, was born long before the time' yet 'my lord his father says it is none of her husband's, and makes him absent himself from her'. Her second letter complained that her father-in-law was always 'lying in wait' to 'put her to shame'. While she lay recovering from a traumatic delivery, describing herself as a 'prisoner' and 'comfortless', she urged Cromwell to mediate, as 'nothing but the power of God had preserved' her and her child.[14]

As Bessie awaited the birth, surrounded by the Augustinian friars going about their devotions, probably removed from the support of friends and family, she may have turned to Catholic texts for support. Her composition proves she was literate and religious and devotional books were a common feature of the lying-in stage. Birth was the conventional opening of many popular hagiographies and miracle stories, widely circulated since Caxton's 1483 English edition of Jacobus de Voragine's *Golden Legend* had become a bestseller. The majority of these authors were male or abstaining females with no direct experience of birth, although accuracy was not their priority. Instead, the intention was to exacerbate their subjects' piety and glorify God, so their tales are prone to exaggeration, implausibility and the employment of iconography for dramatic effect. Such narratives frequently dwell on the signs and holy manifestations that accompanied saints' births, such as comets or holy flames and the allegorical dreams informing mothers of the destiny of their blessed offspring. Typical is the birth account of the twelfth-century recluse, St Christina of Markyate. According to the story, on the day 'when the faithful pay particular honour to the mother of God', a dove, 'whiter than snow', flew out of a monastery and settled in her pregnant mother's bosom: 'such a sign was evidently meant to show that the child within her would be filled with that Holy Spirit', so she carried the child 'with joy' until the day of its birth. The rituals of delivery that followed were predominantly religious: the expectant mother went to church at daybreak to hear matins and Mass, commending herself devoutly to God, his Virgin Mother and St Leonard, whose nativity was celebrated that day. She gave birth between *prime* and *terce* (six and nine in the morning), 'bravely bearing her hour of pain in anticipation of her child'.[15] Such descriptions may have been uplifting for Bessie but essentially misleading.

On his visits to Newhall Place, Henry may well have visited Bessie at nearby Jericho. Some evidence may suggest the affair was already waning by this point or would conclude soon after the birth; did Bessie sense she was losing the king's interest? Perhaps conscious of her fragile status as his mistress, she may have resorted to some of the remedies suggested for a pregnant woman keen to preserve her looks. To keep her breasts pert, she may have worn a chain of gold about her neck, a piece of steel hanging between them or held a bit of cork under her armpit to prevent them 'hanging down like bags'. Equally she may have bathed her breasts in periwinkle, sage, ivy and hemlock boiled in wine, or else a little rose vinegar; a quarter of an hour in the morning was supposedly best, before wrapping them in 'reasonable' warm clothes. From the third month onward until the birth, she should wear a supporting swathe to prevent wrinkling and distortion of the skin. This could be anointed with goat suet, sow fat, goose grease, stag marrow and rose water. The concoction cannot have smelt too pleasant as it was then perfumed with a few drops of musk or civet. Alternative ingredients included dog's grease, sheep's kidney, spermaceti, duck fat and wax; these could be applied on a clean, dry dog skin. As her time approached, an expectant mother should bathe for half an hour in the morning, then lie in her bed and be anointed with salves of mallow, motherwell, lily, camomile, linseed, fenugreek and hen's fat; she should drink white wine and almond oil, bound by an egg. Ill humours might cause Pica, already identified by the Tudors as a desire for either salt, sharp tastes such as vinegar and citrus fruits or strange substances like coal, ash and wall plaster! This was supposedly caused by the growing of the child's hair. For the last-minute pains and practice contractions, Bessie may have chewed fennel, aniseed or cinnamon; to relax her bowels and prepare for the birth, sorrel, spinach and beetroot were added to the existing list of herbs.

Just like for queens, the aristocratic Tudor woman's lying-in process was one of seclusion and ritual. The chamber was made as dark, warm and comfortable as possible, to keep out draughts and evil spirits at a time when a mother was considered beyond the usual protection of the Church. Daylight was thought to be dangerous although some manuals recommend one window being left uncovered while the others were hidden behind hangings; the cradle was placed well away from natural light and under no circumstances was permitted to stand in moonlight. Darkness was considered physically beneficial too, as birth was thought to strain the eyes and repeated childbirth could lead to blindness, so the room's keyholes were stopped up, although this may have been borne out of the need to maximise privacy in smaller homes, shared with family and servants. The comfort and whims of a labouring mother were taken seriously, with food and supplies being brought in for those involved and their visitors during the long days of delivery and recovery, running up bills with traders and shopkeepers, causing disputes. There were no royal kitchens to ensure the average mother was kept well fed. In Chester in 1540, local authorities ruled that 'great excess has been caused by the costly dishes, meats and drinks brought to women in childbed, which they repay at their churchings. Therefore it is ordered that in future no such dishes and wines shall be brought to women in childbed nor to churchings, and that no woman but the midwife and mother, sisters and sisters-in-law shall enter the house with her that is churched'.[16] The penalty was a fine of 6s 8d against the house owner and 3s 4d for every person in attendance. This would be unpopular with midwives who were following the recommendations of Rosslin that women should be refreshed with good meat and drink; again provision would depend very much upon social class and degrees of disposable wealth.

In cases of illegitimacy, midwives were called upon to put pressure upon a mother at the moment of her greatest suffering. The women attending the unmarried Ursula Cleveland in 1588 at Shalford, Essex, asked her pressing questions to determine paternity, later giving evidence in court. The main midwife, Elizabeth Callys, was supported by Catherine Crosse, Rose Ringer and Bytteris Burles in charging her to clear the reputations of two men she had accused, although Ursula held out as long as she could, only naming one William Sympson when she was in 'great peril of her life' and believing herself about to die. A Richard Perrie of the same town told the justices how he had given Urusla cakes and a pot of beer when she confessed to him that the father was one Thomas Noble, although her sister had encouraged her to name Sympson instead. When examined, Ursula's sister Joan Malte stated that she had long suspected Ursula of living a 'lewd life' with Sympson and had once followed him back to her house, where she stood under a window and heard the pair having 'carnal knowledge' before emerging from a bedchamber. When she confronted Sympson he accused her of being mad and offered her a bribe, after which she had encouraged Ursula to tell the truth regarding the paternity. Ursula then confessed Sympson had threatened to kill her if she spoke against him, which appeared to sway the justices. The court found Sympson culpable, ordering him to pay maintenance weekly for its upkeep, until such time that another man was later proven to be the child's father. Ursula was to be stripped to the waist, tied to a cart and receive twenty lashes before the village church and in the street.[17] Rule-breaking was considered a manifestation of sin rather than the product of social circumstance and as such, sinners needed to be harshly punished to cleanse the community and dissuade others.

More midwives helped identify the father of the illegitimate child born to Susan Babye of Coggeshall, Essex, in 1582. Agnes Trewe, a widow, and Agnes Howlett had attended her labour, where she would only claim there was no other father of her child than her half-brother Edward. Shocked, the women pressed further and Susan confessed that one John Fletcher had lain with her at Witham fair, another William Dagnett had had 'to do with her divers and sundry times' and a Richard Howe had slept with her once, all around the time of conception.[18] The phrase used in most recorded cases of bastardy is that of a 'child begotten on the body' of the mother, suggestive of a passive female role, even when the evidence shows collusion. Those women unfortunate enough to conceive during an act of violation were considered complicit, as mutual enjoyment was believed essential to conception. Therefore, pregnancies arising from rape were seen as evidence that the woman had enjoyed herself, invalidating any accusation she may have made. Legally, sex and the creation of a child was considered to lie within the control and responsibility of men, although women could lure and tempt a man to sin. Paradoxically, they were seen as morally weak and yet strong in terms of determination and depravity. Socially, the stigma was more lastingly endured by the woman as men could always deny paternity while pregnancy and birth outside marriage were illegal and difficult to conceal. It was usually the men of the parish where the illegitimate child was born who alerted the assize courts, mindful of the expense to the community if those involved shirked their responsibilities. Justice was a male preserve; women's involvement was determined by male perceptions of their character and reputation. In such cases it was crucial to establish who the father or legal parent was, which could require a confession. Court records show this was not always forthcoming.

While Bessie and her son were to incur the stigma of illegitimacy, her royal connection raised her above open censure and afforded her considerable protection. There would be no awkward questions for her to answer, even from the Church, as Wolsey took charge of all the relevant arrangements. As a result, it must have seemed that even God was sanctioning her liaison with the king and subsequent pregnancy. It is likely that the late spring and early summer days passed pleasantly enough in the priory, punctuated by visits from the king, staying nearby. Henry must have been especially eager to see the arrival of a son, even one not born to his wife. If nothing else, it proved his abilities to father a healthy child and shifted the perceived failings of his marriage firmly onto Catherine. It is unclear exactly when Catherine herself learned of the imminent arrival, whether before or after his birth, yet she cannot have been unaware of his existence once Henry started heaping him with titles and inviting him to visit the court. His presence must have been a constant reminder to her of her own dwindling fertility and the precariousness of her daughter's inheritance. For Catherine, it may have seemed that everyone else was able to produce surviving sons. That spring, news had arrived at court of the birth of a male heir to Henry's great rival, Francis I of France, and by June, ambassador Thomas Boleyn had written to Wolsey describing the boy's christening and the reception of the English gifts presented to Queen Claude in Henry's name, including a salt cellar, cup and layar of gold, which were much praised. It was the French king's fourth child and second son. Francis was greatly pleased, and said whenever it should be the king's fortune to have a prince, he would 'be glad to do for him in like manner'.[19] The implied comparison cannot have but piqued the English king, as it was intended. Meanwhile, Bessie was counting down the days and making preparations for the arrival of her child.

Henry Fitzroy's birth, probably in June 1519, was shrouded in secrecy. Initially the event had little impact at court. It certainly bypassed Venetian ambassador Guistinian, who wrote that 'nothing new has taken place' that summer. No record survives of any resulting court celebrations that Catherine may or may not have been required to endure. It has been suggested that a feast that August at the queen's nearby manor of Havering-atte-Bower may have afforded Henry an opportunity to display or acclaim his son; such behaviour would not seem untypically tactless in the light of his later treatment of Catherine, but there is no evidence to support this either way. Henry certainly did not deny he was the child's father. Thomas Wolsey stood as godfather, specifically stating the king's paternity as he bestowed the royal name at his baptism. He would have control over the arrangements of this event, as well as Bessie's churching, which probably took place in the adjacent church of St Laurence.

A new mother was not supposed to emerge from her lying-in chamber until around a month had passed, which meant mid-July for Bessie. Prior to this religious cleansing, a mother or 'green woman' was expected to remain inside, neither entering her community or church, nor looking upon the earth or sky or meeting others' eyes, assuming childbirth to be a period of sinfulness, tainted by sex and delivery. Technically, she was supposed to refrain from sexual activity until the rite had taken place although conception intervals inferred from baptismal records show this was not always the case, although it must remain unclear just how much control women had over this: according to parish records, at least one Essex wife was already pregnant at the time of her churching. In order to re-establish her social and sexual identity, a woman was led from her chamber to the church porch, veiled, in a parody of marriage which seems ironic in its suggestion that the enforced abstinence of her lying-in induced a return to a near-virgin state. The veil also stresses the association of the mother with depictions of the Virgin as well as an extension of the privacy of the birth chamber until such time as her seclusion was publicly ended. In pre-Reformation days, the priest would be waiting outside in the church porch to sprinkle the woman with holy water before proceeding inside, where some churches had a special pew or stool for churching, although illness might necessitate churching at home. Payment for the ceremony was often the child's chrism cloth, made from fine linen or its equivalent in money. The mothers of illegitimate offspring had to repent in front of the whole village and do penance before partaking in any religious ceremonies, although it is unlikely Bessie had to submit to this humiliation and quite possible her churching took place in seclusion, arranged by the Prior himself.

Later, the ritual of churching came under attack. The main objection that arose during the Reformation was the proper performance of the purification rites and the Protestant rejection of the connotations of sin and uncleanliness in the mother. The medieval *Sarum Missal*, translated into English in 1526, contained a prayer for churching at the porch: 'O God who hast delivered this woman thy servant from the peril of childbirth, and hast made her to be devoted to thy service …' The priest then sprinkled her with holy water, saying, 'thou shalt purge me O Lord, with hyssop', before leading her inside with the promise of eternal life. Unscrupulous priests could also extract bribes and penalties from those women who had conceived out of wedlock by insisting on payment or offerings at the altar. When the Sarum rite was replaced by the Book of Common Prayer in the reign of Edward VI, churching ceremonies were forced to revise their rituals and definitions. The contrast is shown in Bentley's 1582 *Monument of Matrons*: 'O My Lord God, I thank thee with all my heart, wit, understanding and power, for thou hast vouchsafed to deliver me out of this most dangerous travail and has sent unto this world, out of my woeful womb, this child, for which I am not worthy, to give thee condign thanks, praise, honour and glory.' Emphasis has shifted from the priest to the mother, taking a more active responsibility for her own salvation in director communication with God. The importance of the ceremony was secular, as well as religious: it reminded the community of the enormity of this rite of passage: as mothers and attendants, women were engaged directly with the struggle between life and death. In the post-delivery euphoria, among those often living under hard conditions, a successful birth was a welcome occasion for celebration. For Henry, the arrival of a healthy son gave him food for thought: it may have been around this time that he concluded that his marriage to Catherine was unlawful but that God might bless him with sons by another woman.

Interestingly, Henry does not have appeared to have considered marriage to Bessie. Even after the onset of Catherine's menopause, such a union would have allowed him to legitimise his son and any subsequent children. In fact, the timing for such an event was not in Bessie's favour: in 1519, Henry's divorce and remarriage to a commoner were still only theoretical, no matter what Bessie's fertility had proved, and by the late 1520s, she was unavailable and a more formidable rival had appeared in the form of Anne Boleyn. Instead, a suitable match was arranged for her, to Gilbert Tailboys, first Baron Tailboys of Kyme, who was at court under Wolsey's protection following the emerging insanity of his father. It is probable then, that Wolsey arranged the marriage as he had the lying-in and the christening. The timing of Bessie's next pregnancy gives rise to doubts recently cast on the paternity of their eldest child Elizabeth, who appears to have been born before the couple appear in official records in 1522, perhaps as early as 1520. This would place her conception back in 1519.[20] With the exact date of the ceremony unclear, such a brief interval of recovery between lovers invites the interpretation that Henry was in fact, the father of her daughter Elizabeth. But was Henry himself aware of this? Following the pride he felt in Fitzroy's arrival, it seems likely he would have acknowledged or at least provided for an illegitimate daughter if he had been certain of her identity. Her gender made her less desirable in terms of succession but she may have been useful in future dynastic negotiations. Perhaps the arrangement of Bessie's marriage was provision for mother and both children; Henry may have visited her bed again that August as he stayed nearby, resulting in Elizabeth's birth in the summer of 1520. Significantly though, no mention was made of this possibility at the time and without knowing the date of the Tailboys marriage, definite conclusions cannot be reached. In the coming years, Bessie had little involvement with her son, Henry Fitzroy, who was raised in a separate establishment befitting the status of an illegitimate royal. In 1530, the French Ambassador remarked on Henry's fondness for his good-looking, red-haired son; later he would be introduced to Francis I and represent the king in his absence.

Bessie's marriage resulted in the births of three more children before she was widowed in 1530, as did a second union around 1535 with Edward, 9th Baron Clinton. During Henry's short-lived marriage to Anne of Cleves, Bessie returned to court as a member of the queen's household but ill health probably dictated her swift retirement as she died the same year. While not as significant as any of Henry's wives, her importance lies in providing the king with proof that he was capable of bearing a healthy son: Fitzroy's existence provided the justification Henry needed that the failure of his marriage lay with Catherine. Soon after his birth though, a new mistress would supplant his mother.

Popular history has Mary Boleyn down as an 'infamous whore'. Was she really either? Centuries of confusion concerning the identities and activities of the Boleyn sisters have added to the myths about both girls, intensified by film portrayals and fiction. The result has been a tangle of misinterpretation, gossip and romantic imagining. In fact, little is known about the elder sister who caught Henry's eye as early as 1520. Traditional assertions of her reputation have recently been analysed and discredited, with Mary emerging as a far less lascivious or controversial character. Typically described as blonde, pliant, disappointing to her family and unintellectual, there is actually no evidence to suggest Mary was any of these. She may have had a brief liaison with Francis I of France while in the service of Mary Tudor, Queen of France, but this does not necessarily imply the disgrace she has been accused of. She appears to have received less education than her sister, who was sent into the household of Archduchess Margaret in her teens, yet the reasons for this are unclear. Descriptions of her beauty have compared her favourably and poorly with her more famous sister and surviving portraits are of dubious attribution. She may or may not have borne the king one or two children, although he did not acknowledge either. Little is certain about the role Mary played in Henry's life; recent scholarship has overturned centuries of assumptions about her promiscuity with the suggestion that his attentions may even have been forced upon her against her will.[21]

Mary had been attached to the court of Mary Tudor for several years before she became Henry's mistress. She had been born around 1499 at Blickling, Norfolk, into the influential Boleyn/Howard family who were soon to acquire Hever Castle in Kent. Her father Thomas was well embarked on a diplomatic career, having escorted Princess Margaret to Scotland in 1503 and served as ambassador to the Netherlands and France. As a teenager, Mary had travelled to France in the retinue of the future Queen Mary Rose and remained in her service for the duration of that marriage: returning to England in 1515, in Mary's household, she would have been required to attend her mistress at the Field of Cloth of Gold five years later, an event organised by her father. On this occasion, she was a newly married woman, having become the wife of courtier William Carey that February, an event which the king attended. Mary would have been present in the specially erected banqueting house at the English camp in Guisnes, or else when the French king, Francis I, went to dine with Catherine of Aragon. No doubt Mary would have taken pride in the splendid temporary village that sprung up out of the fertile Norman fields; after all, her father had been responsible for its organisation. She may have taken refreshment from one of the two magnificent fountains decorated with flowers and topped with statues of Cupid and Bacchus, spouting white and red wine continually. Or else she was dazzled by the banqueting house, built with brick walls on stone foundations, hung with tapestry of gold and silver interlaced with white and gold silk. It contained four great rooms, eight saloons, chambers, wardrobes and a chapel in blue and gold with rich cupboards full of plate. A sea of smaller tents made up the English camp, coded by colour, fabric and design according to rank. Henry must have cut an impressive figure: still tall, fair and athletic as he departed to meet Francis, dressed entirely in gold, his mantle and sleeves set with diamonds, rubies, emeralds and large pearls. Mary would have witnessed him take part in the numerous tournaments, jousts, masquerades, feasts and dances that took place over the ensuing days. The subsequent expenses betray the extent of the occasion's opulence, including £1,568 spent on supplying drink, £1,374 on poultry alone, £22 on sauces including mustard, wine sauce, capers and verjuice, over £600 for wax and £344 for spices and subtleties. Total estimates for royal consumption that month reached over £7,400.[22] While Henry may have been aware of Mary

Boleyn during this month of festivities, it is unlikely that, as has been suggested, their affair began then. With so many activities and such a lack of privacy, the Field of Cloth of Gold would have hampered rather than assisted the beginning of any liaison; perhaps the attraction had begun, but Henry would have waited until returning home to pursue Mary more discretely.

Mary may have become the king's lover before dancing in the Château Vert pageant in March 1522. If not, it is most likely that this was the occasion that drew them together. Dancing in the role of 'Kindness', Mary and the other women wore white satin gowns and Milan bonnets of gold, encrusted with gems, embroidered with their names. The occasion marked the betrothal of Holy Roman Emperor Charles to the six-year-old Princess Mary. As part of the festivities, Henry had taken part in a joust bearing the motto 'she has wounded my heart': now he followed William Cornish in the pageant, who danced as 'Ardent Desire'. These may well have been indicators to a chosen lady that she had gained his affections. If it was Mary, she had already been married two years, dispelling the myths popularised in film and fiction that she was hurriedly wed in order to cover the liaison. However, this was the last recorded appearance of Mary at court for a number of years. As part of the Duchess of Suffolk's entourage, she may have only been at court intermittently. If she was meeting Henry, it may have been at locations away from the royal palaces, at Jericho or the moated hunting lodge overlooking Greenwich Park. Perhaps Henry visited her at Hever when staying at nearby Penshurst Place, or they met at William Compton's house in Thames Street or else she was conducted in secret into the king's lodgings.

Finding a location for illicit sexual encounters was difficult for Tudor men and women of all walks of life. While it is impossible to delineate patterns of sexual behaviour within marriage beyond the evidence of conceptions, it is apparent that relations took place on a frequent and informal basis among unmarried and adulterous couples, especially those living under the same roof, like fellow servants or masters and female servants. Bedrooms were rare luxuries; most people shared a bed or at least slept in the same room. Servants Davie Cox and Alse Mathews, working together at Tilbury-near-Clare, had sex 'divers and sundry' (many different) times in the space of nine months, before she fell pregnant in 1588.[23] Susan Babye, of Coggeshall, confessed that she had slept with John Fletcher once at the fair in 1582, as well as with Richard Howe who lay with her once at Midsummer and William Dagnett, who 'had to do with her ... divers and sundry times'.[24] Servants Thomas Mathew and Elizabeth Browne had sex on a journey between Witham and Cressing in 1582, although they were 'hinderd by rayne' and later resorted to using their master's chamber in his absence.[25] Joan Collen and William Rothman made use of a 'rye stubble field', a stable and an apple store in 1592[26] while in 1589, Agnes Jolley witnessed Margery Hawles and Thomas Dooe of Chapel going together into a thicket of bushes, after which Dooe emerged, incriminatingly 'tying his points'.[27] Such examples are typical of the opportunistic encounters resulting in illegitimate births dealt with in the legal courts; conversely, when the doors to the marital bedroom were closed, or when royalty were involved, patterns of behaviour were less clear. For Henry's unmarried subjects, the great outdoors provided their best opportunity for illicit sex: Essex parish records list March and April as consistently the most common months for baptisms, indicating conception dates in the abundant midsummer when the temperature and undergrowth were higher. By late summer, before the harvest, food prices would rise and workers would be exhausted by long working hours once the gathering in began. Conception cycles support this theory, with the birth rate tailing off between May and July, suggesting that less conceptions took place in August and September.[28] As poverty and dependence dictated sexual practices, money could buy a degree of privacy and choice. Free from such agricultural commitments, Henry's numerous hunting lodges and country manor houses must have provided him with opportunities. A king could also rely on the discretion of those involved, who would turn a blind eye or even facilitate his amours.

It was unlikely that Mary and Henry's affair was conducted in her marital home or conflicted with her marriage in any way. Just as Henry continued to sleep with Catherine through the duration of his relations with Mary, so she would have been a wife in the fullest sense to her husband William Carey. Modern, romantic sensibilities have attempted to separate two sexual narratives in

1. Modern statue of Edward IV from the exterior of Canterbury Cathedral.

2. Tudor portrait of Edward IV, father of Elizabeth of York and grandfather of Henry VIII.

3. Elizabeth Wydeville, wife of Edward IV. A companion Tudor portrait to 2. with the same rich black and gold colouring. A plain gold wedding band is visible on her left hand.

Above left: 4. Henry VIII and Henry VII, detail from the Whitehall mural of 1537, by Holbein.

Above right: 5. Modern statue of Henry VII, from the exterior of Canterbury Cathedral.

Right: 6. Henry VII, the first Tudor king, in a portrait that perpetuates later interpretations of his miserliness. He holds a Lancastrian red rose in his right hand.

7. Elizabeth of York, the white rose, whose marriage to Henry VII united warring factions and produced the Tudor line. She wears regal red velvet, gold and ermine.

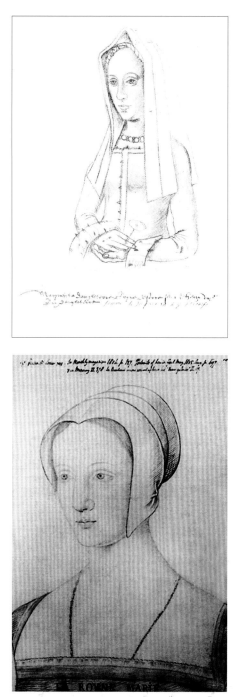

8. Margaret Tudor, eldest daughter of Henry VII and wife of James IV of France. Henry VIII excluded her from his will but her Stuart descendants inherited the throne in 1603.

9. Mary Rose Tudor, younger daughter of Henry VII and Queen of France by her marriage to Louis XII. Grandmother of the unfortunate Lady Jane Grey.

Above left: 10. Prince Arthur, whose premature death allowed Henry VIII to succeed to the throne. The combination of piety and chivalry in this modern window epitomised the early Tudor ideal.

Above right: 11. Modern statue of Henry VIII from the exterior of Canterbury Cathedral.

12. Henry VIII: the most iconic image of a Tudor majesty, his gaze directly confronting the viewer in a departure from previous portraiture (by Hans Holbein).

13. Catherine of Aragon as queen. Henry VIII's Spanish Catholic first wife who refused to move aside quietly, insisting she was his wife until her death.

14. Medieval carved underside of a window in Kent, depicting the 'underside' of life; the female figures attract and repel with their overt sexuality and suggestive fecundity, warning the passer-by to keep their mind on the spiritual and avoid the perils of temptation.

15. Ruins of St Augustine's Abbey, Canterbury, Kent, dissolved by Henry VIII. It was rapidly changed into a royal palace ready for Anne of Cleves to stay there on her journey to meet Henry late in December 1539. In the end, she only lodged here for a single night.

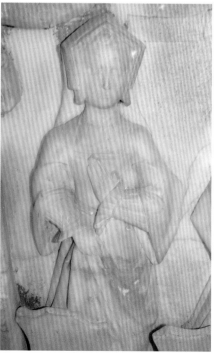

Above: 16. Canterbury Cathedral Chapter House window depicting Henry IV and Archbishop Cranmer flanking another version of the Holbein Henry VIII.

Left: 17. Funeral effigy of Elizabeth Blount, Lady Tailboys, Henry's mistress and the mother of his son, Henry Fitzroy.

Right: 18. Anne Boleyn, Henry's second, ill-fated wife; pen-and-ink drawing by Holbein.

Below: 19. George Cruikshank's depiction of Henry VIII's reconciliation with Anne Boleyn.

Above left: 20. Beheaded statue from a tomb in Canterbury Cathedral; this was the easiest and most symbolic way for iconoclasts to strip Catholic images of their power: even the golden eagle to the right has lost its head too.

Above right: 21. Jane Seymour, the demure and modest replacement for fiery Anne Boleyn. Her rapid marriage to Henry VIII has divided opinion since.

Left: 22. Anne of Cleves, the Holbein miniature that convinced Henry VIII to enter into a short-lived marriage with her in 1540.

23. Window in King's College chapel, Cambridge, depicting Catherine Howard as the Queen of Sheba.

24. Catherine Parr in stained glass at Sudeley Castle.

Left: 25. Modern statue of Edward VI, from the exterior of Canterbury Cathedral.

Below left: 26. Edward VI as a child, playing with a pet monkey. A painting by Holbein in the Kunstmuseum at Basle.

Below right: 27. Painting of Edward VI as a child by Holbein.

MARIA : REGINA.

28. Mary I, an austere but human portrait. Most of her life was spent waiting for an uncertain inheritance that brought her personal triumph and tragedy.

29. Elizabeth I, the longest-reigning Tudor monarch, whose notorious virginity ended the dynasty.

Left: 30. Mary Queen of Scots, heir to her cousin Elizabeth and focus of Catholic discontent until her execution in 1587.

Below: 31. Tudor woman and child.

her life although they were likely to have been concurrent, with no shame to Mary's reputation. In this lies the clue to the suppositions arising regarding the paternity of her two children, Catherine, born around 1524, and Henry in 1525/26. If Catherine and Henry Carey were the children of Henry VIII, he did not acknowledge them as such. From the moment of Henry Fitzroy's birth, there was little doubt of his royal paternity from his christening onwards; in 1525, at the age of six, the boy was created Earl of Northumberland and Duke of Richmond and Somerset; Henry appeared to have every intention of including him in the succession, possibly through a marriage to his half-sister Mary. Yet the birth of Fitzroy differed from that of the Carey children in one key element. Their mother was already married. The law automatically recognised a woman's husband as the father of any children born during or shortly after, a marriage. To alter or contest paternity would cause considerable scandal at significant legislative difficulty. However, this was the king; other reasons may have prevented their recognition. Firstly, if Mary Boleyn was sleeping with Henry and her husband simultaneously, paternity was by no means attributable to either: given the difficulties of ascertaining conception dates and predicting delivery, it is possible that Mary herself was unsure exactly who was responsible. If Henry had chosen to recognise either child, the implications for inheritance became more complex, potentially jeopardising the succession. Additionally, to admit he had impregnated a married woman would have conflicted with the chivalric image Henry had of himself: a king's adultery with an unmarried woman was acceptable while that with another man's wife was something else entirely. If either child was Henry's, it was more likely to have been Catherine, conceived in 1523. A portrait of her from 1562 shows an undeniable physical likeness to many of the Tudor family line, particularly Elizabeth I, although this may easily be through the Boleyn line. Possibly Mary's pregnancy motivated Henry to distance himself from her and brought about the end of the affair; equally, the conception of a child by her husband may have provoked the same response. The most likely solution appears to be that Henry was possibly the father of Catherine, although he was unaware of the fact or in his mind there existed reasonable doubt that he was not. His affair with

Mary may not have lasted until the advent of her sister Anne; in fact, the 1523 pregnancy is more likely to have ended it.

Mary later incurred the wrath of her family by conducting a secret marriage to William Stafford, a soldier far below her in rank. In this, she was following a pattern of many aristocratic women whose first arranged matches had ended through the death of their spouse; now like Mary Rose Tudor, she chose to marry for love. Appealing to Cromwell for financial assistance she claimed she 'would rather beg my bread with [Stafford] than to be the greatest queen in Christendom'. Reappearing at court in December 1534, Chapuys reported that she was pregnant but no record of this child survives; she may not have carried it to term or it may have died in infancy: alternatively Chapuys may have been mistaken, as he often was. She lived in obscurity in for the remainder of her life and died in 1543. Her children, Catherine and Henry, provided her with twenty-eight grandchildren, a record her king would have envied.

6

Anne Boleyn & Elizabeth
1526–1536

Miscarriage & Misogyny

In the King's royal head
Secret displeasure bred
Which cost the Queen her head.[1]

On a summer Sunday at the start of June 1533, Londoners in all their finery converged on Westminster Palace. The Mayor and Aldermen, dressed in crimson and scarlet, arrived by barge; bishops and abbots in their ceremonial copes and mitres; Knights of the Bath with their distinctive white lace on the left sleeve; barons and viscounts in their parliamentary scarlet robes; noblemen in powdered ermine, all awaiting the arrival of their new queen. Her sexual magnetism was legendary, her name scandalous: everyone wanted to see the woman who had held their king in thrall for seven years and displaced the popular Catherine. Between eight and nine that morning, their patience was rewarded. Anne Boleyn, granddaughter of the Duke of Norfolk, emerged from the royal lodgings. Her audience saw a tall, lithe, pale-skinned, raven-haired woman in her early thirties, with enchanting large dark eyes, not traditionally beautiful but unusual and captivating. She was splendidly dressed in a robe of purple velvet lined with ermine, over a kirtle of crimson and on her loose dark hair, sat a gold circlet set with pearls and other precious stones. The accounts for her clothing at that time included over thirty-two yards of crimson velvet, costing 13s and 4d a yard, 19 yards crimson damask costing 7s a yard and 3 yards of scarlet at 9s: considerable expense given that the daily wage of an unskilled labourer was around 7d, a poor woman to wash dishes or a boy to turn a spit could be had for 4*d* and a carpenter could command 1*s*, 2*d* for a day's work.

Under the folds of sumptuous fabric, Anne's swollen belly showed that she was pregnant, carrying the longed-for heir that had precipitated her rival's downfall. As Cranmer wrote later 'the condition thereof did well appear, by reason she is somewhat big with child'. Among her attendants were her triumphant family but also those supporters of Catherine, who had little choice but to fulfil ceremonial roles, like the king's brother-in-law Suffolk, who was High Steward of the day, dressed in crimson, pearls and precious stones. Anne's kinswoman, the Duchess of Norfolk, bore her long train, her ladies wore scarlet with the more fashionable narrow sleeves, while borne above her was carried a canopy of red and blue. She was led to St Peter's Church, Westminster. and sat in the 'seate riall', a platform elevated on two steps, covered with tapestry, where she was anointed by Archbishop Cranmer, who placed the traditional crown of St Edward on her head, although this was later substituted for a lighter one made especially for her. She took Communion and made an offering at St Edward's shrine before processing out to the sound of trumpets. The following feast for 800 guests, was held in the Palace's Great Hall, where the newly anointed queen sat under the cloth of estate. Two ladies sat at her feet throughout, to 'serve her secretly', and two others nearby to lift cloths and conceal her in case she wished to spit or wipe her face. An enclosure around her ensured nobody could approach except those assigned to attend her and there was 'good order' despite the four great tables below hers, extending the length of the hall. Conduits flowed with wine at every door, the kitchens were commanded to give meat to everyone and vast quantities were consumed. Anne, though, ate little of the spices, subtleties and 'other delicacies' presented to her on golden plates, along with wafers and hippocras wine. The mayor of London presented her with a gold cup to drink from before she departed to the sound of trumpets and hautbois, to spend the night at York Place.[2] It was hardly the 'cold, meagre and uncomfortable' affair that Imperial ambassador Chapuys reported to Catherine's nephew Charles V. Yet this is what the old Aragon faction would have hoped to hear. As the dishes were being cleared away, the tapestries and arras taken down and the crowd outside the abbey dissolved, the awkward question still remained. England had a new queen. But what was to be done about the old one?

Few historical figures have attracted such a persistent, fascinated following as Anne Boleyn. Her appeal, then as now, lies partly in her personal charisma and partly in the hold she exerted over Henry, with all its attendant consequences for English royalty and religion. Her dramatic fall from grace on blatantly trumped-up charges, and the shocking execution of an anointed queen, have made her a figure of sympathy and romance for readers of history and fiction, as well as more recent portrayals in film and television. Five centuries on she is still able to provoke powerful and dichotomic responses. Yet for someone so controversial, the basic facts of her life are sometimes unclear. Sources disagree about Anne's birthdate; 1501 and 1507 are usually suggested, with modern scholarship tending towards the earlier. The daughter of a union between the ambitious Boleyn and Howard families, her early years were spent at Blickling Hall, Norfolk, and then at Hever Castle, in Kent. Educated as a teenager in the refined Netherlands court of Margaret of Savoy, then as maid to the unfortunate Queen Claude of France, she acquired a polish that set her aside from her English counterparts, despite not conforming to contemporary standards of beauty. Hindsight has often coloured the accounts of her early years but when she first came to the king's attention, she was little more than another potential mistress: her arrival at court in 1522, dancing as 'Perseverance' in a masque in a caul of Venice gold, hardly gave any indication of the serious threat she eventually posed to Catherine of Aragon and the ultimate event of her coronation.

For aristocratic young women of ambitious families, one route for securing an influential husband was to take a position in the household of the queen or Mary Tudor. In this, Anne did not differ from Elizabeth Blount or her sister Mary, yet early in her career she found herself at the centre of one such scandal. Although she did not become one of Catherine's ladies-in-waiting until 1527, she was probably in attendance on Henry's sister Mary, the French queen, now the wife of Charles Brandon, Duke of Suffolk. One early reference places Anne with Mary at York Place, where

Thomas Wolsey arranged the pageant Château Vert to be danced before visiting Imperial Ambassadors. Around 1523, Anne again came to attention, this time through the secret betrothal she had entered into with Henry Percy, future Earl of Northumberland. Sent to court as a teenager, he became a page at Wolsey's court and would have had ample opportunities to woo the young Anne. If, as Wolsey's nineteenth-century biographer George Cavendish believed, the pair had exchanged formal vows, the question of their physical closeness arises. An informal handfasting between people of noble blood would only be considered binding by the Church if the union was then consummated. As Wolsey was able to dissolve the match, the likelihood is that this final step had not been taken and Anne's virginity remained intact. Cavendish's suggestions that the union was forbidden due to the king's fledgling interest in the bride are unlikely this early; he was at that point in a relationship with Mary Boleyn and if he had desired Anne, her marriage would have only been to his advantage; equally, Wolsey had already dissolved one match made by Percy in 1516. Anne was banished to the country, to re-emerge in 1526, already in her mid-twenties and comparatively old in terms of marriage.

It is not clear exactly when Henry fell in love with Anne Boleyn. The passionate love letters he wrote, dating from 1527–8, leave little doubt that by then his feeling for her was genuine, as was his desire to make her his wife. Crucially, her rise was a question of timing, coinciding with the king's resolution to divorce and remarry. Catherine's menopause occurred around 1525–6, after seven childless years, convincing him that she would not be the one to bear him a male heir. For a short while in 1527, he considered Wolsey's scheme for a union with the French princess Renee, although he rejected her after the Hungarian ambassador told him her inherited limp suggested she would be incapable of bringing 'forth frute, as it apperith by the liniacion of her body'.[3] He had determined to remarry, citing Leviticus 20:21 that a man taking his brother's wife upon his death would remain childless: if he received clerical support, he could simply announce the marriage had been null and void in the first place and no divorce would be needed. He would have been living in sin with Catherine and was free to take a wife of his own choosing. It should have been a straightforward matter but Henry had not reckoned with his queen.

By 1527, Anne had secured Henry's attention, which she maintained by refusing to become his mistress. The following year, he told Cardinal Campeggio, the papal legate, that he had not had intercourse with Catherine for two years, although they shared a bed for the sakes of appearances. Was Henry, therefore, celibate for the entire six years, from 1526 until the end of 1532, when Anne finally succumbed? No doubt he was enthralled by her and their letters testify to their passion and a degree of intimacy but such a claim seems hard to believe. Barely months after their marriage, after Anne's pregnancy was apparent, Henry was seeking out other women; did this king, with his reputation for a 'lewd life' and well-known love of women, really refrain from even the casual encounters with women of lower classes, with whom aristocratic men were expected to find relief? It seems implausible, yet few historians have questioned this. An episode at the end of September 1537, after Jane Seymour had entered her confinement, illustrates how Henry was prepared to initiate casual encounters with women who took his fancy. One William Webbe was out riding with his lover a month before, when the king came upon them, desired the woman, kissed her and 'took her from him' to live in 'avowtry' (adultery) where she remained.[4] In 1592, a John Perrott claimed to be the son of Henry VIII, born in Pembrokeshire in November 1528, placing his conception in February. Despite Perrott's resemblance to the king in appearance and temperament, the claim seems unlikely, as his mother Mary Berkeley spent that period of her life in Wales and the West, while Henry remained further east and had little chance to encounter her. However, the arguments that he cannot have fathered a child during this period due to his devotion to Anne must be reconsidered. Romantic, chaste devotion to a woman he hoped to make his wife would not necessarily preclude casual encounters for a king such as Henry, especially as the years passed with increasing frustration. Unfortunately, the nature of such liaisons, conducted in secrecy and of a short-term duration, leaves little trace in official surviving documentation; yet while many can be discredited, the sheer volume of rumours regarding his activities suggest he was very sexually active. The reports of other illegitimate children, such as Thomas Stucley, Richard Edwardes and a daughter named Ethelreda, all born in the late 1520s, indicates a possible lost oral tradition of the lusty king's encounters.

Yet between 1526 and 1532, Anne denied Henry full consummation. A degree of physical intimacy is suggested by their letters but it is clear they stopped short of the final act, increasing his desire and frustration. Over the following years, a battle of wills between him and Catherine resulted in stalemate. As England's anointed queen and Henry's wife, Catherine would not make way for a younger, more fruitful rival and fought his attempts to dissolve the marriage on the grounds of her previous union with Arthur, insisting that the earlier match had remained unconsummated. The pair maintained a dignified public façade while fighting an increasingly desperate private battle. Catherine's powerful European connections ensured continuing Papal hostility towards Henry's pleas for divorce, and the Legatine court held at Blackfriars in 1529 under Cardinal Campeggio proved lengthy, obstructive and provided Catherine with a forum for dramatic displays of piety and wifely devotion. From 1531 onwards, though, the queen was banished from court and the presence of her husband and daughter, ending up in residence at Kimbolton Castle, Cambridgeshire, still protesting her rights as queen and refusing to compromise. Ultimately, Catherine was to prove the loser, as Henry's split from Rome allowed him to put the matter of his marriage into English hands, while the Boleyns secured the appointment of the sympathetic Thomas Cranmer as Archbishop of Canterbury in October 1532. Shortly after this, Henry and Anne's relationship was consummated and depending upon Elizabeth's conception, suspicions of her pregnancy may have precipitated their secret marriage. A few sources suggest it occurred as early as November but better known is the second, formal ceremony conducted on 25 January 1533. Even this was a quiet, secret affair, officiated by Rowland Lee, future bishop of Coventry in a tower at York Place, witnessed by three of their close companions. By the time of her coronation, Anne was eagerly anticipating the birth of their son.

In the later stages of her pregnancy, Henry showered his new wife with gifts and ensured she was well provisioned as a queen. A week after her coronation, the keeper of the royal wardrobe, Edward Flowde, received a warrant to deliver various items for her use, a number of which must have been previously owned or used by Catherine. It sounded very much as if Anne was feathering her nest, making provisions for her lying-in. She was to receive a cloth of estate made of gold tissue, embroidered with children and the Tudor arms, chairs covered and fringed with gold and crimson velvet, Turkey carpets, woollen blankets and animal hides. The list included a pound of fine white thread for mending sheets and a pound of thick white thread for mending beds; she also received the hand brushes, hammers and hooks essential to maintain a large Tudor bed.[5] Anne's chambers at Greenwich were still a centre of activity though, as on 9 June, Sir Edward Baynton wrote to her brother George of the 'dancing and pastime' that went on there. On another occasion Henry bought Anne a black satin nightgown edged with black velvet.

Henry was less generous to Catherine, though, informing her that the king could not have two wives and that she, the Dowager, widow of his brother Arthur, must desist from calling herself queen and hand over her jewels. There would be 'danger' if she attempted to contravene this, which would only 'irritate' the people against her, and her arrogance would compel Henry to punish her servants and 'withdraw her affection from his daughter'.[6] When his messengers attempted to deliver this commission, Catherine put on a powerful show of sympathy, refusing to rise from her pallet bed and insisting she was the king's true wife and would not damn her soul by behaving otherwise: Henry had not reckoned with the fact that Catherine's religion allowed her to obey a higher authority than his. He did not receive her resistance well but by this time, only weeks remained until the birth of his heir. Even the Pope's sentence of excommunication could not detract from the impending event.

Elizabeth's conception must have taken place sometime in early December, assuming that she was full term. This could suggest Anne was as much as six weeks pregnant at the time of the official marriage; at least she was two or three weeks gone; neither of which scenarios would have allowed the couple to be certain conception had taken place. It is unlikely that the union was consummated before the autumn visit they made to France, so Anne had proved herself fertile, having fallen pregnant quickly and appearing to deliver on the promises that had kept Henry dangling for six years. Later advice was quite explicit regarding the sexual act. One French doctor's manual advised that at the moment of conception a man would feel 'extraordinary contentment' in the company of his wife or a sort of 'sucking or drawing at the end of his yard', which when he withdrew, was not 'over-moist'. The woman should experience a sort of 'yawning or stretching' in the womb or a 'shaking and quivering' as when she passed water, a chill in shoulders and back or a rumbling in the belly as the womb contracted. Within a few days, she should fall vomiting and spitting and disdaining of her meat, although this may not have afflicted every woman, as in February 1533, Anne hosted a sumptuous banquet for Henry, sitting symbolically on his right-hand side and appearing to eat well. Into her second month, the manual claimed, her eyes may grow pale and wan and her eyeballs show less while the veins there would swell, then her breasts would grow hard with milk and her nipples prickle; they would be reddish if she carried a boy and blackish if it was a girl. Other diagnostic tools including mixing a woman's urine with wine or making her drink rainwater at night, or honey and aniseed, which would bring pain to her stomach if she had conceived. If Anne and Henry followed contemporary advice on maternal nutrition and well-being, they would have ensured she resided in 'good and well-tempered air', not too hot, cold, dry or moist. She should not go out in any fogs or winds, especially winds from the south, which were considered especially harmful. Her diet may include meat and wine, with good long periods of rest at night, the better to digest it, for staying awake could engender disease in the foetus; prunes and sugared apples could alleviate discomfort as could broths made of borage, parsley, lettuce and patience. Linen or flax soaked in distillations made from calves' or sheep's heads, violet oil, sugar, aniseed and fennel were convenient and could be applied with discretion to sore areas. She should avoid riding in carriages, especially in the first three months, all forms of strenuous exercise and just as Elizabeth of York was advised, all loud noises, extremes of passion and distressing emotions. Bloodletting and purges were forbidden from the sixth month onwards, around the time of Anne's coronation.

In childbearing terms, Anne Boleyn's heritage looked promising. Her paternal grandmother Lady Margaret Butler had borne ten children, eight of which had survived infancy and her mother Elizabeth Howard was pregnant at least seven times, although only three of her children survived to adulthood. Mary Boleyn's daughter Catherine Carey went on to have fifteen children with her husband Sir Francis Knollys, while her son provided another twelve grandchildren. Mary Boleyn's granddaughter, Anne West, bore thirteen children, delivering on average every eighteen months between 1571 and 1592: only one died young and Anne lived to the age of fifty-three, when her youngest was sixteen. The family were indeed prolific and fecund; there was little in the new queen's family tree to suggest that she would not be capable of bearing many healthy children of both genders. However, Anne's most fertile years were spent in abstinence; from her mid-twenties to her early thirties, she held the king at a distance, when she was old enough to be married and have borne several children. Apparently worried that she would never be wed, she is supposed to have spoken of her concerns that her time and youth would all be spent for nothing. She was old by Tudor standards when she conceived in December 1532 and after an interminable interval of fourteen years, Henry could finally anticipate the arrival of a legitimate male heir. At forty-one, he could no longer rely on his fading youth yet this new match had proved his ability to still father children.

Despite Catherine's continued insistence of her royal status, the new marriage and pregnancy were made public in the spring of 1533: Anne reputedly dropped hints at her condition by stating aloud her craving for apples. The scandal rocked Europe; everyone was taking an interest in Anne's pregnancy, yet the strain of it may already have been causing tensions in the marriage. Denied his wife's favours in order to protect her growing foetus, Henry's eye was straying according to Chapuys: he 'shows himself in love with another lady and many nobles are assisting him in the affair. This unidentified woman, sometimes referred to as the 'imperial lady' or possibly Madge Shelton, with whom Henry was involved the following year, came to Anne's attention. Her unqueenly protestations were met with savage retorts and threats. Chapuys claimed that on 3 September, days before she gave birth, Anne had cause to be jealous of Henry's behaviour, for which he chided her to 'shut her eyes and endure' as more 'worthy' persons had, for it was in his power to 'humble' her as much as he had raised her, with the result that they had not spoken for several days.[7] However, this is not necessarily trustworthy. Given Henry's desire for a healthy male child, it is unlikely he would have risked Anne's composure so close to the birth; Chapuys' reports could be notoriously unreliable and he was clearly writing with sympathy for Catherine: Henry's secretary Sir William Paget described him as lacking honesty or truth; 'he is a great practiser [plotter], tale-telling, lying and flattering'.[8] On the contrary, one witness wrote that the king and queen were in 'good health and merry'. However, it must also have been a difficult time for Anne, knowing the extent of her unpopularity; that week Thomas Cromwell received reports of commoners speaking against her marriage, like the priest in Rye, against whom allegations of defamation were made only two days before Elizabeth's arrival. In the same week, men in Flanders were reporting that Anne had been 'brought to bed of a monster', or that her child was dead; according to them, the king was abused by her and scarcely dared go out 'for the rumour of the people'. Further rumours of discontent had reached Cromwell's ears, as his scribe recorded in June, that some people in the realm 'be not in their minds full pleased and content' at the match.[9] One anonymous writer in Rome predicted the child would be weak because of his father's complexion and 'habits of life'; it may suffer physical debilities because of his rampant sexual appetite[10] while at the end of the month, an English priest named Gebbons was reported to have called the queen a whore and harlot and claimed many burnings at Smithfield would herald her downfall.[11]

Yet courtly preparations went ahead in spite of the possible marital discord. Margaret Beaufort's arrangements for previous royal confinements changed hands; Catherine's chamberlain was forced to hand over all the relevant papers to Cromwell, in an act of such bitter personal symbolism for the defeated queen and her triumphant rival. The lying-in chamber was prepared at

Greenwich, along the same lines as those made ready for Catherine of Aragon, although at this turning point in the country's religious history, it is unknown whether the full complement of images, crucifixes and icons were at hand. Anne's sympathies lay firmly with the Reformed faith, yet the use of such icons in churches would not be fully banned until the reign of Edward VI. Catholic talismen may or may not have been present at her delivery and she may or may not have used them: Dr David Starkey is confident of their inclusion[12] and Anne was known to use other superstitious charms and aides such as cramp rings and to request the presence of the sacrament during her incarceration. Her chambers probably contained an altar and religious texts even if she had rejected the images and relics of Catherine's faith. The floor was carpeted and a false ceiling lined with tapestries. A special cupboard had been built to house the queen's plate, an important mark of status replicated in lying-in chambers throughout the country, to house whatever the household could afford, from wood and pewter up to silver and gold. Some families even commissioned new ceremonial plate for the occasion, marked with images, dates and names. Henry's physicians and astrologers had predicted a son; the Duke of Norfolk reported to Francis I that Henry was planning to christen him Henry or Edward and that elaborate tournaments and jousts had been planned. Some of Anne's favourites were so confident of the baby's sex that they had already sent to Flanders for horses on which to compete. Chapuys reported that one of the most 'magnificent and gorgeous' beds, once given in ransom for a Duke d'Alençon in 1515, had been removed from Henry's treasure room in July as preparation for the birth, and the chamber walls were hung with tapestries depicting the life of St Ursula and her 11,000 virgins.

The 'magnificent and gorgeous' bed that awaited Anne was typical of those of Tudor monarchs yet they would not receive much use. A king or queen would often sleep on a simpler, smaller bed in a back room while such elaborate pieces of furniture were reserved for ceremonial or State occasions. Four-poster beds were a Tudor invention, often the largest and most expensive item in the house. They were constructed around solid wooden frames, carved and decorated, topped with an elaborate headboard and furnished with luxurious and colourful hangings and bedding. The mattress lay on bed strings, or rope, threaded from side to side, often saggy in the middle, necessitating constant tightening, which is the origin of the phrase to 'sleep tight'. Six carvers worked for ten months on the walnut frame of Henry's new bed at Whitehall in the early 1530s. The canopy and tester were made from panels of cloth of silver and gold, edged with purple velvet ribbon, embroidered with the royal arms, Tudor roses and the French *fleur-de-lys*. Five curtains hung round it, of purple and white taffeta edged with gold ribbon.[13] He slept upon eight mattresses, which had previously been checked for daggers and sprinkled with holy water. Beds were an important sign of status and wealth, usually the largest and most expensive piece of furniture in a house; everyone from the monarchy down desired an impressive bed. Anne's brother George slept on a soft feather mattress with down pillows, on a gilded bedstead draped in cloth of gold and white satin, with embellishments in tawny cloth of gold, fringed in white and yellow silk. Privacy was ensured by pulling closed the red and white damask curtains.[14]

Beds were emotive and powerful. The inventoried goods of Bishop Fisher of Rochester, April 1534, included a bedstead with a mattress, a counterpoint of red cloth lined with canvas and a tester of old red velvet, while in another room stood a joined bedstead, a turned bedstead with bedding, bedstead with mattress, an old folding bed, bedstead and two mattresses; Fisher's cook must have been a valued servant to have had her own feather bed and bolster. In her 1515 will, one Catherine Levynthorpe, a widow of Hatfield Kings, left to her son William and his wife Jane a feather bed with a bolster, pair of fustian blankets, red and yellow coverlet and two pillows; to her daughter Anne, she gave a feather bed and bolster with a counterpane and to a Cicely Thornehill, a mattress and bolster, a pair of flaxen sheets, pair of blankets, red and yellow counterpane.[15] The 1520 inventory of Lord Darcy's household accounts included thirty-four beds and many more mattresses; his spectacular bed linen included separate tapestry counterpoints worked with the story of St George, three naked children in a chariot, lords and ladies, vines and grapes, biblical stories, legends, family names, coats of arms, organs and lions. The materials used included yellow silk lined with green buckram, green velvet and black satin, yellow and red sarcanet, tawny velvet and tinsel satin.[16] Good-quality bedding was so highly prized it was often the target of thieves. In 1583, John Seymer of Shalford was accused of breaking into the house of the widow Joan Fytche and stealing, among other items, two pairs of sheets worth 6s 8d and curtains, worth 3s, for a bed[17] while in 1587, another felonious pair, labourers at Coggeshall, were found guilty of stealing a feather bed worth 3s 4d, a coverlet worth 2s, a pair of sheets worth 2s 6d and a bolster worth 2s.[18] At the lowest end of the social scale, servants would sleep on simple pallets or truckle beds, often in the same room as their masters. Bedrooms, anterooms and passageways in Tudor palaces would have been full of gentlemen and maids of honour spending the night on duty, ever alert for potential dangers or royal commands.

Anne went into confinement comparatively late on 26 August, the day of her arrival at Greenwich. This would have suggested to the court that she anticipated giving birth at the end of September, as the customary month dictated, implying she believed in a conception date around Christmas. However, she had scarcely been settled in when her labour began. On arrival, the midwife would have questioned her as to the nature of her pains and felt her womb to discover to what extent the child's head had engaged. She may have anointed her hands with animal fat or herbal oils and examined the neck of the womb to establish her dilation or encourage the waters to break, had they not already done so. Anne did not lack female relations; possibly her mother and sister-in-law Jane were present as well as her ladies-in-waiting, although her sister Mary may still have been absent from court. Equally, the early arrival might have caught them by surprise. Hurrying to be by her side, Anne's relations would have entered a rich, darkened chamber where pleasing scents were burned, such as ambergris, musk and civet, in the belief that they would soothe Anne during her labour, and the fire would have been maintained regularly to prevent the cold closing up her body. In the event, such preparations may have had a similar placebo effect to the clasping of religious artefacts, and represent a step closer to the rituals and practices of modern delivery rooms, often made more relaxing with candles, music and small homely comforts. It is possible that Anne would have still called upon the saints for assistance: St Felicitas was usually invoked to ensure the child was a boy, which she was well aware was Henry's greatest wish. If she did, it was to no avail. A daughter was born after a straight-forward labour, about 3 o'clock on the afternoon of Sunday 7 September.

Exploring the 'what-ifs' of history is always a cul-de-sac that lends itself better to fiction. However, in this case, the immense significance of the newborn's gender, dictated purely by chance, was to have such an impact that the alternative scenario cannot help but provoke questions. How different the course of Tudor history may have been if Anne had borne a boy, not to mention the duration of her own life. The random allocation of genitals was, in this case, to irrevocably shape the future of a nation, as her parents were quickly aware. Chapuys reported that the arrival of a girl was 'to the great regret' of both and great 'reproach of the physicians, astrologers, sorcerers and sorceresses who affirmed that it would be a male child'. Initially, Anne was determined to call her Mary, to supplant the existing princess; Chapuys even reported that was to be her name on the actual day of the Christening the following Wednesday but later corrected himself; the Venetian ambassador thought the name Elizabeth had been chosen in honour of their mothers, Elizabeth of York and Elizabeth Howard. Still, Anne had delivered a healthy child and survived, which was cause enough for gratitude. Celebratory bonfires were lit across the country and free wine flowed in London to the sound of ringing church bells. Three days later, the baby was carried in procession from the great hall at Greenwich along a carpet of green rushes, past Arras hangings, accompanied by 500 lit torches, to be christened at the church of observant friars. Henry had another legitimate heir; surely now sons would follow?

Anne considered children a blessing; 'the greatest consolation in the world'. According to one source, she was determined to breastfeed her daughter but had to give way to the pressure of her role. Instead, Elizabeth was set up in her own establishment at Hatfield. If this account is true, it shows Anne's unconventionality; knowing the traditions of wet-nursing for royal and aristocratic infants must have served as a reminder of the distance she had travelled in becoming queen. Noblewomen would not normally breastfeed, sending their babies instead to a wet nurse and regaining their fertility sooner. Babies born to the nobility, aristocracy and royalty were quickly established with a wet nurse, usually of good and healthy appearance, who had recently borne a child of the same gender. It was thought that a child absorbed the nurses's qualities through her milk, so careful attention was paid to character and social degree: also the wet nurses's food; her garlic and alcohol consumption were carefully monitored, with some serving aristocratic families receiving generous allowances. This allowed noblewomen's fertility levels to return to normal more quickly and queens to resume their public role. It meant that the relationship between a royal parent and child was significantly less close than those established with their immediate carers. In this, as in so many aspects of her life, a queen's personal feelings must have been set aside.

Middle- and lower-class women were more likely to suckle their infants themselves. While breastfeeding might come naturally, especially to an experienced mother, the feeding of first babies could be tricky and required the support and encouragement of women who had themselves been through the process. Folklore remedies had advice to offer the breastfeeding mother; she should wear a gold or steel chain to stop milk curdling and to aid her milk flow, should sip milk of a cow of a single colour, then spit it out into running water, swallow a mouthful of that water and recite a charm. Hemp and henbane were used to soothe sore breasts, while barley water and dried powdered earthworms were reputed to increase milk supply. Unchaste women were believed to have a decreased milk supply, making abstinence desirable, hence the contemporary disapproval of sex during breastfeeding. Receipt books drew on local herbs and ingredients accessible in a domestic context to make poultices and dressings:

For a soare breste:
Take mallowes and chopp them smale and seeth [boil] them tender in running water till the water be consumed so the hearbes doe not burne; put thereto a quantity of deare sewett [deer suet] or for want thereof sheeps sewett, take also a bottle of good ale dregs and

a quarte of white wine, cromes [crumbs] of leaven bread made of wheat, then seethe altogether till it be thicke, so spread itt one a linen cloth and lay itt upon the breast, so hott as the patient may suffer itt, so dresse it every day twise.

Take these following for a soare breast that is swollen:
Take a handfull of mallowes, another of wormewood, seeth them in running water with a softe fyre, till thye bee tender, then take them from the water and coppe [chop] them upon a bourd mingled with boores [boar's] grease to the quantity of half the hearbes and lay as much to the soare as need shall require.

For vaines [veins] in womens breasts wherin is much heate with overmuch mylke which often happeneth after they be delivered:
Take cleane clay without stones, mingle itt with vinegar and the yolk of an egge plaister like, so spread it upon a linen cloth to the soare breste, so let itt ly till itt bee dry, the remove itt and lay to another and so again if neede require.[19]

Paradoxically it was the richest and poorest members of society who did not breastfeed; the children of servants were also put out to nurse in nearby villages, so they could resume their duties. When Marcy Dethecke's servant Joan Bartholomew gave birth to an illegitimate child at Stanford-le-Hope in 1595, she paid fifteen pence a week for it to be nursed at nearby Horndon-on-the-Hill.[20] Christopher Tompson of London sought the help of a vicar in 1575 when attempting to place a male child of five or six weeks out to nurse, although the nurse was afraid to take the child for fear of the sickness in the city so the baby was then sent to Hertfordshire to be nursed temporarily and brought back a couple of months later when the sickness had subsided.[21] Many died in infancy before returning to their parents. Deservedly or not, wet nurses had a reputation for carelessness, for 'overlaying' or falling asleep while feeding, and smothering their charges. Familiar accusations were those of drunkenness or infanticide. In the parish of Good Easter, Essex, the burial of Henry Coot, a nursling child from Chelmsford, was recorded on 18 April 1590 and that of Thomas Watt on 28 November 1596;[22] the names of the high-born mothers and the village nurses are not listed. In the parish of St Mary Magdalene, Great Bursted, Essex, the burial was recorded of an unnamed nursling child in 1599 'being a man chylde of a saylors' while 'Dorrothe Person, a nurse child of London' was buried at Chelmsford on 11 July 1550.[23] Sometimes the decision to put a child out to nurse was made for its own protection. The notoriety of a Mary Webbe, recorded as having lived a 'wicked life', despite now repenting and willing to enter 'honest service', influenced Coggeshall parish to separate her from her newborn illegitimate child and put it out to nurse in 1580, for which the father, John Sawnder, was made to pay 16 pence a week.[24] When a mother was unavailable, ill, poor, dissolute or deceased, the parish took charge of the infant's nursing, drawing from what must have been a pool of suitable women: it was important though, that the child was supported at the location of its birth. Just as with labouring women, infants incurred expenses that drained the resources of smaller communities: in 1602, the Chelmsford assizes ruled that a child named Ruth must be returned to its birth parish of Copford, from whence it would be sent out to nurse at Aldham, placing the charge for its upkeep firmly in the Copford coffers.[25] In many cases of illegitimacy, though, court records state that children were to remain and be nursed by their mothers, which alleviated the parish of additional expense.

Conversely, other wet nurses must have grown attached to their charges and experienced a considerable wrench when the time came to return them to their parents: in some cases, they provided better care than the mother could. A considerable industry of wet nurses in regular employment must have existed, their reputation spread by word of mouth. John Dee's diary records the payments given to those who cared for his children: a Nurse Darant was given 10s, a whole quarter's wages in April 1580 for weaning the nine month old Arthur, while their daughter Katharine was sent home from Nurse Mapsley of Barnes, for fear of her maid's sickness; in the interim she was suckled by Goodwife Benet before being sent on to Nurse Garret in Petersham. Another nurse they used for their son Rowland was also rewarded with extra money for the candles and soap[26] intrinsic to her duties. By placing their child in the care of another woman, Tudor mothers may have distanced themselves a little from the inevitable losses of the first dangerous year of survival. It could be seen as prioritising maternal health and sexuality over the welfare of the child, although this is a more modern view and sixteenth-century parents would have considered they had made perfectly good arrangements for their offspring. If it survived, their child would be returned, weaned and more self-reliant than a helpless baby, ready to become the miniature adult of contemporary portraiture. Without this degree of natural contraceptive protection, noblewomen could also fall pregnant again more quickly.

Anne appeared to conceive again only weeks after Elizabeth's birth. That Christmas, her gift to Henry was a fertility symbol; a gold fountain flanked by three naked women whose nipples flowed with water; rumours of a new pregnancy were already circulating the court by the new year, reaching Chapuys by February.[27] Two months later, orders were being given to the court goldsmith, Cornelius Hayes, for an elaborate silver cradle decorated with Tudor roses and precious stones; he had probably executed a similar design for Elizabeth in 1533, having received a part payment that June, of a considerable £300. Arrangements were also made for the provision of gold embroidered bedding and baby clothes made from cloth of gold. On 27 April, a George Taylor was able to write from Greenwich to Lady Lisle that the queen 'hath a goodly belly, praying our Lord to send us a prince'[28] and a planned trip to Calais that August was intended to take place after the birth, as Anne was 'so farre gon with childe';[29] witnesses saw the queen making merry at Hampton Court as late as 26 June. A possible conception date in November would have led Anne to anticipate lying-in that August, so the pregnancy must have been considerably advanced by the summer. But nothing happened. There was no move to enter confinement, no baby arrived and the matter was mysteriously dropped. By September, rumours were circulating that she had never been pregnant at all. No official records were made of her lying-in or miscarriage, while unsubstantiated gossip hinted at the delivery of a premature son while the court was on progress at the end of June. It is possible that had Anne lost a child following a visible pregnancy; her enemies would have made much of the matter, even if it was handled with the utmost discretion.

Although the king sounded confident when ordering the cradle in April, that summer's silence suggests this was a false alarm. One modern suggestion that she was actually pregnant twice during this period, miscarrying in April and in the summer, barely allows time for Anne to realise her condition.[30] That September, Chapuys reported that she was 'not to have a child after all', which sounds more like a mistake than a miscarriage. Perhaps, like Catherine, she had experienced an infection or other symptoms of illness that were misinterpreted. Professor Dewhurst supports the theory of pseudocyesis or phantom pregnancy, with physical symptoms stemming from Anne's desire to prove her fertility, as does Muriel St Clair Byrne, who identified a similar condition in Honor Lisle in 1536–37.[31] It is unlikely the shame and disappointment of a miscarriage at eight months and the threat of king's wrath would have been enough to silence the most vitriolic wagging tongues. It seems that a mistake had been made. For Henry, the situation felt alarmingly familiar.

In Tudor times, a miscarriage was often called a shift, a slipping away or mischance, and was considered an act of God in the most literal sense; a judgement or punishment passed on the morality and sexual practices of the parents. It could be used to refer to premature stillbirth while today, it is a specific term used only to refer to the 'expulsion of a foetus before twenty-eight weeks of pregnancy'.[32] Physicians considered a miscarried child was either too weak, sickly or large or that the mother was either undernourished or had too much 'fullness and moistness'. The danger signs were milk running out of the breasts or the nipples changing colour or looseness in the belly, back and groin pain; to prevent this, a woman must eat well and rest; occasionally she should be bled or purged, must be merry and not fret, and anoint her navel with mixture of red wine, roses, coral and cinnamon. Interestingly though, it was not until after the death of the final Tudor, Elizabeth, that patterns of miscarriages were observed as having some physiological connection. In 1612, Guillemeau wrote in *The Happie Deliverie of Women*, 'those that have been delivered once before their time, for the most part, they miscarry with the rest of their children about the same time'. Henry VIII may have indeed observed the start of a pattern repeating itself, as did the explanation he could not put aside. In his view, Anne's failure to produce a son, just like Catherine's, was a condemnation of his marriage by God.

It is possible, as a few historians suggest, that Anne had a third pregnancy in the summer of 1535, which again ended in miscarriage, but consensus appears to support the idea that she did not conceive again until autumn 1535. The previous year had been difficult, with Henry's attentions again straying to an unnamed lady whose loyalties lay with Catherine of Aragon and Mary, but by December 1534, Chapuys was forced to admit this affair was not serious and the royal pair were again reconciled. That summer, Anne accompanied Henry on his progress through the Severn Valley and Hampshire; in early September, they visited Wulfhall, home of the Seymours, and in late October when they returned to Windsor, she was pregnant; the royal pair were described by onlookers as being 'merry'. At this time, Henry stopped being clean-shaven and adopted a beard permanently; in the Tudor psyche this is an important indicator of sexual prowess, with facial hair being equated with the production of sperm and may have paralleled his desire to successfully father a male child. In the same month a John Horwode sent a 'book of physicke for the queen' via Thomas Cromwell, in hope of some financial recompense but it was unlikely to relate to her new condition. Chapuys wrote that Henry was still dominated by Anne, claiming she governed everything and he was unable to contradict her, yet this was, again, an exaggeration, as his next claim that Henry was almost 'utterly ruined' suggests. In the same month, the Spanish Dr Ortiz cited Anne as saying that Princess Mary was her death and she was hers, referring to Anne as the 'wench'. Yet neither of these hostile sources knew what the queen was beginning to hope: that this time, she would bear a son and secure her own future. The mood that Christmas must have been one of optimism.

At the end of December, news of Catherine's failing health reached court. It was clear from the doctors' reports that she would not live long; she was in the final stages of what was probably cancer, suffering from pain in her stomach, had lost all her strength, and couldn't eat or drink. When she died on 6 January 1536, Henry and Anne's choice to dress in yellow was considered callous by many at the time and since: Anne was to justify this by claiming it was the Spanish colour of mourning. Other sources claimed they wore regal purple. However, Catherine's death removed a vital safeguard to the new queen's position; while she had lived, if Henry had chosen to separate from Anne, foreign and religious expectations were that he would return to his first wife. With Catherine out of the way however, any rupture in the new marriage might precipitate Anne's replacement and the queen was already aware of a serious rival on the horizon. On the day of Catherine's funeral, 29 January, Anne went into premature labour and miscarried a son of about fifteen weeks. Chapuys later reported that she laid the blame with 'the duke of Norfolk, whom she hates, saying he frightened her by bringing the news of the fall the King had six days before' or that she was afraid of being cast aside like her predecessor, while other voices at court began to doubt her ability to bear children. He named a Mistress 'Semel' or Seymour, to whom Henry had lately given many presents.[33] By January, Jane Seymour was already the king's favourite and accounts of Anne discovering her sitting on his knee may have precipitated her loss. The *Life of Jane Dormer*, a later Catholic biography of one of Mary's waiting women, describes frequent scenes of conflict between the two women, ranging from 'scratching and bye-blows between the queen and her maid', to the incident where Anne supposedly snatched a portrait of the king which Jane wore about her neck.[34] The impending sense of history repeating itself cannot have helped her composure or pregnancy. With hindsight, this loss was to prove a turning point for Anne, a sign to Henry that this marriage, like that to Catherine, was flawed in God's eyes. Stunned, he told her on her lying-in bed that he would speak with her when she was up. In a phrase commonly repeated by twentieth-century historians, Anne had 'miscarried of her saviour' and Henry went to spend Shrovetide alone at Whitehall.

At three and a half months, the miscarried foetus would have been partially developed, about the size of an avocado or goose egg. Later hostile sources sought to justify Anne's later fall by claiming it had some physical defect or deformity but this was not mentioned at the time, nor during her trial and appears to be what Eric Ives calls historical 'newspeak'[35] or later Catholic defamation. The key to these rumours lies in the contemporary belief that a child's healthy appearance was God's comment on the sexual morality of its parents: Martin Luther wrote that birth of deformed children was a personal criticism and political omen. Contemporary medicine identified varying types of deformed or malformed foetuses, called a mola, false conception or moon calf. The false conception was a lump of flesh gathered together like a bird's gizzard, usually expelled between the second and fourth month. A mola could exist in the womb for longer; up to a year or in extreme cases, even as long as a woman lives. It was an 'unprofitable mass of flesh, without shape or form, clinging to the inside of the womb', either conforming to the windy type, watery or a collection of the humours. There were some living and some dead molas, thought to occur when the man's seed was weak, barren or imperfect; or that it had been choked through the abundance of menstrual blood.

Yet there was a mystery surrounding the process, a misogynistic fear of feminine territory that manifested itself in the abhorrence of potential disaster, or the birth of 'monsters'. The short-lived child borne by Alice Rospin of Little Clacton in August 1552 was described in the parish register as 'Creature', in the absence of a given name, perhaps descriptive of its unformed status. Eamon Duffy unearthed similar cases in Morebath in 1564, when the same record was made one of James Goodman's twin sons in the birthing room, who did not survive[36] and that of William Morrse in 1560. London diarist Henry Machyn recorded the news of a 'monster birth' at Middleton Stony, Oxfordshire in 1552: of 'forme and shape as you have sene and hard ... both the for parts and hynder partes of the same ... sam chylderyn havyng ii heds, ii bodys, iiii arms, iiii hands, with one bely, on navel ... they have ii legs with ii fett on syd, and on the odur syd, on leg with ii fett'.[37] They lived only nineteen days. Often, the emerging child's head – or indeed any visible part of their anatomy – was baptised before birth and the gender observed, as was the case when a baby was stuck or clearly failing. 'Monsters' were often perceived as punishments for a couple's indulgence in lewd practices or at forbidden times such as Lent; one of the few supposed indicators of sexual practice within marriage.

What women feared most, possibly even more than the death that promised eternal salvation to the faithful, was the production of a 'monster'. The early Elizabethan period in particular saw a flurry of pamphlets reporting on such births, which today would be classified as conjoined twins or genetic abnormalities. While the Tudors were not unsympathetic to these children as individuals, many of whom were short-lived, they interpreted their birth as a divine signal of disapproval, directed towards the parents for immorality or, more worryingly, towards the State. Abnormal births were interpreted within the tradition of misrule and the subversion of the natural world order, portending catastrophes just as comets and social transgressions did. Prayers existed against the prevention of such occasions and customs forbade certain behaviours in expectant women, such as looking upon deformed and terrifying creatures, which could affect the development of the foetus. Such a birth could not remain concealed; communal networks would ensure the spread of news until its fame became national, upon which the parents could expect scrutiny and censure. Popular news sheets and medical manuals contained sensational illustrations of abnormal birth: at least twelve pamphlets survive from the Elizabethan period alone but these represent a fraction of the total probable output. The most famous cases were the conjoined twins of Herne in 1565 and Swanburne in 1566 and the child born with folds of flesh about its neck, in Surrey, also in 1566, judged to be God's criticism of the fashions of the day. Multiple births were seen as a divine infliction: the female narrator of a ballad criticised a woman who came begging at her door with twins as having lived a lewd life; many believed that twins were conceived through intercourse during an existing pregnancy:

> Thou are some strumpet sure I know,
> And spends thy days in shame
> And stained sure thy marriage bed
> With spots of black defame.[38]

Ironically, the wealthy but currently infertile narrator was punished for her cruelty towards the beggar woman by bearing 365 children: 'was by the hand of God most strangely punished, by sending her as many children at one birth, as there are daies in the year.'[39]

To return to Anne's story: even if the deformed foetus theory was true, it would have been prohibitively difficult to fully investigate the circumstances under which she had conceived without opening the question of Henry's responsibility for creating the supposed monster. Cromwell later admitted much of the evidence gathered could not be used; some may have related to Henry and Anne's sexual practices. At his trial, George Boleyn was accused of having spread rumours that the premature child had not been fathered by Henry as well as having criticised the king's prowess with his sister. However, no word was mentioned at the time of the foetus's appearance. Assuming the mola theory to be a later attempt to discredit Anne, it was still important that blame should not be attached to the king for her misdelivery, especially as her pattern of gynaecological failures was beginning to look very much like that of Catherine. The common factor was Henry; therefore, the miscarriage in January 1536 needed to be attributed to another father.

Once Anne had been identified as a viable target that following May, her enemies used every available anti-female insult to discredit her, from adultery and incest to witchcraft and murder. Her trial and those of her co-accused on the grounds of adultery and incest has long been discredited; Alison Weir has conclusively proved that the supposed dates of her illicit encounters fail to tally with her whereabouts at the time and even coincide with her period of lying-in or pregnancy. Her midwife Nan Cobham was questioned extensively, as were the women of her household, in an attempt to uncover irregular behaviour. Once Henry had decided she was going, whether he believed in her adultery or not, there was no turning back. With miscarriage and the birth of deformed children considered indicative of her poor morals, and as Tudor women were defined sexually and maternally, Anne's femininity was attacked, using every means of justifying her sentence. Widespread misogyny was common during the sixteenth century. Those who transgressed clearly defined boundaries, such as overreaching commoners who married kings, were popular targets. Female inferiority was reinforced in every aspect of life, from the law courts to medicine, familial relations to lyrics, jokes and sayings. Women's subordination and otherness from men permeated mass-market culture through sermons, manuals, treaties, popular literature, proverbs, folklore, charms, rhymes, song, ballads, anecdotes, jokes, superstition, seasonal crafts and customs, festivities, religious iconography, medicinal and herbal practices, emblem books, woodcuts for ballads and broadsheets, engravings and illustrations. They were considered to have a particular talent for being subversive: feminine intelligence was often presented proverbially as cunning: 'women in mischief are wiser than men', they were 'necessary evils' and, through intercourse and pregnancy, were 'made perfect by men'; a woman was 'the weaker vessel', 'the woe of man' and 'a man of straw was worth a woman of gold'. Popular culture identified them with noisy, silly geese, deceitful and insatiable cats, slippery eels, angry wasps and inflexible swine.

One common joke told how a Tudor man was asked why he had married a tiny woman and replied, 'because of evils, the least was to be chosen'. Some pamphlets and chapbooks showed emblems of women lacking heads, in the sense of flawed intelligence but also decapitation as a symbol of the loss of power, the seat of wisdom, an inversion of patriarchal and therefore political power. Disobedience to a husband was small-scale treason, almost as threatening to society as uncontrolled sexuality: one pamphlet's caption reads 'a headless maid is the worst of all monsters', punning on the unsanctioned loss of virginity and sexual appetite that conflicted with the notion of female submission. Assuming Anne's trump card during her courtship was her virginity, later slanders of sexual lasciviousness highlight just how fragile and short-lived her main bargaining tool had been. Her appeal for Henry had partly lain in her denial and abstinence; as she refused to conform to the role of submissive wife, she was redefined in the terms of a sexual predator. The fear of female disobedience to male authority was apparent in popular maxims: 'a woman does that which is forbidden her', 'women are always desirous of sovereignty' and 'all women are ambitious naturally'. The new queen represented the epitome of Tudor men's most deep-rooted fears. Set within this context, the terminology of Anne Boleyn's fall, with all its sexual and moral slurs, underlines a new truth about her condemnation.

Her innocence in May 1536 was an irrelevance; by then, Henry had another wife and potential mother-of-an-heir in his sights. Anne's fate turned on her inability to produce a male heir. Even with all the political and religious upheavals that were concurrent with her rise, Anne's experiences as a mother, like Catherine's, proved the defining factor of her life. Anne's appeal to Henry was founded in fantasy; over the course of seven years of courtship, her attraction was rooted in the promise of her fertility. And as a woman, even a queen, she was vulnerable, a scapegoat of contemporary beliefs, which ultimately cost her her life. She was executed on 19 May 1536. As the Spanish Ambassador put it: 'the entire future turns on the accouchement of the queen'.[40]

7

Jane Seymour & Edward
1536–1537

A Son at Last

Although I have no desire to put myself in this danger, yet being of the feminine gender I will pray with the others that God may keep us from it.[1]

Early one May morning, Anne Boleyn was led from the confinement of her rooms in the Tower of London towards the little green outside. There, a temporary scaffold had been erected, on the orders of Sir William Kyngston, Constable of the Tower, to 'such a height that all present may see it'.[2] Anne's brother George, accused of incest, homosexuality and adultery, along with four other supposed co-conspirators, had met their deaths the day before; they must have been in Anne's mind as she prepared to join them. The Venetian ambassador commented that she looked 'exhausted and amazed' and 'kept looking behind her' as if in disbelief, although John Hussee wrote that she died 'boldly'.[3] Dressed in a black damask gown and ermine mantle, she mounted the steps to stand before the crowd, which may have numbered as many as a thousand. She dispensed the traditional alms, made a speech putting herself in God's hands and thanked her ladies for their service. Before her were ranged the familiar faces of courtiers, councillors and London officials, who had gathered three years previously to witness her coronation: now they had come to see the first public execution of a Queen of England. Anne knelt, blindfolded, and the hangman from Calais raised his sword.

Technically, her death was unnecessary, even if Henry believed in her guilt. Three days earlier, at Lambeth Palace, Cranmer had pronounced the royal marriage 'null and void'. It was impossible, therefore, for Anne to have committed adultery if her union with the king had not been valid in the first place. This was not enough to save her life though, as Henry had previous experience of a wife who would not step aside; now he was keen to marry again. Even before Anne had been executed, Holy Roman Emperor Charles V, nephew of Catherine of Aragon, was proposing the Infant of Portugal or the Duchess of Milan, as Henry's third wife. The Queen of Hungary was also suggested but she was thought to be in ill health and not capable of bearing children. Approaching his forty-fifth birthday, still lacking a legitimate male heir, the possibility of securing his dynasty was apparently slipping away; yet these international brides did not merit the king's consideration. He had already decided on his next queen, having discussed marriage with her before the sentence on Anne had been passed; her marked differences from her predecessor appearing more attractive as his relationship with Anne disintegrated. Jane Seymour was the daughter of John Seymour of Wulfhall, Wiltshire, a descendant of Edward III and distant cousin of both Henry and Anne. Chapuys described the prospective bride as aged over twenty-five, 'of middle stature and no great beauty', so fair as to be pale. She was 'proud and haughty' yet of 'no great wit' and was a great supporter of Princess Mary. Her appeal may have lain in her virginity, although Chapuys questioned this, as she was so advanced in years and had spent time at the licentious Tudor court. He punned on the possibility of her possessing a fine *enigme*, meaning a riddle or secret but also slang for the female genitals. According to Anne Boleyn, Henry had 'neither vigour nor virtue' in his sexual performance, so Chapuys concluded 'he may make a condition in the marriage that she be a virgin, and when he has a mind to divorce her he will find enough of witnesses'.[4] Other chroniclers confirmed this interpretation of her colouring and appearance, while some, like Polydore Vergil, found her 'charming' or considered the match had taken Henry from Hell to Heaven.

If Anne had contradicted conventional notions of feminine behaviour by overreaching her status and being proud and argumentative, Jane conformed. The 1534 *A Treatise of the Nobilitie and Excellencye of Woman Kynde*, by German 'magician' Heinrich Cornelius Agrippa, translated into English by David

Clapham, described the females as delicate and pleasant, their flesh soft and tender, their colour fair and clear, the head comely and dressed with hair soft as silk. Like Jane, the ideal woman's skin was white as milk and her eyes shone like crystals. Her voice would be small and shrill, her speech low and sweet. In movement, she was right and comely, her deportment and cheer were honest and commendable. This beauty was so superior to all other of God's creatures, according to Agrippa, that the children of God took earthly women to be their wives. It was a description which would have pleased Henry, as God's appointed representative on earth and Supreme Head of the Church of England since 1534. In contemporary terms, he had struck gold with Jane Seymour.

The shadow of the block hung over Jane and Henry's wedding. Henry's behaviour since Anne's arrest had been giving rise to criticism, according to Chapuys: while his proposed union with Jane remained secret, he had been 'banqueting with ladies', returning after midnight by river and showing 'extravagant joy'. These visits were probably made to Jane, whom he had established in a house by the river, 7 miles from court, facilitating regular visits and offering her the services of his own cook. Henry must have believed to some degree in Anne's guilt or allowed himself to be convinced by a situation that suited his current need. He allegedly wept before Henry Fitzroy that his son had escaped her attempts to poison him, although ironically, Fitzroy was to die a month later. The callousness he displayed towards Anne was little different from that already shown towards Catherine of Aragon and his previously cherished daughter Mary: once a woman had been excluded from his favour, he was absolute and unyielding in his treatment of them. The willingness of Jane to enter into marriage in such circumstances has given rise to dichotomic historical interpretations of her as ruthlessly ambitious, or else as the passive pawn of her driven family. Tudor factional politics was brutal. Opportunities were seized in the wake of rivals' falls from grace. David Starkey has commented on the seeming impossibility of the 'plain Jane' of Holbein's portrait gaining her position as Henry's queen without the driving force of her faction determined to bring Anne down.[5] Jane was a means, not an end, to the pro-Mary group. Their success lay in their timing. Just as Anne had been, Jane was a player in a complex, heartless game, snatching the opportunity to rise that was borne out of the jaws of death. On the day of Anne's execution, Cranmer issued a dispensation permitting Henry and Jane to marry in spite of their relation in the third degree: the following morning, Jane travelled secretly by barge to Henry's lodgings, where they were betrothed. Five days later, rumours had already reached the Continent that he had taken another wife. Mary of Hungary wrote about the ease and speed of Anne's replacement that 'wives will hardly be well contented if such customs become general'.[6] While speedy remarriage following the death of a spouse was relatively common in Tudor England, Henry's record as a widower of eleven days can have rarely been beaten. The wedding ceremony was conducted by Stephen Gardiner, Bishop of Winchester, on 30 May, in the queen's closet at York Place.

Jane first appeared as queen at Whitsun, which fell on 4 June. Her brother Edward was elevated to Viscount Beauchamp around the same time, receiving many properties, entitlements and lands. To celebrate, she may have worn some of the twenty-eight score (560) pearls that had been ordered to adorn her clothes or those embroidered into her kirtle, for which receipts were submitted at court ten days later.[7] Henry intercepted her first conversation with an ambassador, claiming she would earn the title of 'pacific' as she was so peace-loving, while a few swift alterations transformed her personal badge from the inappropriate peacock to the self-sacrificing phoenix. Ultimately, as the device suggested, she would regenerate the Tudor dynasty at the cost of her own life. A pageant planned for early in the marriage featured Jane's motto 'bound to serve and obey' among devices of true love knots, heavenly bodies, roses, olive trees, a lily among thorns and the well of life. Yet having married in speed, Henry was already experiencing doubts. That August, after famously asserting he was a man 'like any other', he confided to Chapuys that he was not convinced he would have any more children by the queen and was reported to have regretted not having seen two new beautiful women of the court before he had wed. That summer was spent in feasts and celebrations, while Henry hoped that Jane would fall pregnant; one witness reported seeing him put his hand on Jane's belly saying, 'Edward, Edward' months before Jane conceived. The imperative for a son was even more intense after the death of Henry Fitzroy from consumption that July; while he had lived, the possibility of his legitimisation or inheritance of the throne acted as a safeguard against Henry's failure to produce a male heir by any of his wives. Daily, he hoped to hear Jane confirm his hopes, yet the weeks passed. Perhaps it was desperation that prompted his last pilgrimage. While in the process of investigating and suppressing the monasteries, with the destruction of hundreds of saints' shrines, Henry undertook a journey along the Pilgrim's Way across Kent's North Downs, through Rochester and Sittingbourne, to the shrine of Thomas Becket at Canterbury. With Jane, he prayed and left offerings to the very saint whose bones he would burn and name obliterate two years later. The programme of religious reforms in England was already so dramatic and destructive to centuries-old comforts and traditions, that the North rose in rebellion that autumn and Henry was much occupied by risings in Yorkshire and Lincolnshire which came closest to threatening his throne as any in his reign. Promising leniency to the ringleaders of the Pilgrimage of Grace, he later extracted a savage revenge of mass public hangings the following February. However, Henry must have soon believed himself vindicated in his reforms and suppressions as the queen had conceived a child and he was convinced it would be a son.

A number of Henry's actions in 1537 show him to be mindful of the impending arrival's importance in the continuation of the dynasty. Two years earlier, under the patronage of Anne Boleyn, German artist Hans Holbein had become the court's official painter; now Henry commissioned him to create a huge mural to decorate the newly completed Whitehall complex. What had been Wolsey's old York Place now became an impressive, regal complex along the European lines of Richmond Palace, after over £10 million had been spent designing new apartments, tilt yard, indoor bowling green, tennis courts and cock-fighting pit. Hanging in the privy chamber, the mural measured 3 metres by 4 and depicted Henry's parents standing behind him and Jane, flanking a marble plinth, whose inscription compared the king most favourably with his father: 'how difficult the debate, the question, the issue of whether the father or son be the superior. Each of them has triumphed. The first got the better of his enemies ... the son, born to still greater things ... with him on the throne the truth of God has begun to receive due reverence.'[8] Henry's depiction appears to answer his difficult debate. His life-size image, twice as wide as his father who appears a pale shadow behind him, overwhelmed some onlookers who were seen to tremble in its presence; the unusual pose, facing front with legs open, in deliberately heroic style, was effective propaganda for an ageing, obese and increasingly ill king. His eyes stare out directly to meet those of the viewer, as if challenging them to question or defy him. The mural was destroyed in the 1698 fire that razed all but the banqueting house to the ground but many copies had already been made.

During the 1530s, Henry also undertook a series of alterations at Hampton Court, which he had received as a 'gift' from the increasingly desperate Wolsey in 1529. Thousands of pages of building accounts survive for the period, detailing the three main phases of development that reworked Wolsey's already impressive house into the most imposing of Henry's surviving palaces. The royal apartments, stacked up on several floors, were abandoned in favour of a pair of matching lodgings for the king and queen, all on the same floor, sharing a grand staircase that connected with the privy gardens. This marked a significant shift away from the publicity of the old chambers, which were now used entirely for formal business, while the new rooms allowed for greater privacy. An impressive king's lock, symbolic of the increased distancing between royalty and the court, was transported between houses on progress and always used for the king's bedchamber. There was a much stricter access policy than in the old days, when smaller wheeled beds were used for gentleman attendants to sleep in the king's own room at night: now they needed permission to enter. Jane was also intended to benefit from the private gallery overlooking the Thames and gardens, built in 1537 to connect her accommodation with that of the new royal nursery.

The pregnancy was officially announced at the beginning of April and, that May, Jane appeared at Hampton Court in an open-laced gown to announce her quickening. Special Masses were said at St Paul's and the already delayed plans for a summer coronation were again put on hold. The queen passed a quiet summer at Hampton Court as the plague raged through London. Attended by the royal physicians, she was exhibiting a large belly by mid-July, her gown unlaced to the full. On 16 September she took to her chambers, which had been intended for Anne Boleyn, their interlaced initials of H and A hurriedly adapted for the new queen. Henry remained at nearby Esher, for fear of plague being brought to Hampton, awaiting the arrival of messengers. Jane's bed would have followed her into confinement, with its wooden roundel bearing her coat of arms, to ensure her comfort before and after the delivery. Three weeks after retiring, her labour pains began. Unusually, despite having her waiting women present, she was also attended by Henry's male doctors, including the most famous Sir William Butts, which is perhaps indicative of the importance the king placed upon this birth and his certainty of the child's gender. Yet this was little surprise, as the vociferous and numerous prophets of the Tudor era would always proclaim the imminent arrival of a male heir. Mary and Elizabeth were boys until they arrived and proved the predictions wrong. Perhaps at the age of forty-six, the presence of male physicians said more about his increasing desperation for a healthy heir that would survive infancy. For this, he was prepared to overturn the usual rules; it indicated a significant shift towards the later very public accouchements of seventeenth-century queens.

Jane endured a long, hard ordeal before her son arrived at two in the morning on Friday 12 October, the eve of St Edward's Day. Later rumours that a Caesarian had been performed and that Henry was forced to choose between mother and child are unfounded, despite their perpetration in places ranging from popular ballads to Papal documents. Such procedures were not practised in England at the time; living foetuses were removed surgically but only from dead or dying mothers: the first recorded maternal survival following such a procedure was in Switzerland in the 1580s. Following the birth, Jane was weak but appeared to be recovering well and Henry rode to Hampton Court delirious with joy. Hugh Latimer wrote that there was no less rejoicing at his arrival than that of John the Baptist and that God had 'overcome all our illness with his exceeding goodness'.[9] Pamphleteer Richard Morison felt a 'wonderful force, an inerrable strength of gladness', making his heart 'leap' for joy, his blood pump faster and filling him with the desire 'much lighter to run'.[10] When the news reached the city, the Tower shot off 2,000 rounds of ammunition and impromptu celebrations broke out: banquets were held, banners and garlands hung, bells rung, torches lit, wine ran freely and parties filled the streets. It was the first surviving male heir to be born in England since Henry himself in 1491 and the last until Charles II in May 1630.

The following Monday, Prince Edward was christened in the chapel at Hampton Court. The renovations to Wolsey's old chapel had been completed only two years before; the hammer-beam ceilings, painted blue, decorated with angels and inlaid with gold stars, still recognisable today, were fresh and new overhead but a special temporary screen had been set up to hide the child from prying eyes and create a sense of secrecy about the ritual. A fire pan of perfumed coals filled the air and a special basin had been set aside to wash the child if necessary. Torch bearers led the way before the procession of dignitaries, two by two. Little Elizabeth, aged four, carried the chrism and the Earl of Essex carried the salt, traditionally used in the Catholic ritual of placing a pinch in the infant's mouth. The baby, dressed in a white gown, was brought in under a canopy carried by six gentlemen of the privy chamber, surrounded by bearers of burning wax tapers; the twenty-one-year-old Lady Mary followed, in the role of godmother. The company took spices, wafers and wine and gifts were given of silver and gilt pots and bowls before they departed to the sound of trumpets. Anne Bassett, one of Jane's new waiting women who had been present during her lying-in and confinement, wore a specially commissioned dress of black velvet 'turned up with yellow satin' which was hurriedly worked on to be ready on time. Edward was then returned to his parents to be blessed; Jane sitting upright in bed, dressed in red velvet lined with ermine and Henry later distributing 'great largess'.[11] Jane seemed to be recovering well and plans were being made for her churching: Anne Bassett was to have a new satin gown. However, things were about to dramatically change for the queen.

A surviving letter addressed to Cromwell, describing Jane's last days, was signed by six doctors who attended her, including

William Butts, Henry's leading physician, and George Owen, who became Edward's chief doctor. It describes how her delivery had lasted two days and three nights and that she had seemed well immediately after the birth. Within days, though, she worsened and a procession at St Paul's was made to pray for her health, as one had while she was in labour, after which she seemed to rally. Five days later though, the doctors were concerned again: 'all this nyght she hath bene very syck', worsening rather than improving. Rumours flew about that she was already dead. On 24 October the Earl of Rutland wrote to Cromwell that the queen had suffered 'an natural laxe', probably a heavy bleed, after being very sick all night. Her confessor was with her in the morning, preparing to administer the final rites of extreme unction. Sir Thomas Palmer hoped that 'if good prayers can save her, she is not like to die for never lady was so much plained [complained] with every man, rich and poor'. Others, though, saw the imminence of the threat. Norfolk, recently prominent at Edward's christening, wrote 'there is no likelihood of her life ... I fear she shall not be on lyve at the tyme ye shall read this' and urged Cromwell to 'be here tomorrow early to comfort our good master'.[12]

Jane's end was sudden. The same day, Henry VIII wrote to Francis I of the joy of his son's birth coupled with the 'bitterness of the death of her who has brought me this happiness'. Yet Henry was not even there: he continued to delay his departure from Esher, citing the plague as an excuse; it is uncertain whether he managed to reach Jane's side as she died, or if he even attempted to. Chris Skidmore places him there at eight in the evening, four hours before her death.[13] Cromwell attributed her demise to 'the neglect of those about her who suffered her to take cold and eat such things as her fantasy in sickness called for', and later sensational rumours abroad suggested Henry was damned for having caused Jane's limbs to be stretched and broken to allow the child to emerge. Like the caesarean accusations, this certainly was untrue, although Cromwell may have been partly correct regarding the apportion of blame. Jane's death was probably caused by ignorance rather than neglect. With no understanding of the benefits of hand washing, germs easily entered the mother's bloodstream, causing fatal results. Neither was there any co-ordinated system of separating and delivering clean water and disposing of waste; in London all water was recycled through Thames, thus tainted by sewage and decay. Hampton Court was exceptional in having water brought in along lead pipes from springs 3 miles away but it was not enough to save Jane. With no idea that hygiene was significant, amoebic dysentery, tapeworms, whip-worms and bore-worms must have been common. There would have been occasions when the dirty hands of well-meaning midwives may have cost many maternal lives, yet Jane was attended by male doctors rather than the traditional female midwives with their wealth of practical experience. Puerperal fever has traditionally been held responsible for her demise, although descriptions of her end have given rise to recent theories that part of the placenta had been left in Jane's womb, leading to serious haemorrhaging. Midwives would routinely inspect the placenta for any ruptures but less experienced practitioners might have overlooked or misdiagnosed this essential safeguard. With the majority of births of all classes still attended by women, it is impossible to speculate on a male doctor's experience of placentas in the 1530s. The queen's untimely death may be attributable to the imbalance of gender – and therefore gynaecological knowledge – in the birth chamber.

Henry was upset but sanguine, his sorrow offset by the continuing health of his son. Sir John Wallop reported on 3 November that the 'king was in good health and merry as a widower may be'.[14] At the time of Jane's funeral almost a week later, he retired to a 'solitary place to pass his sorrows' while her body was interred at Windsor. A surviving account details the preparations. She had been embalmed by a wax-chandler, who had removed her entrails, which were interred in the chapel, and prepared her body with 'searing, balming, spicing and trammelling in cloth' before the plumber soldered her in lead. She was conveyed to Windsor in a hearse surrounded by twenty-one tapers, while her ladies left off their colourful clothes and 'rich apparel' and wore mourning clothes with 'white kerchers hanging over their heads and shoulders', held Masses at the hearse and watched over it day and night. The chapel was prepared in advance, along with all the chambers leading to it, hung with black cloth and 'images'. On Monday 12 November, 200 poor men wearing the queen's badge lined the route with their torches while the solemn procession passed into the castle walls and on to the chapel for the funeral. Following the internment, the mourners were 'sumptuously provided for' in the castle, with all being concluded by midday.[15]

Edward, on the other hand, was thriving and according to Cromwell was 'sucketh like a child of his puissance (power)'.[16] Initially he stayed at the new nursery that had been built to receive him at Hampton Court, connected, sadly now, by a corridor to the queen's empty chambers. An extra wash house and kitchen had been built at the palace to cater for his needs and ensure there was no cross-contamination from the daily court business. Strict guidelines governed the roles of those in his household, forbidding any under the degree of knight from entering and barring all serving boys and dogs as naturally clumsy and prone to infection. Henry regularly checked the list of employees. All food was tested before being given to the prince and his clothes were washed, brushed, tested and tried on before being worn; new clothes were to be washed and perfumed before use and dried by the fire. Walls, floors and ceilings were also washed down several times a day for fear of infection and those in direct contact with the little prince were required to be scrupulously clean. The precautions seemed to work. At New Year, the thriving boy received gifts of pots and cups of gilt plate totalling 616 ounces and, soon after, a new nursery was established for him at Richmond. Every indication suggested he would be a strong, long-lived boy, a powerful future King of England.

8

Anne of Cleves &
Catherine Howard
1537–1542

The Rules of Attraction

God send me well to keep.

No other will but his.[1]

For the first time since 1509, England lacked a queen. The ramifications of this went beyond the personal; not only would Henry lack the officially sanctioned sexual relationship that became increasingly important to him as he aged, along with the possibility of more heirs, it meant that a whole section of the court were out of a job. No queen meant no queen's household and no attendant ladies. No attendant ladies meant fewer, if any, beautiful, willing young ladies to divert the eye of the king or his gentlemen. There would be no assignations with aristocratic teenagers in the palace gardens or late night feasting and dancing with all its possibilities of flirtation and snatched embraces. Traditionally, this had been the pool from which Henry selected his next wife: Anne Boleyn had served Catherine of Aragon and Jane Seymour had in turn served Anne. Daily titillation was made possible through visits to his existing wife's chambers and the routine coming together of both households under one roof. The lack of available court ladies may partly explain the unprecedentedly long delay before Henry remarried. The situation needed to be remedied. Jane's death was inconvenient on many levels.

Yet one person was of the opinion that it could have been prevented. Tudor women did die in childbirth, even royal ones. Henry knew this from his own experience, recalling the loss of his mother thirty-four years earlier, yet Jane's departure still came as a shock. While the overall survival rates were good for straightforward births, unexpected complications could claim the lives of mother and child but Jane's apparently successful delivery and delayed death gave rise to the legend, suggested by Cromwell, that she had been neglected, then indulged. It has fuelled historical interpretations of Henry as a callous, selfish husband, in addition to his treatment of his wives and daughters, through the lens of modern behavioural analysis and expectations. Yet it is impossible for a modern audience and even a Tudor one to be certain of his motives at this time. In a society where protocol dictated that kings and queens did not attend each others' coronations or funerals, mothers did not attend christenings and parents often were absent from their children's weddings, such behaviour cannot fairly be evaluated. Following this psychological analysis, modern hypotheses have suggested that the occasion stirred Henry's memories of his mother's death or that his presence in the sick chamber may not have been considered appropriate; perhaps he did not believe she would die or else his abhorrence of illness and death may have stayed his hand. It has also been used in various arguments about Henry's changing character, with some historians identifying the year 1536 as a major turning point; some see Jane as another victim of an increasing monomania. The truth may have been more complex. It may not have been.

With three surviving children by three different wives, Henry's succession was by no means secure even if he had the longed-for son. By the time the court came out of deep mourning at Candlemas in 1538 he was forty-six, no longer the handsome youth whose energy had set the tone of his chivalric court. Traditionally, medical texts placed the onset of old age between thirty-five and forty-five, a threshold Henry had now passed, and in this may lie the key to his increasingly despotic and extreme behaviour. His health was clearly failing; the fall he suffered early in 1536 had left him unconscious for hours and may have caused some permanent damage; if nothing else it left him unable to joust and hunt, after which he rapidly put on weight. Two years on, he suffered from serious illness when the skin on his ulcerated leg closed over, projecting the excreted matter inwards instead of weeping out into its dressing. For a while his life was despaired of and his Privy Councillors argued over whether their loyalties should lie with the infant prince or the adult Princess Mary. Then, Henry rallied and soon after, the search for a new wife was back on. Through the following years, his health intermittently failed; as the Cleves ambassadors arrived to conclude the treaty for his fourth marriage, Henry was suffering from a cold which his doctor treated with a pill and a glister; there was no need to use the powdered unicorn horn that had been sought for his medicine. Soon after, a chill confined him to bed after he was purged with a laxative and enema, probably administered through a pig's bladder. Such regular incidents must have been a difficult reminder that he was no longer the dazzling, slender Sir Loyal Heart of his youth, admired in all the European courts. His attempts to find a fourth wife were rooted in the desire to forget his advancing age but would show just how far his courtly, gallant reputation had altered for the worse.

Since the age of seventeen, Henry had been secure in the affections of the women of his choosing. After all, he was the king; no matter how long they may resist, few women could deny the benefits of an association with him, either as a short-term mistress or more permanent fixture. Anne Boleyn and Jane Seymour had won their status by holding out for their position in the full intention of the ultimate surrender. His wives had overlapped, making transition between them easy. He was a romantic, driven by chivalric impulse and in a very modern sense, wished to enter into a companionate marriage and be in love with his spouse, who would be his confidant as well as his bedfellow. In this, he was following the pattern of the early years of his marriage to Catherine of Aragon, a significant departure from the dynastic unions of most European royal houses, including that of his own parents. Now, with no replacement lined up, he was open to suggestions, both domestic and international. They came thick and fast, with Cromwell as chief matchmaker. A number of eligible princesses, duchesses and women of the European nobility were considered but, mindful of the past consequences of Catherine of Aragon's connections, England would need to tread carefully. Additionally, Henry's poor reputation as a husband had spread, meaning that at least one suitable wife, Christina of Milan, was unprepared to run the risk of placing herself in his hands, reportedly saying that if she were possessed of two heads, she would gladly give him one. This was unfortunate for Henry, as by 1538 he believed he had fallen in love with her.

Yet the beautiful young widow had not been Henry's first choice. Even before Jane's funeral, Cromwell's mind had turned to her possible replacement. This is not necessarily as callous as it sounds; the careers of Anne Boleyn and Jane Seymour proved that whichever court faction presented a suitable candidate at the right moment could secure the fortunes of those involved. With religious reforms well underway, besides his own political future, Cromwell had much to lose if a prospective new wife was disposed to favour the old religion headed by the Lady Mary or to dislike him. It was a matter of survival. For this reason, he turned his search outside the country, hoping a swift diplomatic foreign union would be the answer. Luckily, his first candidate, Marie of Guise, seemed to meet Henry's approval. Born in 1515, Marie had already proven her ability to bear sons and was rumoured to be strong and healthy, which appealed to the king's desire for a large wife to match his large frame, as he told the French ambassador Castillon in December 1537. However, Marie had already caught the eye of Henry's nephew, James V of Scotland, and their marriage treaty was moving towards conclusion. To prevent such a union between England's old enemies and snatch Marie from under his rival's nose would have been a considerable triumph for Henry and a feather in the cap of his servant.

James V was a recent widower. The only surviving child of Margaret Tudor and James IV, he had inherited the throne at the age of one, following his father's death at the Battle of Flodden Field. Now he was twenty-six, young and handsome; with the Tudor blood flowing through his veins, he was not only Henry's rival but a potential heir to his throne. Previously betrothed to Mary of Bourbon, he had travelled to France in 1536 and fallen in love with Madeleine, the daughter of Francis I. Still only sixteen and frail since birth, the girl had already contracted tuberculosis, yet despite her father's protests, was keen to marry James. The ceremony took place in January 1537 at Notre Dame and the couple departed for Scotland that May. By July, she was dead. Now, to continue the French alliance, James sought the hand of Marie of Guise. Hearing of the intended match, Henry could hardly believe his Scottish rival could be preferred to himself, even though, like Christina of Milan, Marie had heard of his reputation and supposedly commented that she had only a little neck, referring to a similar statement made by the condemned Anne Boleyn. The treaty was concluded in January 1538, forcing Henry to accept the inevitable and look elsewhere. Marie and James would become the parents of Mary Queen of Scots and grandparents of James VI, future heir to the Tudor line, yet all this lay well in the future, after Henry's time. By the time of their marriage that May, he already had a number of other candidates in mind, namely Marie's two younger sisters. Neither of these proved any more successful: the eighteen-year-old Louise would marry Charles, Duke of Arschot in 1451 and die soon after, while her sister Renee would enter holy orders. Henry was also rejected by Francis' cousins Anne of Lorraine and James' intended bride Mary of Bourbon, even if she had not suffered from the ill health that led to her death in 1538. Holbein had travelled to France and painted the portraits of both, although neither image survives. Perhaps it was rumours that James V had been considering Christina of Milan as a possible bride that sparked his rival's interest.

Famous now for her Holbein portrait and supposed spirited rejection of Henry, Christina of Milan was born in 1521. At sixteen, she was five years younger than Henry's own elder daughter when he sought her as his wife. She had already been married young, by proxy, to the Duke of Milan in 1534 and his death the following year left her a widow and probably still a virgin at fourteen. English Ambassador John Hutton described her as 'very tall; taller than the Regent, of competent beauty, soft of speech, and gentle in countenance'. She wore Italian-style mourning and 'resembles one Mrs Sheltun that used to wait on Queen Anne', a reference to the beautiful Madge Shelton, a Boleyn cousin who had once diverted Henry. This must have been a deliberate attempt to encourage him. Hutton continued: 'there is none in these parts for beauty of person and birth to be compared to the duchess. She is not so pure white as the late queen, whose soul God pardon; but she hath a singular good countenance, and when she chanceth to smile there appeareth two pittes in her cheeks and one in her chin, the which becometh her right excellently well'.[2] Furthermore, she was accomplished, which Henry found essential in a wife, able to speak French, Italian and high German. The reports were pleasing enough for Henry to send his court painter Hans Holbein to Brussels, where with astonishing speed he produced the well-known portrait after only a three-hour session. When it arrived back in England, with its rosebud lips and dimples, Henry fancied himself in love. Christina, however, was less keen and made her dislike of the match clear.

In the same year, Cromwell suggested a match with Cleves, an Erasmian state in the Holy Roman Empire, comprising a series of territories in Northern Germany with its capital at Dusseldorf. John, Duke of Cleves, known as the Peaceful, had two unmarried daughters, Anne and her younger sister Amalia, both in their early twenties. Cromwell had already instructed his ambassador Christopher Mont to examine the ladies and report back as to their appearance and qualities, 'their shape, stature and complexion'[3] to judge their suitability for marriage. Mont reported that Anne eclipsed the beauty of Christina of Milan as the sun did the moon and was universally praised. Ambassadors Nicholas Wotton and Richard Beard were dispatched to make overtures at the court of Cleves, but were unable to view the ladies' faces or figures under their veils and layers of clothing. When requesting a closer look, they were indignantly asked by the Cleves minister whether they wished to see the women naked! Once again Holbein was dispatched to paint a potential queen, this time to the Castle of Duren, in summer 1539, where both Anne and Amalia sat for him. Anne's well-known image survives, upon which Henry based his decision to marry her, but only a sketch may depict her younger sister whose portrait has been lost. In many ways, Anne seemed highly suitable. Wotton reported that she had been raised by a strict mother to be docile, obedient and respectful; she liked cards and was good at needlework but otherwise her education had been neglected; when she arrived in England she could still only speak German although the ambassador insisted she would learn quickly. This had not been a barrier when Catherine of Aragon arrived in England back in 1501. Holbein was back in England that August and the Cleves ambassadors arrived soon after, on 14 September. French ambassador Marillac was mistaken when he wrote to Francis I that there may be some coolness towards them and that the king was considering reopening negotiations for Christina of Milan.[4] The portrait and reports clearly appealed to Henry, as he received the visitors warmly at Windsor and practical questions regarding Anne's journey were discussed. The king's recent wardrobe expenses indicate some of the finery in which he may have received them; a coat of engrained violet trimmed with a marten fur was made, as were alterations to enlarge Henry's jackets and doublets, to accommodate his expanding girth.[5] Marillac got closer to the truth on 3 October, when he reported that repairs to the king's main residences had renewed the usual repairs and ornaments, especially in the queen's apartments, and that quantities of gold and silver cloth had been ordered. Ships were also being assembled and equipped to fetch the Princess of Cleves to England. In following days, the treaty was signed. A few weeks later, Anne had left her childhood home forever.

The journey was full of ceremony and expectation. The young princess, sheltered in her strict Erasmian parental home and wooed by proxy, had little experience of the intrigue and protocol of the English court. She must have been nervous, knowing that the weeks of travel were to culminate in her union with a man she had never met, almost twice her age, three times married with a daughter only months Anne's junior. The formal receptions at almost every stage along the route must have given her a taste of what she could expect as queen and no indication that her long-awaited presence would be anything but welcomed. Travel across land in the sixteenth century could be cumbersome, yet it was far safer than trusting such a precious cargo to the vagaries of the tides. Initially Henry's plan had been to send his fleet to collect her from the Cleves-ruled port of Harderwijk on the Zuiderzee, to avoid the necessity of asking Emperor Charles V for permission to travel overland through his territories. Cleves favoured the overland route, as a sea voyage might spoil Anne's complexion. After all, they were travelling in mid-winter when the weather would be considerably worse: at least on land, the party could pause and shelter for as long as necessary. Once embarked on the water, Anne's fleet would find no relief and increased the danger of illness, injury or even death. To give an indication of the size of the company, 263 people travelled with Anne, ranging from her waiting women and translators to those performing the essential services of care of her wardrobe and horses. By mid-October though, Imperial permission had been granted and the land route finalised.

The first stage of the journey was between the Cleves base of Dusseldorf and Antwerp; on arrival there, Anne was met by English merchants four miles out of the city, dressed in velvet coats and gold chains, waiting to conduct her to English lodgings in the town. From Antwerp, merchants accompanied her towards Gravelines, where she was received by the town captain amid a volley of gunshot and, by 11 December, she arrived at Calais. This was where the waiting began. Unsurprisingly for the time of year, the weather was terrible. Grounded for fifteen days, Anne was entertained by Governor Lord Lisle and his dignitaries in their all finery: cloth of gold and purple velvet, gold chains, satin damask and yeomen in the king's colours of blue and red. At the town's Lantern Gate she viewed the waiting English fleet of fifty ships, including Henry's famous flagships the 'Lion' and the 'Sweepstake', decked with 100 banners of silk and gold. Trumpets sounded and a 'double drum' never seen before in England was beaten, followed by so much more gunshot that her train could not see each other for smoke. The mayor gave her a gift of 100 gold sovereigns and escorted her to the feasts and jousts that helped filled the days. Watching the turbulent seas each day, Anne must have mused about her future husband and the possibility that she might soon become a mother. After all, that was what queens did, even if she wasn't quite sure how. Her mother had neglected that part of her education, too.

Finally the tide turned. Early in the morning on 27 December, the fleet set sail from Calais and soon had the coast of Kent within sight. As they approached, Anne may have caught a first glimpse of the rolling chalk-white cliffs of her new home or the impressive grey stone castles that stood out proudly and defensively along the shore. They landed that evening between six and seven and were conducted to Deal Castle for a banquet and change of clothes, then on to Dover Castle with the Duke and Duchess of Suffolk, Henry's former brother-in-law Charles Brandon and his fourth wife Catherine Willoughby – Henry's sister Mary Rose, Brandon's third wife, had died in 1535. Predominantly Plantagenet, Dover castle had Norman, Saxon and even Roman elements, staring out formidably into the Channel. After Deal's compact, squat six bastions, it must have been an impressive and well-provisioned stronghold; Henry had been here two years previously and added the bulwarks of the moat. Anne would spend a couple of days here to recover from her journey and ready herself for the first meeting with her husband. It was to come sooner than she anticipated.

Anne's route then took her through Canterbury and Sittingbourne, ending at Rochester on New Year's Eve amid stormy weather. Although Rochester Castle still dominates the town, chroniclers have variously stated that she stayed at the Palace or Priory. This might have been Bromley Palace, residence of the Bishops of Rochester containing a holy well in its grounds or Rochester Palace in the present nearby village of Halling; most likely though, was the fifteenth-century palace within the cathedral precincts, home to Bishop Fisher. Anne still had a fair way to travel before the planned reception at Greenwich but Henry had other ideas. Unable to contain his excitement, he imagined a meeting along the lines of courtly love and the conventions of court entertainment, whereby his bride could not fail to recognise him in spite of his unscheduled, masked appearance. It was his test of true love; the vital test that Anne must pass. Always a romantic, in spite of his experiences, Henry set off to ride to Rochester, intent on playing out a role in a chivalric tale that had already proscribed Anne's response. In common with the heroines of troubadour legend, she would instantly recognise her betrothed and the spark of love would ignite. After all, his majesty and prowess could leave no one in doubt as to his identity. Decades of masked balls, including the Château Vert, had been played along these lines, with canny Tudor courtiers colluding in the king's deception and feigning surprise when his disguise was revealed. The unsuspecting Anne, unfamiliar with such games, was resting from her journey. So far as she knew, the king she had never seen was days away. It was a scheme that was doomed to fail. Henry himself had created an unrealistic scenario which would determine the course of his most unsatisfactory marriage.

As Henry and his courtiers sneaked into the castle, Anne was watching a bullfight. Assailed by unknown masked men, she wisely and virtuously repelled one who tried to kiss her, cursing in German, the only language she knew. Factors influencing sexual attraction can be random and unpredictable; circumstances and accidents can cause initial interest to flourish or be stunted due to conditions beyond the control of those involved. Anne's failings as a wife have traditionally been held to lie in her appearance and manners, yet something almost inexplicably subtle had prejudiced her chances right from the start. She had lost a game she was unaware she was playing. For Henry's exacting requirements, ever difficult to satisfy as he aged, her non-conformity was fatal. He could not see her in any other role than that he had precast for her. Optimistic chroniclers such as Holinshed, who reported how lovingly they addressed each other, were not present to witness this in person. With his personal rules of attraction so dependent upon a code of conduct that excluded his future wife even before their meeting, Henry's disappointment, while a blow to his ego, was of his own making. Yet Henry was by no means the first ruler to pre-empt an official meeting with his future spouse: Henry VII had insisted that he and Arthur met Catherine of Aragon *en route* to London, even when they had been refused entry and she had tried to escape by retiring to bed; likewise James IV of Scotland had hurried to meet Margaret Tudor unexpectedly before their wedding. There were precedents for Henry's actions yet none of these had involved the bridegroom arriving in disguise.

The surprise had failed. Henry unmasked and Anne was made aware of her mistake, yet the damage was already done. After dining together, he departed to brood on her supposed unresponsiveness while she travelled on, unaware, through Dartford and Blackheath, arriving at Shooter's Hill on 3 January. Here, the couple met a second time, more formally, with Anne dressed in impressive cloth of tissue of gold and a German headdress set full of Orient pearls, a coronet of black velvet and a necklace of sparkling stones. Perfumed fires were lit and all the trees and bushes were cut down;

city dignitaries in furs and chains of gold lined her route towards the tents where she and Henry would dine. According to Hall's chronicle, repeated by Holinshed, she had a most 'amiable aspect and womanly behaviour' while Henry embraced her 'with most lovely countenance and princely behaviour'. This was intended to have been their first encounter. Dressed up to look her best, with the correct formalities and procedures in place, willing and responsive, Anne may have made a more favourable impression had Henry stuck to the original plan. Yet Henry's mind was already made up: the more he saw her, the less he liked her. Using her appearance, manners and foreign costume as his first excuse, he started looking for ways out of the marriage even before it had been conducted. In this, he was different from many of his predecessors and European contemporaries. Traditionally, kings and queens had put aside personal feelings in order to honour matches that were diplomatic and usually international. The match of Henry's parents had been conducted primarily for political advantage, as had that of his elder brother Arthur and sister Margaret: Henry himself had arranged his younger sister's marriage to the ageing Louis XII of France. Such was the lot of royalty. With luck, the couple may be able to co-operate, with mutual respect and friendship developing; if love were to blossom, it was an unexpected but welcome bonus. Most foreign princes could not hope to escape this ritual, either to strengthen their own claim or reinforce important foreign ties. Francis I had married the daughter of his predecessor and cousin, Louis XII, on his accession while in 1533, Catherine de Medici had married Henri, Francis' second son, in a notoriously loveless union. In rejecting Anne of Cleves, Henry VIII could cause an international scandal and alienate the powerful German states; in allowing his initial personal dislike to overcome all other concerns, he was adhering to romantic aspirations that were at odds with the nature of the match.

Taken by surprise, Cromwell could not find his master a way out. The pre-contract between Anne and Anthony, Duke of Lorraine, was raised, although it had been arranged when she was below the age of consent and dissolved in 1535; the surprised Cleves ambassadors could not produce paperwork to prove this, although they promised to deliver it imminently and Anne herself swore that the betrothal was now invalid. The net was closing in. Despite expressing his distaste, Henry was forced to go through with the ceremony on 6 January 1540. Thomas Cranmer officiated at the service in the queen's closet at Placentia Palace, in what was to be Henry's most public marriage. They exchanged vows and Henry placed on Anne's finger a wedding ring engraved with the legend: 'God send me well to keep'. The couple then processed into Greenwich Park where the dignitaries of the city were gathered to receive them. Seeing her for the first time, French ambassador Marillac described her as 'tall, thin and of medium beauty and of very assured and resolute countenance'. Overestimating her age at around thirty, when she was in fact twenty-four, he wrote, 'according to some who saw her close, is not so young as was expected nor so beautiful as everyone affirmed' and that 'the turn and vivacity of wit supplies the place of beauty.'[6] Following the ceremonies, the couple spent their wedding night at Greenwich. In the 1530s, Henry had made considerable improvements to the old medieval palace, building tilt yard towers and stables for jousting as well as a great wardrobe to contain the king's 'standing beddys', with long presses for Arras, carpets, cushions and hangings: one such press measured 55 feet and seven ladders were required to manage the hanging of the huge tapestries.[7] Greenwich also boasted a specially upholstered close stool for the king's use and magnificently curtained beds, in one of which Henry would have visited Anne that night. The encounter itself cannot have been anything less than a disaster: Henry's dislike was concealed from the court but made plain to his close servants. Famously stating that he liked her even less after their attempted union, he questioned her virginity because of the 'flabby belly and breasts' he took as signs of sexual experience. There can be no question though, of the sheltered princess's innocence, even ignorance. Strictly supervised at the Cleves court, she later proved herself unaware of the processes of reproduction. Three of her ladies – Rutland, Rochford, and Edgecombe – deposed that upon questioning the queen, they had uncovered her naivety in believing that mere kisses were sufficient, while Lady Browne judged Anne to have 'such fashion and manner of bringing up so gross that in her judgment the king should never heartily love her'.[8]

In some cases where marriages had not been consummated, a bedroom trial might be instigated. This went back at least as far as the twelfth century, when Thomas of Chobham advised a physical examination of a man's genitals by a panel of matrons who would then observe the couple in bed over a number of nights to see if the 'member is always found useless and as if dead'. This could hardly constitute encouragement to perform! In Canterbury in 1292, twelve matrons found the member of Walter de Fonte to be 'useless' and berated him for not being 'better able to serve and please' his wife. In fifteenth-century York, a husband was submitted to such an ordeal before witnesses: his wife 'exposed her naked breasts and with her hands warmed at the fire, she held and rubbed the penis and testicles of the said John ... and stirred him up ... to show his virility and potency (yet) the whole time aforesaid, the said penis was scarcely three inches long ... without any increase or decrease'.[9] There was little danger of Henry being forced to submit to such a trial.

Henry's repudiation of the unfortunate Anne was finalised that summer. The queen appears to have received little advice from those close to her as to how to try and please her husband or what to expect from him. Whilst she gradually learned the English language and ways and set aside her foreign clothes, she did not become any more attractive to Henry who could not overlook his initial dislike of her body or what he described as its strange odours. Women at the time, wishing to remain sweet-smelling in their heavy clothes, may have carried scented herbs and spices in bundles or pomanders about their person; nutmeg, lavender and mint were common. Trotula of Salerno recommended women to rub their breasts, nipples and genitals with a mixture of dried roses, cloves, nutmeg, laurel and galingale before sex. All forms of mint were strewn among clothing and bed sheets, for its scent as well as the ability to repel fleas, with pennyroyal a particular favourite. Crushed camomile was also used to scent laundry and flowers such as lavender and rose, and formed perfumes and waters to freshen the body. Sage, balm, liquorice and angelica were chewed to freshen the breath and whiten teeth. The mouth could also be cleaned with salt, rosemary or powdered cuttlefish administered on sticks or linen cloths, although the arrival and popularity of sugar did little to improve dental hygiene. A late fourteenth-century lyric predates Shakespeare in comparing a mistress's charms to herbs and flowers:

> Your breath is sweeter than balm, sugar or licquorice
> And yourself as sweet as is the gillyflower
> Or any lavender seeds strewn in a coffer to smell.[10]

Many contemporary receipt books included recipes for personal hygiene and appearance alongside those for illnesses and dishes for the table:

To make a Sweete Smellinge Breath:
Lett a man use to drinke verven (vervain) tempered with wine, itt drives away the Stinke of the Mouth and maketh thee a Sweete breathe.

For the Same:
Take Garden mynte, seeth them in Vineger, wash thy mouth therewith, then rubb thy gummes with powder of Minte.

A Water to putt away the Redness of the Eyes:
Take an ownce of Quick Brimstone, whyte Frankencense 2 drames, Mirra 2 drames, Camphora 2 drames, make all these in powder by themselves, then putt them in a Stillatory and take Rosewater 1 pint and therewith wash your face and you shall perceive your coullor to abate.

Other personal problems experienced by the Tudors were the parasites that could infest bedding, clothing and rushes. Fleas found homes in clothing, particularly favouring the rich furs of the court. One solution was to seal the garment up in a closed bag, suffocating the pests, as the usual washing with lye did not help; rooms were scattered with alder leaves and slices of bread smeared with glue were left as traps. More feared were the lice, which could thrive in 'sweat and foul odours', necessitating the removal of the court at regular intervals so that the royal palaces could be cleaned. Fleas were inevitable but to be infested with lice carried definite social stigma. Removing vermin from hair and beards was an intimate act, performed by those close servants that had access to the royal person. Combs were an essential personal item. Most Tudor palaces were equipped with a bathroom of some sort; at Hampton Court, Henry's Bayne Tower contained a round wooden bath which was lined with linen to prevent splinters. Sometimes the linen sheets were lifted to make a steam bath and hot stones were added, with cinnamon, mint, cumin or liquorice. Water was pumped underneath the Thames through a lead pipe from a spring three miles away; two large bronze taps delivered it either hot or cold. Such luxuries were beyond the reach of most, though, for whom washing was a less frequent, communal activity. London's public baths or Southbank stews became increasingly associated with brothels due to their mixed bathing and were closed down by Henry in 1546. Even before this, the fear that water spread disease, especially syphilis, began to curtail even the most regular bathers, who rubbed their bodies with oil to close up the pores before indulging. Medicinal baths for the more fortunate might be liberally sprinkled with hollyhock, mallow, fennel and camomile. However, even had Anne resorted to such hygienic, herbal and floral remedies, she could not compete with the new apple of her romantic husband's eye.

Ironically, the establishment of a new queen's household had brought fresh young female blood to the court and the king's head had quickly been turned by a petite, plump teenager who could not have been much more different from Anne. The red-haired Catherine Howard, a Boleyn cousin, may have been aged between fifteen or twenty-two, depending on various sources, by the time she left the household of her step-grandmother to serve the new queen. That spring she and Henry became lovers; once he decided to free himself from Anne and marry her, events moved very swiftly; perhaps there was a possibility that she had fallen pregnant or that, at least, Henry believed she had. On 24 June the queen was commanded to leave court and retire to Richmond, with the promise that Henry would follow soon after. It was a promise he did not keep, citing fear of the plague, although according to at least one contemporary source the area was relatively safe that summer. A commission of the clergy was established to examine the marriage and depositions taken from various sources among those who had witnessed the king's displeasure.

The statements of court gentlemen give some indication of their access and proximity to the king as well as his expressions of dislike. Even had he held his tongue, it must have been impossible for him to keep the details of his sexual activities secret from his closest male attendants. The court was a hotbed of scandal. According to the Earl of Southampton, Henry had been displeased with Anne's person from the start but said little: 'when he saw her first, the king considered it was not time to dispraise her who had been so extolled by others, so waited and proceeded coldly.' Eight days after the marriage, the Earl of Essex told Southampton that the queen was still a maid and the king had no affection for her; the marriage was still unconsummated at Easter by which time Henry had become Catherine Howard's lover. Lord Russell, Lord Admiral, said that the king was 'astonished and abashed when he first saw Anne' and asked Russell 'if he thought the woman so fair and of such beauty as report had been made of her': he was 'ashamed that men hath so praised her as they have done'. Sir Anthony Browne, Master of the Horse, had been present with Henry at the unfortunate Rochester meeting, where he had noticed on the king's 'countenance a discontentment and misliking of her person, and the King tarried not to speak with her twenty words' and 'deferred sending the presents that he had prepared for her'. Sir Thomas Hennage reinforced the sexual slurs Henry had already made: 'he mistrusted the queen's virginity, by reason of the looseness of her breasts and other tokens; and the marriage had never been consummated', which was supported by Anthony Denny, gentleman of the king's chambers and his secretary Thomas Wriothesley.

Still, this was all Henry's opinion; it was hardly equable with the fabrication of evidence that had brought down Anne Boleyn or the theological case Henry had compiled against Catherine. Yet, in the intervening years Henry had discovered he could bend the law to his inclination and had put aside two burdensome wives in order to follow his romantic desires. The queen's behaviour could not be faulted and she found many admirers at court but Henry's age and aversion, fuelled by the surrender of Catherine Howard, placed his imperative to father more children at the centre of the debate. He could not perform with Anne, although he was capable of the act, as testified by his physician Sir William Butts, who swore to the effect that Henry experienced two nightly ejaculations. He might also have prescribed wild purslane and blue iris to remedy this excessive 'waste'. Literally, the precious royal seed was being spilt to no good effect. Therefore, Anne must step aside.[11] When Anne was first informed of Henry's intentions, she took the matter 'heavily' but after the initial surprise, perhaps mindful of the fates of her predecessors, declared to commission that she was 'content always with your majesty'. Her swift recapitulation resulted in a generous settlement. She was to be given Hever Castle, Richmond Castle and other various houses and would thereafter be known as the king's sister. The marriage was annulled on 9 July; Henry married Catherine Howard, his 'rose without a thorn' on 28 July.

Catherine Howard is most famous – or infamous – for committing adultery while married to the king. It may be the case though, that the marriage itself was adulterous or bigamous, as according to practices of the time, she was technically someone else's wife. Nor may she actually have had intercourse with anyone else after her marriage to Henry. Her behaviour prior to arriving at court gives a good indication of the casual sexual encounters that occurred between young people living under the same roof. Unsupervised as a teenager, she had an early liaison with her music teacher Henry Manox, during which he came to have an intimate knowledge of her body while stopping short of full intercourse. This was due more to his lowly social status than her youth. Sharing a dormitory which was supposedly locked securely at night, Catherine found a way to entertain her new lover, Francis Dereham, whose status as a gentleman gained him access to her bed. While the women slept in the crowded chamber, Dereham and a friend crept in using a duplicate key and spent the night there in feasting and merrymaking. It is clear from the descriptions of the 'panting and puffing' as well as witness statements, that Catherine and Dereham had full sex on a number of occasions, in the belief that they would be married in the future, 'hanging together by the belly like sparrows'; a bird that was considered especially lascivious. By calling each other man and wife, they had entered into a pre-contract or handfasting, which was as good as a ceremony in the eyes of the Church, thus legally invalidating Catherine's union with Henry. Catherine's later condemnation for adultery, therefore, had little basis in reality.

Catherine's promiscuous past must have been fairly typical of Tudor youth. It was common practice to place young people either in an apprenticeship or position of service in a large household. Often with scant regulation, prey to their fellows or masters, young women grew to maturity in environments where sexual opportunity was available and sometimes inescapable. Service did not necessarily denote low social class; often these were girls from good families who had fallen on hard times, like Catherine herself. Servants in particular were vulnerable to exploitation and censure, especially as the child's father might be their master or a fellow servant in the same household, in whose interest it was to apportion blame elsewhere. In such cases it was important to ascertain exactly what had happened. Sometimes this was necessary to prevent an unwed mother feeling the full force of the law, especially when things went wrong during delivery. When spinster Margaret Hilles, servant to Bartholomew Skerne, gentleman, gave birth in his house at Pattiswick between ten and eleven at night on 26 January 1568, fifteen male jurors gave their oath that the child had been stillborn. Margaret had been 'overcome with labour'[12] in Skerne's house, suggesting that this had not been her intended or desired place for lying-in, although it may have been her place of residence. This strongly suggests she was denied the traditional female preserve and assistance of a ritualised lying-in and her labour was a public affair, with all members of the household being informed of its progression at first hand. The extent of the privacy and support offered to servants in her position depended upon the good will of her master and those household members senior to her in age, experience and rank. Who was the father of Margaret's child? Her body may have been the property of her master in every sense.

Cases of servants labouring in master's houses, beggars in fields and barns are sadly plentiful and the penalties for transgressing social codes were felt most heavily by the vulnerable. Their cases come to light most typically when unplanned pregnancy was the result. It was common for masters to dismiss pregnant workers or remove them from sight, perhaps to conceal their own guilt, like Margaret Grene of Fairstead, Essex, who was taken by her master over the county border into Suffolk in 1588 to give birth in anonymity.[13] In the same year, Alse Mathewe of Essex lost her job for conceiving an unlawful child by a fellow servant and was forced to wander the countryside, begging and finally giving birth in Clare, Suffolk, attended by local women and midwives who tried to discover the child's paternity. Mistresses could be more sympathetic, especially when there was no question of the master being implicated in the pregnancy. In the summer of 1591, Alice Perier's mistress paid for her to travel to London to find the father of her unborn child. Alice stayed for a week at the White Horse by Bishopsgate, until she was ejected for being too great with child, then went into labour on the way to find new lodgings in Whitechapel. She delivered her son in the porch of St Botolph's by Aldgate, where a few passing women took pity on her and carried her to the house of a Father Noswell, a water-bearer who lived in a nearby alley, where she remained for a month. On the advice of her mistress, Alice later abandoned the child, for which she did penance in a local church: what became of her son is unrecorded. A similar story is that of Mary Andros, who gave birth in 1599, while having left her employment to seek the child's father. Unsupported and friendless, she had no choice but to lie down on the bare ground and be assisted by local women in an unfamiliar place.[14] Such births cannot have been too infrequent, given the readiness of women to extend their help to a stranger, whose gender and travail overrode any other concerns.

Catherine, though, famously stated that she knew how to 'meddle' with a man without conceiving a child. This implies a significant knowledge of birth control for one of her years, suggesting she had been informed early by the other women of her chamber. Undoubtedly among women of all classes, the usual methods of delaying conception were employed, such as withdrawal, the risky rhythm method and potions of herbs like rue. For new mothers, prolonged breastfeeding could also offer some protection. The parish registers of several Essex villages indicate that conceptions occurring after a birth happened on average between nine and twelve months later, consistent with breast feeding patterns among the lower classes. For young girls like Catherine, an ill-timed pregnancy might spoil their chances of a better marriage later on. In fact, Catherine was keen to distance herself from her 'husband' Dereham once a place at court had been secured for her. Superstition had plenty of contraceptive advice to offer: a hemlock plaster on the testicles could prevent pregnancy, as could the placing of a cockerel's testicles under the bed. Sponges soaked in herbs or vinegar were used as barriers and apparently, some women went as far as to use wax to seal up the uterus! The first quondams, or condoms, made by glovers from linen or animal gut became available in the sixteenth century, named after the cowls worn by monks whose licentious behaviour was often cited as the reason for the Reformation. Early lambskin condoms were known as the Venus Glove. However, these would have been expensive and beyond the reach of most. In addition, certain times were prohibited for sexual activity. Sundays, Lent and saint's days were debarred, although this was clearly not strictly followed as some churches insisted those indulging during that time must be denied Communion or do public penance. Contemporary wisdom advised abstinence at the height of summer, as sexual activity overheated and dried the body, although the parish records show a conception cycle which suggests otherwise. More encounters took place in warmer weather, with young people taking advantage of greater degrees of privacy offered by the great outdoors, resulting in peaks in the birth rate the following spring.

What is perhaps more surprising is that Catherine did not conceive while married to Henry. The rumours in July 1540 of her potential pregnancy proved to be just that. He had been disappointed four year before that Jane Seymour had not conceived sooner; now he was approaching fifty. After his recent claims to have been experiencing 'twice nightly' excretions to prove his ability, and despite lavishing Catherine with public physical affection, she gave no indication of being with child. This may have been embarrassing for the king who would not have liked the implication that he was 'not a man like any other' but it was not just a royal problem. Then, as now, some couples clearly found it easier to achieve conception than others. Baptismal records are inconclusive on this; some wives conceived before or very soon after the wedding, while others did not for several years. In the case of infertility, it would be unlikely for a yeoman, craftsman or labourer to be able to afford the advice of a doctor, even if that doctor had been able to help: medical diagnoses were based on the four humours; hot, cold, wet and dry and imbalances might be addressed by certain foods. Cheaper methods would be passed by oral tradition through the social network: a mixture of chestnuts, pistachios and pine nuts boiled down in sugar and ragwort was a recommended aphrodisiac. A mixture of rabbit's blood, sheep urine, mare's milk and mugwort were also reported to enhance fertility. Alternatively, large winged ants were mixed with the testicles of quail, bark oil and amber and applied to the member; failing that, a tourniquet to the left testicle or the sympathetically shaped Mandrake root was recommended. Bald's ninth-century *Leechbook* suggested agrimony boiled in ewe's milk would provoke an insufficiently virile man, while boiling the herb in Welsh beer would produce the opposite results.

If herbal cures did not work, a variety of other methods were available to the childless couple. Superstition would encourage them both to urinate on a mixture of wheat and bran; if this became 'foul', the infertile partner was identified. A barren woman was invited to echo the reproductive capabilities of a rabbit by drinking a mixture made from that animal's powdered womb; frigid or unresponsive women were to have the 'grease of a goat' rubbed on their private parts. Religion would encourage them to attend their local church, pray, undertake pilgrimage and be sprinkled with holy water. The *Compendium Medicanae*, a thirteenth-century tract by Gilbertus Anglicus, told them to uproot a large comfrey plant, followed by a smaller one within three hours; they must recite the Lord's Prayer three times while pacing, juice the plant and use this to write the prayer on a card, which they then wore about their necks during intercourse. For a girl, the woman should wear the card; for a boy, the man. Other incantations included the repetition of phrases like 'Lord, wherefore are they increased' and 'rejoice, loose their chains O Lord'.[15] Sympathetic magic was also used; one Oxfordshire couple named Phipps were denounced by the Church in 1520 for keeping an empty cradle by their bed in the hopes that it would prompt conception.[16] Infertile couples might also seek to use alchemy or astrology to help conceive a child. The position of the stars was held to be auspicious at conception and birth: if they could afford an alchemist's fees, a couple may be given certain dates to avoid or rituals to follow. In Bury St Edmunds, a white bull festooned with garlands was led through the streets from its paddock home to the gates of the abbey: women who wished to conceive would accompany it, stroking its sides until reaching the shrine and offering prayers, again making the woman responsible for ensuring conception. The eleventh-century female doctor Trotula of Salerno was among the few to state that infertility might be equally attributed to men and women. She suggested a man drink a liquid while reciting the paternoster nine times. This would have hardly been an acceptable explanation for Henry.

Obviously, Henry had to be regularly sharing Catherine's bed in order for her to conceive. As the months passed and the summer of 1541 arrived, bringing the king's fiftieth birthday, even she began to despair that she may never fall pregnant and thus ensure her position. Perhaps it was partly this fear that contributed to the commencement of an adulterous relationship almost under the king's nose. In the full awareness of her predecessor's fates, to smuggle her cousin Thomas Culpeper into her bedchamber at various locations on the royal progress was an act of extreme folly at the very least. Perhaps it was indeed the romantic, innocent liaison they portrayed, fuelled by intention rather than activity. There is a chance that the affair was not consummated in the physical sense at all and that a second of Henry's wives met her death innocent of the charges of adultery. When a servant named John Lascelles came forward with information about the nightly activities of the Duchess of Norfolk's charge, the king was horrified. Just as he had been mistaken over Anne of Cleves' sexual experience, he had naively believed in his young wife's virginity and she had not taken any steps to open his eyes. He had not insisted on any of the contemporary virginity trials, like the examination by a panel of matrons or the waving of a chicken wing over the abdomen. Once again, Henry found his initial impression of a woman did not match up to the reality. Whether or not she had cheated on him after their marriage, his disillusionment over Catherine's past was enough; her days were numbered.

It was incumbent upon a married man to acknowledge, as his own, any children born to his wife, so long as they were living together. However, Tudor men did not always take kindly to being 'cuckolded', especially when it came to the inheritance of money and property. One scandal diligently recorded by the parish clerk of Little Clacton was that of Thomasin Robwood. She had married a Walter Clarke on 15 November 1574, although later events proved that by this time she was already three months pregnant. The question of whether she had known and if she had communicated this to Clarke appears to be answered by the later naming of the 'bastard's' father, Peter Tredgold, who is listed the previous year as a tailor in the village. Their daughter Prudence was born in May 1575, having been conceived in August 1574. Perhaps Clarke had finally realised the truth of his wife's condition and worked out the maths or had gallantly offered her security and later changed his mind. No answers can be found to explain under what circumstances the conception take place but Thomasin and Walter did not go on to have any more children together.[17] For Henry VIII, the all-important succession was dependent upon his wife's fidelity; the possibility of an illegitimate child inheriting the throne was unthinkable. It was this suspicion that had fuelled the vehemence of his rejection of Anne Boleyn: now her cousin was trying to provide him with the 'heir' he needed, possibly with the assistance of another man! There may be the possibility that for the young teenager, romantically in love with Culpeper while married to an ageing, obese man, the question of the succession was not sufficient deterrent. At his examination, Culpeper insisted that they had merely talked, with the intention of infidelity but had never consummated their attraction: it was not enough to save his neck.

The swiftness and severity of Henry's reaction shows the depth of his sudden disillusionment with his beloved young 'rose without a thorn' as well as the blow to his ego. Catherine's promiscuity, like her cousin Anne's supposed behaviour, did not just pose a threat to the succession. Apart from making a fool of the king, it exposed him to the risk of venereal disease. That term was coined in 1527, although syphilis, known in England as the 'French pox' had been common in Europe since the fifteenth century, and other sexually transmitted diseases present in England for centuries. Syringes for injecting the mercury treatment directly into the urethra were discovered aboard the wreck of the Mary Rose, Henry's flagship that sank in 1545. The spread and effects of such conditions was poorly understood, demonised and sometimes deliberately exploited. It sounds ridiculous to a modern audience that in 1529, Thomas Wolsey was accused of blowing in the king's ear in an attempt to give him syphilis yet the overlap between infection, superstition and magic was strong. As far back as 1346, a royal proclamation stated that leprosy would 'taint persons who are sound, both male and female'[18] and a widespread fear that it could be spread through sexual contact contributed to the regulation of London prostitutes or 'Winchester Geese', after that Bishop's role in licensing them. Women might attempt to cover the effects of the disease by applying asses' milk or bean-flower water to the skin; some remedies called for the use of brimstone or dog turds. The city's brothels were located almost out of sight and mind across the Thames in Southwark and Bankside, often closing during the plague and outbreaks of illness, such as the syphilis epidemic of 1504. Henry VIII had attempted to close them entirely in 1535, on the basis that they spread disease, a battle he wouldn't achieve until 1546. Some commentators felt this had little impact, with the spread of prostitutes now less easy to regulate:

> The Stewes in England bore a beastly sway
> Till the eight Henry banish'd them away
> And since these common whore were quite put down
> A damned crue of private whores are grown
> So that the divill will be doing still
> Either with publique or with private ill.[19]

Medieval recipe books carried a range of contemporary and ancient remedies against the effects of sexually transmitted diseases, some superstitious, some herbal. Gonorrhoea was a well-known condition, being treated with soothing remedies for 'burning members' (genitals), while women with the resulting discharge should soak a yarrow and lay it beneath their seat to take away the odour. 'Loin ache' could be soothed with mixtures of nettle, bettany, pennyroyal, groundsel and hound's tooth diluted in wine. Pennyroyal, dill and sage were suggested for genital itching, while infused dock could treat swellings or else a patient could attach henbane roots to the thigh. For leprosy, still considered to be passed through sexual contact, drinking or bathing in the blood of virgins or children was recommended by the Ancient Greeks but even into the eighteenth century, dog blood was listed as an effective remedy. Some of these illnesses could result in infertility or interfere with the birth process. In 1513, Rosslin wrote that if the woman's parts were affected with boils, ulcers or warts, a midwife should take advice from a doctor before the delivery; if unable, she should pour oil and fat into the vagina to make the delivery less painful and try to prevent miscarriage. The possibility of Catherine's infidelity, which Henry was at first reluctant to believe, introduced the possibility of his own infection, fertility and mortality; all issues that were particularly close to his heart.

The details of Catherine's past were written in a letter left by Cranmer for Henry to find in the chapel at Hampton Court. She was accused of living 'dissolutely' and 'using the unlawful company of Dereham'; in the words of Holinshed, they had been pre-contracted. His reaction was swift; the extent of his shock and grief surprising. After the incrimination of Manox and Dereham – who had done little wrong in fraternising with a willing teenager before she rose to become the king's wife – the association of Catherine and Culpeper was uncovered. All were sent to their deaths; the men in December, Catherine in February 1542. The heads of Manox and Dereham remained on London Bridge until as late as 1546. The event afforded a small glimmer of hope for Anne of Cleves, whose brother petitioned Henry to accept her again as his wife, yet Henry was not prepared to re-enter that particular yoke.

9

Catherine Parr
1543–1548

The Virtuous Wife

If they be women married ... wear such apparel as becometh
holiness and comely usage with soberness ... love their children ...
be discreet, chaste, housewifely, good and obedient unto their husbands.[1]

Catherine Parr, Henry's sixth and final wife, is perhaps best known for her history of marriage to elderly husbands and the ageing Henry's appreciation of her nursing skills. The king's ill health is well known and various authors have pictured the devoted nurse drawing on her experience to administer to his aches and pains. In fact, neither of these statements are true. Henry had enough doctors. It would have been highly inappropriate for a woman like Catherine to perform this function, especially when what Henry really wanted was a woman to divert his attention and help him regain his youth; he would go to considerable lengths to prevent his wife from witnessing his worst episodes by barring her from his presence. Marriage to Catherine was for pleasure, not duty. However, the reverse was probably true for her. An intelligent and informed woman, she was already in love with another man when she became aware of the king's preference for her and was forced to sacrifice personal interest and accept a dangerous and unwanted position at Henry's side. Less well known is her status as a published author, a leading proponent of the Reformed faith and that she too, like Jane Seymour, died following complications arising in childbirth.

Catherine was born 1512, probably at her parents' Blackfriars house in London. Although they owned property further north, her mother Maud was an attendant on Catherine of Aragon and would have lived in relative proximity to the court during the periods of her employment. Catherine was first married at around the age of seventeen but some historical confusion about the identity of her husband, Edward Borough, has given rise to the idea that she was espoused to a much older man. The misidentification of grandson for grandfather during the Victorian era may explain this, although it does seem likely that her young husband may equally have been ill, as she was widowed in spring 1533 after only four years of marriage and bore him no children. Later the same year she took a step up the social ladder through a union with John Neville, Lord Latimer, a man of forty to her twenty. He already had two children by his first wife but a second short-lived marriage had produced no more offspring; Catherine was not to conceive during the decade she spent as his wife. Latimer's son would produce only daughters and on his demise, the title would disappear until the twentieth century.

Outside the monarchy, the upper classes were equally keen to secure their succession to gain and retain lands, titles and properties. Sons were essential; primogeniture, or the inheritance of the firstborn child of the entire estate to the exclusion of other siblings, applied only to men. Although Salic law did not prevent the inheritance of females in England as it did in Europe, Henry VIII's struggle to produce a son indicates how undesirable the inheritance of females was to the Tudor mind. Large aristocratic families were the norm. Just as a fecund couple could multiply a dynasty, infertility, ill health and infant mortality could grind one branch of an aristocratic family to a halt. Such a turn of events threatened the stock of the Windsors and demonstrates the unpredictability of conception, despite the best of marital intentions. Of the eight children born to Andrew and Elizabeth in the 1490s and 1500s, only three went on to marry. The eldest, George, died at the age of twenty-four without having become a father; his wife Ursula remarried but did not conceive and died childless. The second son William had no issue by his first wife, so remarried on her death; his new spouse, Elizabeth, was twenty years his junior and would have three husbands in all, only bearing a daughter in her final marriage at the age of forty-two; that daughter had two husbands and no issue. The Winsdors' eldest daughter Eleanor was widowed at the age of fifteen then remarried and bore three children, dying at the age of thirty-one in giving birth to a fourth infant, who shared her fate. Of her offspring, one son reproduced, so the Windsors only had two great-grandchildren, of which one was a boy. He went on to have eight children of his own, perhaps conscious that the lineage was dependent on him. For a Tudor family, such misfortune could only mean that God was punishing them. Some women in these circumstances might have resorted to desperate measures, such as in the life of Hugh of Lincoln, where a gentlewoman, desperate for an heir, feigned a pregnancy with pillows and adopted the child of a peasant.[2] It has been estimated[3] that in the seventeenth century, almost one in five noble families died out from infertility or infant mortality.

Shortly before her husband's demise Catherine became aware of the king's interest. Her first recorded meeting with Henry probably occurred around 1540 when, amid his present marital trials, he may have noticed the short, pale-skinned red-head with a love of bright clothes. John Foxe later described her as 'endued with rare gifts of nature, as singular beauty, favour and a comely person'.[4] In February 1543, after being widowed a second time, she became a member of Princess Mary's household and a regular face at court. A love affair with Thomas Seymour, uncle of Prince Edward, quickly developed. He was dashing, handsome, impulsive and had returned to court that January after a diplomatic mission abroad: they may have even planned to marry but the king intervened and Seymour was sent to Brussels. This was arranged in March, although he did not leave until May, which perhaps gives a framework for Henry's proposal and Catherine's acceptance. In many ways, Lady Latimer was a safe bet. After the death of Catherine Howard, it became illegal to conceal knowledge about a potential queen's past; keeping quiet about previous relationships was a serious matter but Catherine's marital history was known. By marrying a widow, Henry protected himself from any such revelations as had occurred in 1541. He knew exactly with whom she had been previously intimate! Additionally, her apparent infertility was less of a problem given his intermittent impotence, although he still expected a sexual relationship with her. Catherine was still only thirty-one and was privately reluctant to become his wife, although duty and desire to serve the king were engrained in the Tudor woman's being. In February 1543, Henry paid a tailor's bill for Catherine and her stepdaughter of 'numerous items' of cotton, linen, buckram, hoods and sleeves, Italian, Venetian, French and Dutch gowns, totalling over £8; he was already considering her as his next queen and his proposal must have followed soon after, probably in March or April.

Catherine didn't answer at once. She was allowed time to think about it but there was never really any question of refusal. The marriage licence was issued by Cranmer on 10 July and six days later, Wriothesley wrote to the Duke of Suffolk that the king was 'married last Thursday' to a woman of 'virtue, wisdom and gentleness' and was sure 'his majesty never had a wife more agreeable to his heart than she is'. Sir Ralph Sadler claimed that news of the match had caused rejoicing at the 'real and inestimable benefit and comfort which thereby shall ensure to the whole realm'.[5] Later that month, Chapuys wrote that the king had 'espoused the queen privately and without ceremony'. This was typical of Henry's emphasis on the private rather than public aspects of his marriages, with only the ill-fated Anne of Cleves union beginning with a formal, public occasion: all others had been conducted in secrecy. Stephen Gardiner officiated and Anne herself had taken 'great grief and despair' at the news, as Catherine was supposedly not as beautiful as her and had 'no hope of issue, seeing that she had none by her two former husbands'.[6] Plague had again hit the capital that summer so the newly-weds spent an extended six-month honeymoon staying in Henry's numerous manors and hunting lodges, although his increasing girth and ill-health meant that he was watching rather than participating in the hunt.

Catherine was not needed to nurse Henry. He had a multitude of doctors, surgeons, physicians and intimate servants to ensure his bodily needs were being met. Perhaps they, or he, consulted the *Fyrst Boke of the Introduction of Knowledge*, published in 1542 by 'physycke doctor' Andrew Borde. Borde's advice extended to diet, exercise and the arrangement and organisation of the household and daily life. His instructions on sleep give an interesting insight into practices of the time. After daily exercise, moderate rest was required in order to nourish the blood, 'qualify' the heat of the liver, restore memory and quiet all the humours. Excessive sleep was a dangerous path to sin, sluggishness and all sorts of illnesses; according to Borde's application of humour-based theories, seven hours were sufficient for a sanguine man while a phlegmatic one required nine. A sick man was advised to sleep whenever he could, although it was best to do so at night and retain his natural pattern; if he must sleep in the day, he should do so in a chair or leaning against a cupboard! He recommended a fire in the chamber to rid it of foul pestilences and the foul air of man's breath, while the windows should be closed. Sleepers should avoid old rooms where mice, rats and snails might creep in. It was important to lie for a little while on the left-hand side before rolling over onto the right for the 'first sleep'; upon waking, a man should pass water then take his second sleep lying on his left side. The interval between was apparently the best time to conceive children. When they slept again, the head should be raised, in case recently eaten meat should rise, although pillows were considered a luxury and a night cap of scarlet cotton, flock or wool should be worn. Scarlet, originally a cloth rather than a colour, was thought efficacious in the prevention of scarring in illnesses like small pox, when hung in the windows. For the best sleep, a feather bed with white covering was needed. It is surprising, in medieval and Tudor depictions of bedroom scenes, how many times the colours red and white are used in bedding, yet these depictions are often imaginary or idealised; most of Henry's subjects would have slept upon 'pallets' which were sacks stuffed with hay or straw, if they were lucky to have a bed at all. Upon waking, a man should stretch, cough and spit, make his stool, comb, wash, walk a couple of miles in the garden, hear Mass then take some light exercise before a modest meal. Henry may have taken this advice, although Borde's recommendations against surfeit of meat eating, which could cause many illnesses, strangulation and sudden death, may have come too late.[7]

By the time of his last marriage, Henry himself was an experienced medical practitioner. He personally recommended cures to his household and was keen to source unusual (and even fictitious) ingredients such as unicorn horns. To Sir Bryan Tuke, he passed a remedy for curing a tumour in the testicles as 'cunning as any physician in England could do' and devised potions and salves of his own to 'dry excoriations and comfort the member'. However, he was unable to cure the regular pain in his ulcerated leg. Borde urged such patients not to forget to empty themselves when the need arose and ensure they wore stays and that their shoes were not too tight. They should avoid their legs getting cold and not go wet-shod. Prohibited foods included beer, red wine and new ale, new bread, eggs, fresh salmon and herring, eels, oysters and all shellfish, beef, goose, duck and pigeon. Most importantly, they should not commit acts of venery on a full stomach.[8] However, a 1545 *Propre boke of new Cokerye*,[9] containing inventive and extravagant recipes which represented the height of mid-Tudor cuisine, probably depicted more accurately what was being served up in Henry's kitchens. Boiled peacocks were re-stitched into their skin and feathers and made to 'breathe' fire using camphor, roasted chickens apparently sang and hens were presented in six different colours. Omelets were made to resemble flowers, meatballs dressed as oranges, almond cream eggs were served in real shells, as were cakes. No doubt Henry would have celebrated his marriage to Catherine in his accustomed style. In her turn, Catherine's role was to be an ornament and companion, to divert him from his pains and labours and as she herself wrote, in her 1547 *Lamentations of a Sinner*, 'to be a comely, good and obedient wife'. The marriage appears to have been harmonious, even surviving an attempt by Stephen Gardiner to attack the queen on religious grounds. By the end of 1546, as Henry's ill health worsened, he retired to Whitehall and Catherine was not to see him again. On his death in January 1547, she found herself a widow for the third time and retired to her house at Chelsea on the coronation of the nine-year-old Edward VI.

As the king's widow, still young and well provided for, Catherine was a good catch. Her feelings for Thomas Seymour had not changed. Now she was free to remarry and represented, for the ambitious courtier, a far greater prize as the queen dowager than as Lady Latimer. Still, Seymour investigated the possibility of taking either Princess Mary or Elizabeth as his bride before he married Catherine in secrecy that May. The indecent haste caused a minor scandal at court when it was discovered. While enough time had elapsed for Catherine to be certain she was not pregnant with Henry's child, the period of official mourning was by no means over. Her actions offended her stepdaughter Mary in particular, as well as the new king and his regime headed by Seymour's brother, although in their case it was irritation at the overmightiness of Thomas than with Catherine herself. It was a hasty and possibly foolish move but, for the first time, Catherine was married to a man she loved and she was happy.

Catherine had considered herself infertile until falling pregnant in the winter of 1547. Passing the winter between her houses at Chelsea, Hanworth or Seymour Place in London, she must have conceived in early December and become aware of her condition with the approach of spring. As she experienced her first symptoms and physical changes, she may have been reluctant to confront a potential problem developing under her roof in the shape of her fourteen-year-old stepdaughter Elizabeth. Having experienced fluctuating fortunes under her various stepmothers, the slight, red-haired teenager had experienced something like a family life for the first time under Catherine's care. Her last stepmother provided her with security and a Protestant education, with the result that a real affection had developed between them. Now, an attraction between Elizabeth and Seymour began as a form of horseplay, with dancing and tickling sessions, although the ambitious courtier had previously explored the possibilities of marriage with her in order to give him the position he believed that, as the king's uncle, he deserved. With Elizabeth living under the same roof, he would enter her chamber early in the morning before she had risen and slap her familiarly on the back and buttocks, before trying to climb into bed with her. Abstinence during Catherine's pregnancy may have provoked a relatively innocent situation to develop into something more serious but at some point in the early summer, after a bizarre incident when Catherine assisted Seymour in cutting the girl's clothing with a knife, the ex-queen found her stepdaughter in her husband's arms. Elizabeth was sent away that May but later, the hostile Catholic Jane Dormer would hint at the possibility of an illegitimate pregnancy: 'there was a bruit of a child born and miserably destroyed ... only the report of the midwife, who was brought from her house blindfolded thither ... said it was the child of a very fair young lady'.[10] This was the first of many rumours of illicit sex and childbirth to be attached to Elizabeth, whose denial of the traditional feminine role confounded the understanding of her peers. No proof exists for any of them and the balance of probability lies against the majority.

Now, Catherine focused on her advancing pregnancy. A reformist since her teens, her approaching labour would not have been relieved by any of the traditional superstitions of relics or appeals to Mary and the saints: instead she turned her attention to practical preparations, aware that at the advanced age of thirty-five, she was at risk as a first-time mother. She moved first to the relative comfort and seclusion of her house at Hanworth, while Seymour was caught up with court business. Near the present-day town of Feltham in Hounslow, the manor house then stood in a quiet village surrounded by heathland that was good for hunting. The months of waiting did not pass smoothly, either; she was sickly and unwell although she eagerly anticipated the child's arrival. Seymour recorded their child's quickening in a letter: 'I hear my lettell man doth shake hys belle, trostynge, iff God shall geve hym lyff to leve as long as his father ...' Later he asked her to 'kepe the litell knave so leane and gantte with your good dyett and walking that he may be so small that he may krepe out of a mouse holle'.[11] The summer was unusually hot and drought-ridden, which must have added to Catherine's discomfort, as did fears of the outbreaks of plague in the capital. In mid-June, with six weeks to go until the birth, they removed to Sudeley Castle, with a household of over a hundred, where a suite of rooms had been prepared for her lying-in on the south-east side of the inner quadrangle. A covered corridor linked these to the servants' quarters and kitchens, so Catherine could anticipate being well looked after. On 30 August 1548, she delivered a daughter and appeared to be recovering. All was not as it seemed though; after a few days, she became seriously feverish and delirious.

Midwives were aware of the dangers protracted and difficult births could create in recovering mothers. They also knew that even apparently straightforward births, like Catherine's probably was, could conceal underlying problems that emerge days later.

Preparations before and care during and after the delivery were vital. Before the birth, expectant mothers might soak in a bath of softening, smoothing ingredients like mallow, camomile blossom, maidenhair, linseed, fenugreek, dogs' mercury: with many modern mothers opting for water births, the relaxing effects of submersion are still well known and used today. Lubricants were recommended to open the birth canal, including a slime made from quince seeds, linseed, dates or fenugreek, which was smeared on the genitals. Small women whose pelvic measurements were causing concern should have their ligaments and joints anointed and drink oil of almonds, while weak and dainty women were to be fed with egg yolks tossed in wine and sugar and drink cinnamon water. Sometimes it was believed that the bladder may be lying in the way, preventing delivery so the midwife should, somehow, provoke woman to pass water. As with Jane Seymour, sudden flux, blood loss and convulsions were serious indicators of potentially deadly problems but appeared days after the birth, when the mother appeared to be out of danger. As these could kill a mother and child instantly, the midwife must see that all was done to soothe her and deliver the child as soon as possible; some physicians still advised bleeding the mother at this stage but medical opinion was divided and such a move was controversial. Others resorted to physical intervention, actually reaching in to pull out a child and treating the bleeding with vervain or cinnamon drunk with red wine or beer. Contemporary receipt books listed the healing powers of oak leaves to heal 'all manner of flyxes in the wombe', but Catherine was well past this stage. Difficulties in the delivery of the placenta could lead to gangrene, tumours, ulcers or flux of blood; this was treated with pills of myrrh, gentian and oil; also, pepper and cinnamon would encourage a mother to sneeze and expel the afterbirth, as would making her smell bad things such as old shoes and burnt partridge feathers. In the eventuality of tearing, Trotula of Salerno recommended the perineum be washed in wine and butter, sewn up with silken thread and covered with linen cloth before being doused in hot tar! If the mother survived this, the wound should be closed up using powder of comfrey, daisy and cinnamon. She must remain with her feet elevated for eight or nine days and neither wash nor cough.[12] A further cause of difficult or prolonged deliveries was rickets. Deficiencies of vitamin D could deform the pelvis of a growing girl, which in some places was drastically anticipated by the breaking of these bones in infant females. Other fears covered breech birth and the presentation of a foetal limb, which would be sometimes cut off in order to facilitate delivery; some mothers were even shaken or held upside down in desperate attempts to harness the force of gravity.

If Catherine's midwives tried any of these remedies, they were not successful. Raving bitterly about being mistreated, which may have referred to her treatment or her relations with Seymour, she was not strong enough to sign her will. She died in the early hours of 5 September, probably of the puerperal fever which also claimed the life of Jane Seymour. At some point during delivery, bacteria were spread on the hands of her assistants and lay dormant for several days before causing her to develop a fever and deteriorate. Modern hygiene means this rarely happens today and IS easily treatable with a course of antibiotics. Whilst seventeenth-century practitioners would report a death rate of between 20 and 25 per cent from the illness, the death rate among Henry's wives was two in six, or 33 per cent. Catherine's daughter, Mary, was given to the keeping of her friend Catherine Willoughby but does not appear to have survived infancy. The ambitious Seymour outlived his wife by only six months, losing his head for plotting to abduct the king.

Catherine herself was interred in the chapel at Sudeley with all the ceremony of a queen. Miles Coverdale's epitaph to her concluded:

> ... a beauteous daughter bless'd her arms,
> An infant copy of her parents' charms.
> When now seven days this tender flower had bloom'd
> Heaven in its wrath the mother's soul resumed...
> Our loyal breast with rising sighs are torn,
> With saints she triumphs, we with mortals mourn.[13]

10

Henry's Legacy
1534–1553

Reform in the Birth Chamber

Blessings turned to blasphemies,
Holy deedes to dispites.

About these Catholic's necks and hands are always hanging charms
That serve against all miseries and all unhappy harms.[1]

At the end of January 1547, Henry VIII died, leaving his nine-year-old son Edward as heir. After almost forty years of him struggling to secure the succession, it was entailed upon the heirs of Henry's sister Mary Rose, rather than his own daughters Mary and Elizabeth. This was partly for religious reasons but also occasioned by the fluctuating legitimacy and favour of his female offspring. Edward, however, would not live long enough to father children of his own. Proposed marriages were mooted for him to his cousins Mary Queen of Scots and Jane Grey among others, yet he died before his sixteenth birthday, of what was probably tuberculosis. However, it would be a mistake to think that the reign of Edward VI has little relevance in the history of childbirth: ironically it would be a child whose reign had the most impact upon Tudor birth practices.

Major religious changes took place in the sixteenth century. The childbearing history of the family of Jane Yate of Berkshire ran parallel with these. With the dramatic dissolution of the monasteries and attacks upon many superstitions and customs of the time, Jane's experiences and those of her offspring may serve to illustrate exactly what impact this had in the birth chamber. Jane was born in Berkshire in the 1480s, married a William or Philip Fettiplace and bore her first child, Elizabeth, in 1510, a generation before the English Reformation began. Her first pregnancy ran concurrently with that of Queen Catherine's and a range of her female relatives would have been on hand to offer her advice and support, if not to attend her during her lying-in. Her stepmother, Alice, had three small children at the time and was pregnant with her fourth in 1510; one of her sisters-in-law was also a mother and she had nine other immediate female relations to offer their assistance. This, as well as friends and neighbours, formed a substantial body of knowledge based on experience and an oral tradition that encompassed a mixture of gynaecological, superstitious, herbal and quasi-religious practices that had been passed down through generations of women. An upper-class Catholic lying-in would have included all the prayers, blessed candles, holy water and devotional images and objects that the Church had to offer; nearby monastic establishments may also have offered cures and advice. However, new laws meant that by the time Jane's grandchildren arrived, many of these comforts and customs were prohibited. Jane died in 1557, meaning she was potentially witness to the births of sixteen children between 1526 and 1547: did she and her companions really obey the letter of the law when the door to the birth chamber was closed and the lives of her family hung in the balance?

In 1509, Henry VIII and Catherine of Aragon were visible and active leaders of their faith, especially in relation to their desire to produce healthy surviving children. Along with many hopeful parents, they undertook pilgrimages to shrines across the country, offered prayers and gifts to the saints and deployed the relics and rituals of Catholicism. If she chose, Jane Yate could have been among those asking the Virgin Mary for assistance: after all, she bore her first child comparatively late for the times, possibly towards the end of her twenties, and may have sought the reassurance her faith had to offer. Those who spoke out against such practices were rebuked or punished, such as an Elizabeth Sampson of London, who visited the shrine of Our Lady at Willesden in the year of Henry's accession and described the Black Madonna as a 'burnt-tailed elf and a burnt-tailed stock'. Another of the early voices of criticism raised against Walsingham came from the Dutch humanist Desiderius Erasmus, with whom Henry VIII had corresponded since childhood. In 1512, he produced the satire *A Pilgrimage for Religion's Sake* after visiting the shrine, harshly portraying the requests and prayers of pilgrims as absurd and irrelevant. Additionally, rioters in Canterbury had refused to escort the noblemen bringing Henry's annual gift to the shrine of Thomas Becket, instead attacking priory property and ill-treating the monks. Such incidents were isolated, rather than the norm. Those displaying such behaviour could expect to be dealt with severely by their pious king.

For centuries, labouring mothers in England had drawn strength and courage from the religious rituals and superstitions associated with their condition. Women had given birth clutching holy relics and other religious artefacts, praying to saints in symbolic female isolation: they had lit candles for their dead, sprinkled their beds with holy water, and recounted pseudo-religious texts and chants. Then after the traditional month of seclusion, they had processed to church in a veil to be purified and welcomed back into society: churching was Catholicism's protection for women against the pressure of resuming potentially dangerous sexual and domestic duties too soon and for many, it was successful. Nor was the ritual and devotion confined to the reproductive chapters of her life: Catholicism defined every aspect of women's existence until the 1530s. For a modern reader, it is difficult sometimes to appreciate how very powerful and pervasive the influence of the Church was over the rhythms of the rural year and the rites of passage that defined life. Conception, birth, baptism, churching, marriage and burial were the obvious points of personal contact, besides regular procession and prayer for the success of crops, good health, safe journeys, prosperity and the habitual ceremonies of the day, month and year. Hell, Heaven and Purgatory were very real; the divine intercession of saints, the Mass, feasting and fasting, observing saints' days, pilgrimage, offering prayers for the living and dead were all accessible methods of easing the transition to eternal bliss and staving off the fires of torture. Each earthly action was a step closer to heaven or hell. Superstition, custom and religious practice mingled in a Pagan legacy that permeated and defined the medieval and early Tudor consciousness, providing motive and explanation for the mysteries and uncertainties of life.

At the time Jane Yate attended the lying-in of her own daughter Elizabeth in 1526, who was aged only sixteen, these upheavals still lay in the future. Jane and her female relations could draw on the practices they recalled their own mothers using years before. Elizabeth went on to have seven more children, the last in 1534, when things were beginning to change. By the time Jane's daughter-in-law, Bridget, bore her children – one a year between 1540 and 1547 – many of the old comforts had been removed. As Jane and Elizabeth assisted her, they may have been forced to think twice about some of the methods they had previously tried and tested. For women with little control over their gynaecological destinies, the sudden removal of these emotional supports cannot but have left a gaping hole in the lives of many. One example illustrating this sea-change in English culture took place in the year of Bridget Yate's first confinement. A woman from Wells, in Norfolk, had imagined a miracle brought about by the image of Our Lady at Walsingham, an occurrence that would have been lauded and reported a few years before, giving hope to other women and mothers who attended her shrine. Now the unfortunate was set in the stocks at Walsingham on the market day with a paper about her head, calling her 'a reporter of false tales', before she was sent her round the town in a cart, while the young people and boys threw snowballs at her.[2] Walsingham had been one of Henry VIII's targets during his programme of monastic closures in the 1530s: although the prior was one of the first to comply with the new reforms, the sub-prior Nicholas Mileham and another man were hung for conspiring with rebels to suppress the changes. The Slipper Chapel, where pilgrims began the final barefoot stretch, became a farm building; the statue of Mary was taken to Chelsea and burned. A 1530s miscellany *The Court of Venus* included the 'Pilgrim's Tale', probably by Richard Singleton, chaplain to Anne Boleyn, describing the visitors to Walsingham as having 'sprung out of Antichrist' and putting their trust in the 'fabulous vayn' virgin. It also came to be known as 'Falsingham' and the Virgin as the wyche (witch).

Jane's daughter Elizabeth would have been easily able to undertake a pilgrimage to any of a number of shrines in 1526; Bridget, however, would have found it increasingly more difficult and even dangerous to do so. The late 1530s spawned a new series of parodic pilgrim badges, with saints and pilgrims depicted in lewd poses, displaying their genitals to illustrate the supposed sexual immorality of travellers. One by one, shrines were dismantled and pilgrimage censured, under the aegis of Thomas Cromwell. One of his agents described the dissolution of Caversham and dismantling of the shrine of Our Lady: 'I have pulled down the image of your Lady at Caversham whereunto was great pilgrimage. The image is plated over with silver ... I have also pulled down the place she stood in, with all other ceremonies, as lights, shrouds, crutches and images of wax'.[3] At Willesden, as they dismantled the shrine, Richard Mores described how five people were still praying there: two old men, a woman and child and another bearing a gift of flowers. For the crime of being an idolatrous parish, the church of St Mary was fined £13. In 1539, the Lady Chapel of Ely, largest of its kind in England, was dismantled. It had been a popular pilgrim destination, containing a huge carved life-cycle and miracles of Mary made by John de Wisbech under the guidance of master craftsman Alan de Walsingham, which was completely mutilated. In the year Bridget gave birth, zealous locals took the destruction of Ely a stage further by riding horses inside and beheading the remaining statues of saints. The once-popular Suffolk Our Lady of Woolpit, with its supposed healing spring, was jeered as Our Lady of Foulpit. The cult of Mary was particularly attacked because it represented the excesses of idolatry and the perceived hollowness of Catholic guarantees of salvation. Critics saw it as allowing safe conduct for sinners to heaven and specific misogyny directed at the Marian cult became savage and sexually oriented. One Thomas Bilney called Our Lady of Willesden 'a common paramour of baudry' while Bishop Latimer attacked Mary for pride, arrogance, bad manners and reprimanding Jesus. William Thomas, Prince Edward's tutor, said in 1546 that the Romish Mother Church was 'an arrogant whore, a fornicatoress, an idolatress'.

Tudor women, including queens and princesses, had taken comfort from the possession of images, statues and icons of their favourite childbirth saints. These were present in the birth chamber, accompanied them on journeys and were objects of devotional focus: the most famous were lent out to aristocratic ladies but they must have been present in the minds and prayers of many others. Such focus can channel the mind and encourage relaxation and an illusion of control under extreme circumstances, such as labour and birth. After the 1535 proclamation that all false images and relics were 'utterly to be abolished, eradicated and erased out' so there must be 'no memory of [iconography] in walls, glass, windows or elsewhere', the majority of these icons were destroyed. Many statues of the saints were burned in 1538 at Thomas More's old house of Chelsea, as well as at Tyburn and Smithfield. Cromwell organised a system of destruction that removed the most important icons of English Catholicism, in what has been referred to as the 'long summer of iconoclasm'. Bishop Hugh Latimer described the statue of the virgin at Worcester as a 'devil's instrument' as it burned at Chelsea along with its 'old sister of Walsingham and her younger sister of Ipswich'. Statues from Doncaster and Penrhys would not be 'all day in burning'; according to Latimer these had been 'the instruments to bring many … to eternal fire'.[4] Some statues from Canterbury were reportedly being given to local children to play with as dolls, holy bread was fed to dogs, altar stones became fireplaces and sinks and banners were burned.[5]

Shrines were also stripped of their relics, purported health benefits and wealth. Cromwell's agents razed the shrine of St Anne at Buxton, removing the saint's relics, locking and sealing the healing baths so the wells couldn't be used. Among the relics taken were the girdle from Bath Abbey, as well as three combs dedicated to St Mary Magdalen, St Dorothy and St Margaret; an image of St Moodwyn used by labouring women taken from Burton on Trent; St Mary Magdelen's red silk girdle from Bruton in Somerset, as well as girdles from Basedale in Yorkshire, Kirkstall, Rievaulx, Newbury, Kelham, York and Haltemprise. The very girdle from Westminster that Elizabeth of York, Catherine of Aragon and Margaret Tudor had given birth clutching was removed and destroyed. Yet a number of icons and images, pilgrim badges and ritualistic items may have existed within wealthier private homes and the fate of these is less certain. Following the accession of Edward, the rules became even stricter. Jane Yate's daughter-in-law Bridget may still have delivered her children while calling upon assistance from St Anne or St Margaret, in a bed which had been blessed and sprinkled with holy water. This was about to change. Injunctions of 1547 banned the use of rosaries, the undertaking of pilgrimage and prayers for the intercession of particular saints; there was to be no reciting of the rosary, no casting of holy water, ringing of holy bells, or blessing of candles. If Jane had owned a rosary, did she manage to smuggle it under her gown into the birth chamber? Would Bridget have wanted it?

The role of the midwife also came under lasting attack during this period, as recognition of the widespread pseudo-religious nature of birth room practices. In the fabric rolls of York Minster, a condemnation can be found of 'charms, sorcery, enchantments, invocations, circles, witchcraft, soothsaying or any like crafts or imaginations invented by the devil and specially in times of women's travail'.[6] Old chants were replaced by new, religious ones, which often substituted female saints for male ones, an interesting indication of the imposition of patriarchal authority into the traditional female preserve of the birth chamber: if men could not be there in person, their Biblical representations would be:

> There are four corners to her bed
> Four angels at her head:
> Matthew, Mark, Luke and John:
> God bless the bed that she lies on,
> New moon, new moon, God bless me,
> God bless this house and family.[7]

In 1538, Nicholas Shaxton, Bishop of Salisbury, urged midwives not to resort to the use of 'girdles, purses, measures of Our Lady or such other superstitious things', which was echoed in the first midwives' oath of 1567. In Kent, the same year, an inquiry asked women to inform against any midwives who used sorcery, witchcraft, charms, unlawful prayers or invocations in Latin. This perceived overlap between female gynaecological practice and malevolent secrecy was a key step along the road to the witchcraft trials of the later Elizabethan and Stuart eras. One traditional identifying factor of a witch was her knowledge and use of herbs, to good effect or ill. This body of wisdom was yet another casualty of earlier reforming zeal, as prioresses and nuns had been a long-standing repository of oral medical tradition. From almonries and specialist infirmary gardens, medicine and assistance was dispensed that represented the best of ecclesiastical tradition, often after monks and nuns had swapped 'horticultural knowledge' and resources. Scribes copied classical herbals, which were adapted to use native English plants and flowers; the devotional roses and lilies featured alongside traditional cures such a sage, rue, clary and hyssop. Benedictine nuns in particular were known for their curative wisdom and work.[8] The embargo on growing and using herbs and flowers in monastic gardens, as well as the dissemination of their remedies and knowledge in the community, represented an irrevocable loss. While women could still grow their own flowers and herbs at home, this could not compete with the scale and body of knowledge that was lost when monastic infirmary gardens were destroyed along with their establishments. The Church had long encouraged the use of prayers while gathering medicinal herbs, suggesting their efficiency was improved by being picked in a highly ritualistic way, a view which survived long after the Tudor era. It is easy to imagine later interpretations of old women muttering chants as they picked herbs by moonlight.

This is not to condemn the reformers by any means. There is little doubt that Catholicism had been open to abuse for centuries, most famously documented in Chaucer's *Canterbury Tales*. Many fake relics were exposed such as the holy blood of Hailes, topped up by the monks with that of slaughtered ducks, and the proliferation of relics that meant many saints would have posthumously ended up with twenty fingers and several heads! Undoubtedly some undertook pilgrimages for the sake of it, which played on the stereotype of vulnerable women sacrificing their virtue on the journey, either by accident or design. The fourteenth-century writings of Sir John Mandeville, Chaucer's contemporary, had secularised the religious aspects of his travels as a 'feast of delights', reducing the experience to sightseeing by recounting lists of marvels and distractions along the route. Equally, many reformers were female, including Anne Boleyn and Catherine Parr, as well as the Grey sisters, and would have welcomed these changes. Anne herself went into nunneries to berate the nuns about their corrupt practices. However, the theological motives for the reformation of Catholicism are less significant to the history of childbirth than its effects upon Tudor women's lives. For those previously reliant on such important placebo comforts, personal faith could come into conflict with cultural change in unprecedented ways. Even if the girdle they held had never belonged to the Virgin and had indeed been cynically manufactured for profit, what mattered was that women believed it had: this could induce a calmer mental and physical state resulting in conception or an easier birth as well as giving them a feeling of control over an otherwise critical and volatile area of their lives. The belief that God was on their side went a considerable way to dispel terror in the Tudor mind. Just as modern mothers might burn candles, listen to music or use their own talisman and mascots in order to relax, these ancient practices, even if they were abuses, served an invaluable purpose to many women. The annihilation of such Catholic trappings meant the denial of women's 'life-affirming comforts': even for those women who were reformers or Protestants, religious liberation came at a cost.

The implications of these changes for Tudor women were obviously dependent upon personal belief. As such, the story of childbirth during the mid-Tudor Reformation is as much the story of the dissolution of shrines and the banning of Catholic practices and folklore that had formed centuries of female wisdom: the cultural construct of birth would have been experienced differently by an expectant mother withdrawing into her chamber in 1525, to one in 1540 and others in 1555 and 1595. The secrecy of birthing rituals, female illiteracy and the confusion and dangers arising over religious change mean that many more questions regarding mid-sixteenth-century motherhood can be raised than answered. Each case was a matter of health, personal circumstances and conscience, yet as a collective, women's experiences were complicated by the wider national interplay of dynastic and religious change. Only through deliberate acts of defiance and the privacy of documents like wills can it be judged just how far the Reformation managed to turn the tide against traditional childbirth and maternal practices. Where women were prepared to engage in risky acts of open insubordination, they must have experienced few qualms about private rebellion.

So what did Jane Yate and her fellow women do when it came to the lying-in of their daughters and granddaughters? Some may have developed new approaches to delivery in response to religious reforms but for others, attended by their experienced mothers and grandmothers, outlawed traditions simply went underground. Closing the chamber door on the men during lying-in also provided protection and solidarity for the airing of dissenting and heretical opinions and beliefs, for both Protestant and Catholic women. Nor was religion that easily polarised. Religious views and practices didn't just change overnight; shrines were being dismantled as people arrived to worship at them, so in the extremes of pain, overshadowed by the possibility of death, some women must have struggled to determine whether religious conviction or obedience to their sovereign was more important. A sense of female authority and separation from the male-determined culture may have given them confidence to privately override political vicissitudes. Local assize court records in Kent and Essex, dating from the late 1570s to 1580s are full of women who had failed to attend church, such as Jane Wyseman, 'wife of Thomas Wyseman of Wimbish, esquire, [who] doth wilfully absent herself from her parish church and hath not been there at divine service by the space of this whole year last past'[9] and 'Mistress Gonnell who has been in Walthamstowe by the space of a year and a quarter has not in all that time come to church but once and that was before Easter last, neither has she received the Communion since her coming thither'.[10] The Wysemans were in trouble again in 1592 for attending a Mass delivered 'contrary' Elizabeth's acts.[11] The list could go on; dozens of them appear. If women were prepared to disobey religious changes openly, they were surely prepared to do so behind closed doors. If Jane Yate's mother and grandmother had taught her certain 'charms' and 'invocations', and passed her down images and practices for use in the birthing chamber, wouldn't she pass these on to her daughter and her daughter's daughter?

Women clearly did. Of course, the most zealous female reformers would have rejected the practices they saw as abuses, yet for many others, their centuries-old traditions didn't change overnight. Later accounts document the survival of the superstitions and charms that Bishop Shaxton had attempted to suppress in the 1530s. Among the artefacts left by a Jane Daniell of Hackney was an eagle stone used in her labour of 1601. The seventeenth-century midwife Jane Sharp was advising the use of the eagle stone in her 1671 book, and a Canterbury cleric's wife still used such a stone well into the eighteenth century, lending it out to friends and parishioners. There was also the problem of disposal; to reject or destroy such symbolic items out of fear or even religious conviction may have been a step too far for many. The surprising resurfacing of many 'banned' objects during the reign of the Catholic Mary, such as crosses, statues, images and altar cloths, is indicative of many private attitudes towards the Reformation. Many had been simply hidden away until such times as it was safe for them to be used again. Reports of the theft and use of holy water appear frequently, such as Cardinal Pole's instruction that the font should be locked in Cambridge in 1557; priests administering the sacrament were also told to place the Host in the recipient's mouth to prevent them carrying it home and using it for other 'superstitious or wicked' purposes. Long into the seventeenth century, labouring mothers dedicated their children to saints and infertile ones promised to devote them to the Church, if they conceived and bore a live child. In further, rural corners of the kingdom, such practices lasted much longer; recusant midwives produced girdles and artefacts and as late as 1584, one Puritan document claimed 'three parts at least of the people' were 'wedded to their old superstition still'.[12] As Edward lay on his deathbed, months before his sixteenth birthday, frantic plans were made to prevent the accession of his elder sister and the undoing of recent reforms. The terms of Henry VIII's will passed the crown through the heirs of Frances Grey, daughter of Mary Tudor, excluding the Scottish line borne by his elder sister Margaret. The attempt to supplant her with the Protestant Jane Grey was notoriously short-lived. Support for Mary was strong enough, nationally and politically, to override religious concerns.

If any family were determined to adhere to their old faith, it was the Yates. In 1538, Jane's father acquired Lyford Grange – then in Berkshire, now Oxfordshire – an impressive fifteenth-century quadrangular building which had formerly been part of Abingdon Abbey. After his death, Jane's half-brother Thomas inherited the house and, following him, his son Francis. Francis Yate was a well-known recusant; a Catholic refusing to attend Church of England services. In 1580, he was imprisoned for his faith as was his wife the following year. His mother Alice, Jane Yate's sister-in-law, remained in the house; Jane may have attended her during her delivery of Francis back in 1535. Alice invited the Jesuit missionary Edmund Campion to visit her and preach at Lyford but he was captured there, imprisoned and martyred in 1581. In the twentieth century, an Agnus Dei, banned by Elizabeth, was found hidden in the roof at Lyford, dated to 1578. These consecrated wax discs, symbolic of the flesh of Christ and impressed with the image of a lamb, were supposed to extend Papal protection from, among other things, sickness, sudden death and the malice of demons. It is typical of the personal talisman that people retained and concealed in their homes and among their possessions when the law ruled against their faith. Its presence makes the resistance of Jane, Elizabeth, Bridget and Alice to changes in the birth chamber more likely.

11

Mary & Elizabeth
1553-1603

A Dwindling Dynasty

God prosper her highness in every thinge,
Her noble spouse, our fortunate kynge
And that noble blossome that is planted to spring
Amen, sweet Jesus, we hartelye singe.
Blysse, thou sweet Jesus, our comforters three,
Our Kynge, our Quene, our Prince that shalbe;
That they three as one, or one as all three
May governe thy people to the pleasure of thee.[1]

The above lines formed the conclusion to a ballad written to commemorate the pregnancy of Mary I, printed by William Riddell early in 1555. Yet the writer was misinformed, along with numerous chroniclers, citizens, courtiers and even Mary herself. There was no child. Despite the swelling in her belly and supposed quickening she had experienced, despite the elaborate preparations and prepared declarations, despite Mary's prayers and hopes, she was not pregnant. She would never bear a child and would die heartbroken, only months after her final false hope: among the effects she left at her death was a book of prayers, with a page devoted to intercessions for women with child, supposedly stained with tears. On a purely personal level, setting aside other issues of her reign, Mary's life was a tragedy.

Yet it began with a blaze of popular success. Following the death of Edward VI in 1553, months short of his sixteenth birthday, Protestant factions led by the Duke of Northumberland followed the terms of his will over that of Henry VIII, excluding Mary and

Elizabeth whose legitimate status was cast into doubt. Next in line were the heirs of Henry's younger sister Mary Rose Tudor, through her daughter Frances Brandon. The eldest was Lady Jane Grey, famously England's queen for nine days before a surge of support established the Catholic Mary on the throne. The history of the thirty-seven-year-old had been one of uncertainty, ill-health and emotional turmoil under the previous reigns; at times she had even feared for her life or been the focus of plots to flee the country; her religious practices had been curtailed, her faith challenged and her place in the succession dramatically overturned. Separated from her mother and estranged from her father, her religion had made her into a figurehead for the old ways, yet her accession was never guaranteed. Attempts in the 1530s to marry her to the German Duke, Philip of Bavaria, had come to nothing; aged twenty-three, she disliked his religion but saw him as a route out of her unhappy life. He made her a gift of a diamond pearl cross and kisses were exchanged. A marriage treaty was drawn up but never concluded; Henry VIII's deteriorating relations with Cleves may have been a factor. Through Edward's reign, as the Protestant faction pushed through even more dramatic reforms and the possibility of marrying her off to a foreign prince was mooted, her chances of accession appeared very slight. Edward was young and might have lived for years and fathered many children. Then, in a sudden reversal of fortune, due partly to her popularity and the failure of Northumberland's efforts, Mary found herself as queen. Her support was particularly strong in the East of England, the previous Catholic stronghold of the cult of the Virgin Mary. Lauded as the Marigold, she was celebrated in ballads as having shown 'great cheare in heate and cold', enduring storms patiently, and had been brought to her 'estate' though some 'dyd spite this marigolde': she had been saved by God to right all wrongs.[2] She was the English 'jewel and joy' – merciful, meek, good and wise.[3] In spite of all these qualities, though, Mary was the first female to inherit and retain the throne: as such, she could not expect to rule alone. Tudor understanding of gender politics dictated that she swiftly find a husband to guide and support her: she was merely the vessel for the rule of men. Her next duty would to be to produce a male heir.

Mary's choice was predictable but unpopular. Recalling her Spanish roots and having been betrothed as a child to Charles V, Holy Roman Emperor, she was intent upon marriage with Charles' son, Philip II of Spain. He already had a son from a previous marriage, fuelling Mary's hopes of bearing a male heir to the throne. From her accession onwards, parliamentary delegations had been urging her to marry an Englishman, suggesting her kinsman Edward Courtney, Earl of Devon. Born in 1527, Philip was eleven years Mary's junior yet his religion and nationality made the match unpopular in England, causing unrest and contributing to uprisings during 1554. The complete dominance of husband over wife in the Tudor mind led many to fear that England would become an enclave of Spain and sacrifice national interests in order to serve foreign Catholic policies: it was inconceivable to her subjects that Mary might retain any sort of independence or autonomy after her marriage. Some openly rebelled. Wyatt's Uprising, in 1554, was partly fuelled by the desire to prevent the country being 'overrun by strangers', although coincidentally, the ringleaders all happened to be Protestants; their implied intention was to displace Mary and marry Elizabeth to Courtney, a situation which temporarily cost the apparently innocent Elizabeth her liberty. Later playwrights Dekker and Webster reflected the common mood: 'Philip is a Spaniard, a proude Nation, whome naturalliye our countriemen abhor'[4]; English xenophobia reached such a fever pitch that unprovoked attacks on Spaniards were common and a fleet was planned to prevent Philip from landing, aided by the French.

However, land was exactly what Philip did, in July 1554. Amid torrential rain he proceeded to Winchester, where he prayed at the Cathedral and changed into a rich coat embroidered with gold and a matching hat with a feather in order to first meet his future wife. Aged thirty-eight, her difficult adolescent and young adulthood had taken a toll on Mary's health. If he was disappointed, he did not show it. Thin and slight, Mary was afflicted with dental abnormalities, irregular menstruation, anorexia, depression as well as various other complaints. Her repeated ill-health as a girl had developed into regular cyclical suffering: she dreaded the onset of winter for the aches and pains the bad weather could bring. At twenty-seven, Philip was described in a letter written by

John Elder as 'well favoured with a broad forehead and grey eyes, straight-nosed and manly countenance'; his pace was princely, gait straight and upright; 'nature cannot work a more perfect pattern'.[5] By 1563, the Venetian Ambassador saw a man 'slight of stature and round-faced with pale blue eyes and somewhat prominent lip ... [he] dresses very tastefully and everything he does is courteous and gracious'.[6] The mismatch had been arranged by his father and Philip had been raised to follow his imperial destiny: the throne of England was a prize he greatly valued and modern historical assessments of his personal dissatisfaction impose an anachronistic sensibility. The first meeting was described by chronicler Wriothesley as taking place at the deanery, or Prior's lodgings, where Prince Arthur had been born in 1486; Philip was conveyed there late on that rainy night, by a secret route, in order to spend a brief half-hour with his intended. He could speak no English so they communicated in a mixture of Latin, French and Spanish. Whatever the groom's feelings, for Mary, it was love at first sight.

Philip remained tactful throughout the wedding service two days later, in spite of the English insistence that he appeared dressed in the French-style fashions that were popular at that time. It was 25 July, St James's day, the patron saint of Spain. Each proceeded to Winchester cathedral on foot, richly apparelled 'in gownes of cloth of all gold sett with rich stones'[7] designed to match and complement each other, as if this act of couture-sympathy would set the pattern for married life. Mary's outfit was made of rich tissue embroidered on purple satin lined with taffeta and set with pearls; she wore a white kirtle enriched with silver and a long train. The cathedral was hung with arras and cloth of gold and a scaffold had been erected, covered in red carpet, where, in an inversion of the usual order, Mary was to stand on her husband's right. This was a less than subtle reminder of the honour she bestowed on him through marriage and an early indicator that her status meant the balance of power between the couple would not follow the traditional pattern. As she approached the altar and saw Philip waiting, Mary must have been happier than she could have anticipated. It had been a long hard struggle to reach the throne and this marriage reaffirmed her Spanish roots and would have pleased her long-dead mother; did Catherine of Aragon cross her mind as she made her vows? Officiating was Stephen Gardiner, who had been instrumental in the divorce of Henry VIII and Catherine of Aragon, who Mary had instructed to undo his earlier work and re-establish the legitimacy of the marriage and her succession. The past was very much in her mind, as Wriothesley claimed, even extending to her choice of ring: 'her marriage ringe was a rownd hoope of golde without anye stone, which was her desire, for she sayde she would be married as maydens were in the olde tyme.'[8] The couple appeared afterwards, hand in hand, under a rich canopy to hear the Mass, before going on foot to the court and dining openly at one table. The wedding breakfast was held at Wolvesley castle, former palace of the Bishop of Winchester, an important and impressive residence since the twelfth century. It must have been an intimate occasion, as the two of them ate alone on one table while their 140 guests were seated separately. Dancing followed before the king and queen departed and supped separately, then Gardiner blessed the marital bed and they were left alone. The wedding night must have been less than satisfactory for Philip, given the comments of his waiting gentlemen. Ruy Gomez commented that 'she is no good from the point of view of fleshly sensuality'[9], although Philip knew the match was made not 'for the flesh but for the restoration of this realm'.[10] Mary, however, was happy.

Within months, the queen believed herself pregnant. Her menstruation ceased, she felt queasy in the mornings and rapidly put on weight: there seemed little cause to doubt the evidence. Given the history of her step-mothers, Mary was aware of the potential dangers of childbirth; in addition, her triumphal entry into London in July 1553 had coincided with the death of her favourite, Jane Browne, while giving birth to twins. An added danger existed in the scope for Philip's control over her heirs, in the event of her premature death. In January 1555, an ordinance was passed to provide for the education of the children of the king and queen, if the worst were to occur. In the spring of 1555, Mary anticipated her arrival, suggesting a conception date around the wedding night. Froude suggests she retired to Hampton Court at the end of April, with rockers, nurses and cradle at the ready:

circulars were printed and signed by Philip and Mary, ready for the insertion of day and month, spreading news of the arrival of a prince. Retiring to her sumptuously provided chambers looking down to the palace gardens and Thames, all Mary had to do was wait. At the end of the month a false report that she had given birth was recorded by London diarist Henry Machyn: tidings 'came to London that the Quen's grace was delevered of a prynce and so ther was great ryngyng through London ... and the morrow after yt was turned odur-ways to the plesur of God'.[11] The Venetian Ambassador reported that bonfires were lit and bells were rung, while the whole of London feasted in celebration. Embarrassingly, though, no child had been born. Other reports claimed that Mary was not in fact pregnant, but that a plot existed to smuggle a child into the palace and pass it off as her heir. This was a long-established fable, found back in the twelfth-century life of Hugh of Lincoln, where a desperate woman faked a pregnancy by putting a pillow up her dress, then adopting the child of a peasant. Mary continued to wait; in late May she was seen walking about the garden, 'stepping' so well it seemed unlikely the birth was imminent. Her doctors revised her due date but Philip was already having doubts. She remained at Hampton Court through the summer until it became clear there was no child; the decisive failure was sealed when in August she left for Whitehall. Did Mary think of her mother during those months? If so, it must have felt like history was repeating itself. It is unclear how much she knew of Catherine's gynaecological history. Was this an inherited problem, a psychosomatic phantom pregnancy or perhaps an illness? With hindsight, Mary's death, following soon after second occurrence of these symptoms, might suggest some form of ovarian cancer or similar condition. The early onset of ovarian cancer can produce bloating, back pain, tiredness, loss of appetite and constipation as well as the build-up of fluid in the abdomen, all of which can be confused with signs of pregnancy. At such a remove, it is impossible to claim whether this was directly related to her death or whether she was suffering from such a condition by the summer of 1558, but it remains a possibility.

Almost as soon as Mary had accepted there would be no child, Philip left the country. A crisis in the Netherlands required his attention but Mary was heartbroken at his absence and felt it as a personal criticism of her gynaecological failure. It is this combination of circumstances that historians[12] have sometimes used to explain the sharp increase in the persecution of Protestants that then began in earnest: to Mary's mind, God had punished her for failing to restore the 'true' religion and she needed to redress this. The years 1555 to 1558 were witness to a savage campaign using the Spanish inquisition method of burning heretics, rather than the usual English hanging, drawing and quartering. Recorded in Foxe's *Book of Martyrs* of 1563, this earned Mary the popular epithet of 'bloody' and has understandably coloured interpretations of her reign. Women numbered among the martyrs included those who not only held fast to their faith but administered or sheltered others; many of those burned were from the artisan and lower classes such as Alice Driver, who had driven her father's plough, Agnes Potten, the wife of a shoemaker, Joan Trunchfield, wife of a brewer, and Joan Waste, a blind rope-maker. However, in terms of Mary's religious conviction, the remedy was beyond her control while Philip was out of the country. God could hardly bless her with a child while she was unable to conceive; additionally, gossip about her husband's liaisons with women at the Flemish court may have reached her. She wrote to his father, Charles, begging for the return of her 'chief joy and comfort', without whom the kingdom was in a 'miserable plight'.[13] Yet foreign commitments kept Philip abroad until March 1557, when he returned to England to organise a campaign against the French. They were reunited at Greenwich where Mary might have worn the embroidered sleeves of cloth of silver given to her by Elizabeth or the dress of white tissue or the Spanish gown of black velvet furred with sable Mary herself had ordered for his return: no doubt she was keen to impress him after such a lengthy absence. By the time Philip departed to lead the forces against the French in early July, Mary was again convinced she had conceived. This time, few people believed her. It was also the last time she would see her husband.

In January the following year, Mary was convinced that she was drawing towards the end of her pregnancy and anticipated the birth of a child sometime within the next few weeks. Philip learned the news from Reginald Pole, Mary's Archbishop of

Canterbury; Philip wrote to Pole that the news had given him 'greater joy' than he could express, 'as it is the one thing in the world I have most desired and which is of the greatest importance for the cause of religion and the welfare of our realm'.[14] Privately, he was sceptical, as were the majority of her court, although they dared not contradict the queen. Her own doubts are indicated by her claim that she delayed announcing the news until she was herself certain. By the time March arrived in 1558, eight months had elapsed since Philip's departure, yet no lying-in plans had been made nor prayers said for the queen's delivery. That month she made her will; 'thinking myself to be with child ... foreseeing the great danger which by God's ordinance remain to all women in their travail of children'.[15] As the weeks passed and no child arrived, the matter was dropped; courtiers and doctors went about their business with no mention of the queen's latest humiliation, which must have been ignominious enough for the ageing Mary. She begged Philip to return to her but they disagreed over the question of Elizabeth's marriage to the Duke of Savoy and their letters became acrimonious. The country was on high alert in case of invasion by the French, who had regained Calais; seditious anti-Spanish pamphlets flooded the capital and disease struck. Wriothesley recorded that 'divers strange and new sickenesses' were claiming many lives: it has been variously estimated that the death rate that summer was 40 per cent, or 124 per cent above the national average in afflicted places. The illness may have been a form of influenza, which did not act so swiftly as the dreaded plague or sweat, which had last broken out in 1551.[16] It spread rapidly and did not discriminate. Before the disease had run its course, it was to claim a royal victim.

Mary showed the first signs of being ill that August. Travelling from Hampton Court to St James's Palace, she felt unwell on arrival and retired to her rooms. Seized by a fever, she remained secluded as the following weeks saw her briefly rally only to become weakened even further. By October it became apparent that her condition was not going to improve: she and her councillors had to face the likelihood of her death and the succession of the Protestant Elizabeth. At the end of the month she added a codicil to her will recognising that she would not bear 'fruit nor heir' and asking her sister to honour her religious changes: Elizabeth learned of her formal nomination and impending accession at the start of November. Early in the morning of 17 November 1558, Mary heard Mass and then quietly died, surrounded by her ladies. Henry VIII's youngest daughter was now queen. While Mary was notorious for her desperation to have a child, Elizabeth would become known for her efforts to evade it.

Like her father's, Elizabeth's reign was punctuated by the question of inheritance. A number of suitors, English and European, were suggested at varying stages of her life and some appeared to be in with a serious chance of leading her up the aisle but ultimately, she remained wedded to her kingdom, as she famously declared to Parliament. With hindsight, her resistance is consistent and logical: she did not wish to be dominated by a husband's will nor run the risks of childbirth and the policy of flirtatious relations with her male courtiers and suitors allowed her to exploit male expectations of feminine indecision, which she used as a successful manipulative tool. Yet at the time, Elizabeth herself may not have been so certain of her marital future. At certain intervals she promised she would wed and energetically wooed several possible husbands, suggesting that perhaps she was a victim of her own vacillation and found herself surprised by time. Theories of her physical deformation or inability to bear children, ranging from the bizarre claims that she was in fact a man, to the supposed gynaecological blockage preventing intercourse or the existence of illegitimate children have yet to find any basis in historical fact.

Elizabeth's early flirtation with the dangerous Thomas Seymour had exposed her to the dangers of failing to control her behaviour and emotions. The fates of her mother and her step-mother, Catherine Howard, illustrated the potential dangers of marital life while the deaths of Jane Seymour and Catherine Parr were a reminder that childbirth was a very real threat. Her decision not to marry may have been influenced by these factors: equally, there may not have been a conscious 'decision'; motherhood may have been a secondary casualty of her choice that there was 'one mistress and no master' in her realm. Many romantic theories have been spun concerning the supposed secrets of her heart, her wishes and stifled desires, particularly in regards to Robert Dudley, Earl of Leicester. From her accession in 1558, Elizabeth did exhibit many signs of being in love with the already-married Dudley, including moving his bedchamber next to her private rooms a year later. His wife's death in suspicious circumstance in 1560 created a potential threat to her throne that she was not prepared to risk; although some, including Dudley, believed she would now make him her husband. Elizabeth saw the dangers of association with such scandal. No matter what her private feelings were, she was probably too cautious to become Dudley's lover even if the overcrowded court could have allowed them opportunities; Elizabeth herself answered the rumours by saying she was never alone and therefore had no chance to be intimate with any man. As a woman, her private chambers became her sanctuary, removing more of the daily business of government to more public arenas in comparison with the court of her father, yet the constant presence of her women gave them a privileged and exclusive role, meaning an affair would have been almost impossible to conceal.

However, in 1587, a young man claiming to be Arthur Dudley, illegitimate son of the 'lovers' was shipwrecked on the Spanish coast. His age placed his conception early in 1561, when Elizabeth was bedridden with serious illness, possibly dropsy, which causes the body to swell. This gave the theory credence, as had the ability of several of Elizabeth's waiting women to conceal their own pregnancies until the final month under voluminous clothing. Arthur Dudley stated that a servant named Southern had been summoned to Hampton Court at night, to find a nurse for an infant who had been born to a careless employee and needed to be concealed from the queen; Southern raised the child as his own, only confessing the truth on his death bed in 1583. The Spanish believed his claim as it served them in the run-up to the Armada, and it still persists in modern scholarship, but Tudor imposters were common and it seems incredible that no rumours of his existence derive from the 1560s and particularly ironic, as a male heir was the one thing Elizabeth's parliaments urged her to produce. For her to have conceived, carried and delivered a male heir in 1561 seems to stretch credibility to the limits. In all likelihood, she and Dudley were never lovers, as the situation would have placed her under too much political and gynaecological danger, besides having to submit to the will of another and constant fear of exposure. Later events in Scotland demonstrated that she was wise to have done so. When the granddaughter of Margaret Tudor, Mary Queen of Scots, found herself embroiled in a similar situation in 1566, Elizabeth saw her cousin's life unravel as the result of an impulsive romantic match.

Born in 1542, Mary became queen before her first birthday, after the death of her father, James V, at the Battle of Solway Moss. Brought up in France from the age of six, she had been married in 1558 to Francis II, grandson of Henry VIII's old rival Francis I, and became Queen of France the following year. Her dual titles made her an impressive opponent to Elizabeth and one of a pool of possible heirs to the English throne. Her seniority over the Grey sisters, descendants of Mary Rose Tudor, made her the main focus of Catholic hopes throughout her lifetime. Her first husband died young, aged only sixteen; various illnesses have been suggested for his frailty, including his undescended testicles, but ultimately he was killed by an ear infection leading to an abscess on the brain. The widowed Mary returned to Scotland and, in 1565, married her cousin Henry Lord Darnley, bearing him a son, the future James VI of Scotland and I of England. James' cradle from 1566 still survives; a broad semi-circular band of gold jewel moulding and sides inlaid with panels of dark and light wood. By the time of his birth, though, the marriage was already in crisis. Darnley was immature and unpopular; his despotic and irrational behaviour, peaking in the murder of Mary's favourite Italian musician, David Rizzio, while she was heavily pregnant, eventually led to his own murder in 1567. While the palace of Holyrood was blown apart by gunpowder, Darnley's strangled corpse was found neatly lain out on the grass outside. Soon after this, Mary married his supposed murderer, the Earl of Bothwell, an act her opponents could not stomach, which led to her deposition and flight to England. She would spend the rest of her life in captivity and lose her head in 1587 for plotting to gain the English throne. Mary's ungoverned behaviour was a powerful sign to Elizabeth of the dangers of allowing the heart to rule the head. With Dudley forever tainted by his wife's murder, no matter how carefully he established an inquest to investigate matters, marriage to him was too great a risk for Elizabeth. Rejecting the other suitors suggested by Parliament, including the ageing Sir William Pickering and Mary's cast-off, Edward Courtney, as well as outright refusing her brother-in-law Philip of Spain, she turned abroad for a possible husband. Perhaps the miles between the rulers of Sweden, Austria and France were part of her delaying tactics and allowed her to distance herself from the reality of marriage, as well as giving her a powerful bargaining tool in foreign politics.

Elizabeth's most significant suitors were the youngest two sons of Catherine de Medici and Henri II of France. In 1570, it was first proposed that she marry the Duke of Anjou, the future Henri III. He was a rebellious young man who had veered towards Protestantism in youth while still technically Catholic and was beset by rumours of homosexuality, although the biggest stumbling block was the disparity in their ages. She was thirty-seven, he was nineteen, easily young enough to have been her son by Tudor standards and vocally critical of her age, appearance and supposed limp. Inheriting the throne of Poland in 1573, he abdicated the following year on the death of his brother Charles, when he became King of France. All negotiations with Elizabeth were abandoned by the time of his union with Louise of Lorraine in 1575; their fourteen-year marriage produced no children despite one rumoured miscarriage and her numerous pilgrimages and religious offerings. Towards the end of the decade, Catherine de Medici offered Elizabeth her youngest son, Francis, Duke of Alençon. The queen was then forty-six to his twenty-four and he had suffered terrible scarring after a bout of smallpox at the age of eight. Still, there seemed to be a fondness and flirtation between them that her advisers took so seriously as to warn her against the dangers of childbearing at her advanced age. It may have been the closest Elizabeth came to marriage but she gave the duke a decisive refusal in 1581, writing a formal yet passionate goodbye in a short poem entitled 'On Monsieur's departure'. He went on to become King of France eight years later, when Henri III, Elizabeth's previous suitor, was assassinated.

In her final years, Elizabeth increasingly cherished her identity as the Virgin Queen. Concurrent with a lamentation of the loss of sites such as Walsingham, she shrewdly deployed the previous national devotion to the cult of Mary to create a semi-divine, detached and iconic image of her own. Using the heavy cosmetics and dyes of the era, coupled with a typical Tudor appreciation of pageantry and ceremony, she embraced her virginity and gave it mythical status. Her face would be daubed in ceruse, a poisonous mixture of white lead and vinegar; cochineal, madder and vermilion dyed the cheeks and lips, kohl accentuated the eyes and hair, while wigs were dyed with celandine, lye, saffron and cumin. These efforts, coupled with her supposed 'masculine' qualities and the length of her rule gave rise to the theories that have refused to accept her identity at face value, even into the twenty-first century. Just as her mother Anne Boleyn encountered, women were expected to conform to particular types and exhibit certain forms of submissive behaviour. This was not compatible with successful queenship. Some strains of Tudor misogyny dictated that Elizabeth's 'mannishness' must be genuine; the inability of her enemies to believe a woman could have the necessary qualities to rule led them to deduce that she must be either a man or a defective woman. The state of androgyny was feared and women who never married were considered deviant. This is not to suggest though, that all Tudor society regarded her with suspicion; if the anomaly of a female ruler could be embraced, so could that of an unmarried one. The celebration of her virgin state and purity developed over time and retrospectively; it was partly Victorian prudery that gave rise to many theories about Elizabeth's identity that have lingered anachronistically.

So was the Virgin Queen Elizabeth actually a man? Probably not. Perhaps the most persistent theory is that of the Bisley boy, supported by the Gothic writer Bram Stoker. According to the story, the young Elizabeth had died at around the age of eleven, while staying in a local country house. Henry was absent on a French campaign, so she was rapidly substituted for a male playmate of the same colouring, who proceeded to take her place. Most of the 'evidence' for this is based on descriptions of her having mannish qualities and features, such as her long fingers, height and love of hunting and riding, as well as the layers of make-up being used to hide stubble. Additionally, her fashionable high collars and ruffs were supposed to hide her Adam's apple and suspicion was raised by her forbidding an autopsy after her death. Apparently though, this tale was invented by an imaginative local clergyman in the nineteenth century. Following this idea, recent suggestions have been made that Elizabeth had a form of male pseudo-hermaphroditism, now called 'complete androgen insensitivity syndrome'; a congenital defect where suffers develop male and female genitals. Although appearing female at birth, the condition of those affected becomes apparent at the onset of puberty. It affects one in every 20,000 babies, presenting with undescended testicles, no womb or uterus and a body producing testosterone.[17] Many such theories abound, prompted by the inability to accept Elizabeth's qualities or her unmarried status. The truth may have been much simpler, as the queen herself explained; that she was married to her kingdom and would have one mistress and no master. It did not solve the problem of her succession.

The will of Henry VIII had bypassed the heir of the Scottish descendants of Margaret Tudor in favour of Mary Rose and the Greys. The two younger sisters of the ill-fated Lady Jane had been born in the 1540s and stood in line as Elizabeth's immediate successors until their secret marriages lost them royal favour. Forbidden from taking husbands without the knowledge of the queen, Catherine was the first to incur the Virgin's wrath. At twelve, she had been married once before to Henry Herbert, son of the Duke of Pembroke, as part of the Northumberland-Grey power base but after failure of their coup, Pembroke promptly dissolved the match, which had never been consummated on account of the couple's youth. As an older teenager, Catherine fell in love with Edward Seymour, son of the Lord Protector, and the couple determined to marry against parental wishes. Legal marriages could take place anywhere, so long as the vows were properly made, enabling them to wed in secret in his bedroom in 1560 and immediately go on to consummate what became a doomed match. Edward's sister, their only witness, died soon after. Edward went overseas and Catherine found herself trying to conceal her pregnancy at court, unable to prove her marriage was legal. She maintained her secret until the eighth month, finally begging for help from Bess of Hardwick and Robert Dudley, who took the news straight to Elizabeth. Catherine was confined to the Tower, where she delivered a son. She was later allowed secret visits from Seymour by her gaolers, during which she conceived and delivered a second son. Eventually released but living under house arrest, she refused to eat and died, probably of some wasting illness exacerbated by anorexia, at the age of twenty-eight. It was a similar story for her sister Mary, born in 1545. Famously short and hunch-backed, Mary secretly married the royal gatekeeper Thomas Keyes, a very tall man, for which she was imprisoned by Elizabeth in 1565; the couple had no children and Mary died in 1578. Another potential claimant to the throne was Arbella Stuart, the granddaughter of Margaret Douglas, daughter of Margaret Tudor by her second husband. She was born in 1575 and following the death of her mother, lived with grandmother Bess of Hardwick at Hardwick Hall. Elizabeth's advisers never seriously considered her claim however, as the birth of Mary Queen of Scots' only son, James, in 1566 offered a better candidate. In 1594, the arrival of James' first son Henry confirmed the line and it was James who ultimately succeeded Elizabeth as King of England.

Towards the end of 1602, Elizabeth fell ill and retired to her personal chambers. In each of her palaces, sumptuous beds had been dressed with the richest fabrics, like the walnut frame delivered to her in 1581, with its cloth of silver and velvet, lined with Venetian gold, silver and silk; the headpiece made from Bruges crimson satin topped with six huge plumes of ostrich feathers sparkling with gold spangles. At the end, though, she eschewed all her beds and lay propped up on a pile of pillows on the floor, trying to delay the inevitable. It didn't work. She died the following March, at the age of sixty-nine at Richmond. Exactly a century after the death of her grandmother and namesake, she was buried at Westminster Abbey. Her embalmed body in its lead coffin was carried downriver at night on board a boat ablaze with torches. A hearse, drawn by four horses and draped in black velvet, carried a coffin covered in purple, on which lay a life-size wax effigy of the queen dressed in her state robes and crown. Mourners lining the route to the abbey wept and wailed at the sight, pausing only to gasp at how lifelike her effigy was. At the altar, Archbishop Whitgift was waiting to perform the ceremony; almost a thousand mourners followed but one in particular was notably absent. En route to the capital were the new royal family; James, great grandson of Margaret Tudor, his wife Anne of Denmark and their current children, Henry, Elizabeth and Charles; the journey south was slow and they did not arrive until after the event. By then, the old queen had been interred alongside her sister but James did order a magnificent tomb to be built in her honour, designed by Maximilian Colt and completed in 1606.

Although Henry VIII died leaving three legitimate children who might be expected to marry and bear a host of heirs, no Tudor royal delivery took place after the arrival of Edward in 1537. Although predominantly it was the dynasty's men who were the ones to win battles and reform national churches, female fertility shaped their dynasty. The question of succession was an inescapably pressing one right from the start. Henry VII needed to establish his line in the uncertain days after Bosworth, Henry VIII became a serial husband in the quest for a son, Edward VI died young, Mary was unable to conceive and Elizabeth chose not to. These factors shaped the course of over a century of English history. It was in the bedroom rather than the council chamber that the fate of the Tudors was determined.

For Tudor women, queen or commoner, giving birth was rarely a straightforward affair. Undoubtedly class was the most significant factor determining the nature of the experience and although it made richer women's experiences more comfortable, it was still no guarantee against complications and death. Marriage could be very much a lottery; the nature of Tudor society meant that women were subject to the rule of their male relations, whether husbands, fathers or brothers. The quality of their lives, therefore, depended upon the characters and understanding of men they often had not chosen and although some did rebel, the repercussions for divorce, adultery, promiscuity and illegitimate birth were great. Women's sexual lives were also at the dictate of men, denying them the ability to make individual and informed choices about the conception of children. Birth was dangerous and when things went wrong, medicine appeared to have less to offer than conventional wisdom or sympathetic magic. The era was also divided by religious reform; before the 1530s, a greater range of superstitious practices were permissible but the subsequent upheavals of the mid-Tudor era left many women politically and religiously uncertain, especially the illiterate. On the whole, culture-specific factors mean that sixteenth-century women's reproductive lives were vastly different from those of their modern counterparts. Still, their aspirations for marriage and childbirth were not too dissimilar. Just like the twenty-first-century mother, they felt hope and fear, pain and elation: only an accident of time separates them.

Notes

1. Elizabeth Of York & Arthur, 1485–1486:
The First Tudor Heir

1. 'Ladye Bessiye' Anonymous Ballad, possibly composed 1560–80. From Ian Forbes Baird, *Poems Concerning the Stanley Family (Earls of Derby) 1485–1520*, PhD thesis (University of Birmingham, 1989).
2. Venice 1481–1485, *Calendar of State Papers Relating to English Affairs in the Archives of Venice*, Volume 1, 1202–1509, 141–159.
3. Bacon, Francis, *History of the Reign of King Henry VIII* (Cambridge University Press, 1901).
4. Hall, Edward, *Chronicle; containing the History of England, during the reign of Henry the fourth and the succeeding monarchs, to the end of the reign of Henry VIII, in which are particularly described the manners and customs of those periods (Collated with the editions of 1548 and 1550)* (London: J. Johnson, 1809).
5. Jerdan, William (ed.), *Rutland Papers. Original documents, illustrative of the courts and times of Henry VII and Henry VIII* (London: Camden Society, 1842).
6. Okerlund, Arlene Naylor, *Elizabeth of York* (New York: Palgrave Macmillan, 2009).
7. Rutland Papers.
8. Souden, David, *The Royal Palaces of London* (London: Merrell, 2008).
9. Nicolas, N. (ed.), *Privy Purse Expenses of Elizabeth of York; Wardrobe Expenses of Edward IV* (London: Pickering, 1830).
10. Tremlett, Giles, *Catherine of Aragon, England's Spanish Queen* (Faber & Faber, 2010).
11. Thurley, Simon, *The Royal Palaces of Tudor England* (Yale University Press, 1993).
12. Hall, Edward, *Chronicle; containing the History of England, during the reign of Henry the fourth and the succeeding monarchs, to the end of the reign of Henry VIII, in which are particularly described the manners and customs of those periods (Collated with the editions of 1548 and 1550)*

(London: J. Johnson, 1809).

13. Stowe, John, 'Historical Memoranda of John Stowe: The Baptism of Prince Arthur, Son of Henry VII' in Gairdner, J. (ed.), *Three Fifteenth Century Chronicles* (1880).
14. 'Houses of Benedictine Monks: Priory of St Swithin, Winchester' in *A History of the County of Hampshire, Volume 2* (1973) 108–115.
15. Flete, John, *The History of Westminster Abbey* (*c.* 1450).
16. Paden, William D. and Paden, Frances Freeman, 'Swollen Woman, Shifting Canon: A Midwife's charm and the Birth of Secular Romance Lyric', *PMLA*, 125, 2 (March 2010) 306–321.

2. Elizabeth of York & the Future Henry VIII, 1487–1503: The Family Expands

1. Anonymous Ballad, seventeenth century, in *The Union of the Red Rose and the White by a Marriage Between King Henry VII and a Daughter of King Edward IV* (Huntington Library, University of California).
2. Hutchinson, Robert, *Young Henry: The Rise of Henry VIII* (Weidenfeld & Nicolson, 2011).
3. Pelling, Margaret and White, Frances, *Database of Physicians and Irregular Medical Practitioners in London 1550–1640* (Institute of Historical Research, 2004).
4. Millet, B. and Wogan-Browne, J., *Medieval English Prose for Women* (Clarendon Press, 1992).
5. Cressy, David, *Literacy and the Social Order: Reading and Writing in Tudor and Stuart England* (Cambridge, 1980).
6. Schofield, Roger, 'Did the mothers really die?' in *The World we have Lost* (Cambridge papers: 1993).
7. Cressy, David, *Literacy and the Social Order: Reading and Writing in Tudor and Stuart England* (Cambridge: 1980).
8. Bentley, Thomas, *The Monument of Matrons* (1582).
9. Anonymous ballad, details as in note 1.
10. CSPS Spain (April 1503).

3. Catherine of Aragon & Henry, Prince of Wales, 1501–1510: Widowhood & Fertility

1. Guillemeau, Jacques, *The Happie Deliverie of Women* (London: Hatfield, 1612).
2. Spencer, W. G. (trans.), *Celsus de Medicina* (1476) (Massachusetts: Heninemann, 1935).
3. Pelling, Margaret and White, Frances, *Database of Physicians and Irregular Medical Practitioners in London 1550–1640* (Institute of Historical Research, 2004).
4. CSPS (March 1505).
5. Ibid. (October 1506).

6.   Ibid. (April 1507).
7.   Ibid. (August 1507).
8.   Mendelson, Sara and Crawford, Patricia, *Women in Early Modern England* (Oxford: Clarendon Press, 1998).
9.   Burton, R., *The Anatomy of Melancholy* (Oxford: 1621).
10. Lemnius, L., *The Secret Miracles of Nature in Four Books* (1658).
11. CSPS (June 1505).
12. Ibid. (August 1505).
13. B. L., Cotton Mss. Titus.
14. CSPS (June 1509).
15. Public Records Office. Spanish transactions 1, 5, f 119.
16. Donnison, Jean, *Midwives and Medical Men: A History of the Struggle for the Control of Childbirth* (Heinemann, 1988).
17. Essex Record Office (ERO) Q/SR 126/58.
18. ERO Q/SR 160/14.
19. EBBA 20763 Pepys 1.414–5.
20. EBBA 20807 Pepys 2.192.
21. Cressy, David, *Literacy and the Social Order: Reading and Writing in Tudor and Stuart England* (Cambridge: 1980).
22. Guenther, Megan, 'To all grave and modest matrons: Practical midwifery and chiurgery in De conceptu et generatione hominis (1580)' in *Anatomy of Gender* (2005).

4. Catherine of Aragon & Mary, 1511–1518: Saints, Pilgrimage & Infant Mortality

1.   Sarum Missal, volume 2, 162.
2.   Fox, J., *Sister Queens: Catherine of Aragon and Juana, Queen of Castile* (Weidenfeld & Nicolson, 2011).
3.   Quoted in Butler, Derek, *The Quest for Becket's Bones* (Yale University Press, 1995).
4.   Walker, Damian and Walker, Godfrey, 'Forgotten But Not Gone: The Continual Scourge of Congenital Syphilis', *The Lancet Infectious Diseases*, 2, Issue 7 (July 2002).
5.   Hutchinson, Robert, *Young Henry: The Rise of Henry VIII* (Weidenfeld & Nicolson, 2011).
6.   Vail, Anne, *The Shrines of Our Lady in England* (Gracewing, 2004).
7.   ERO D/P 162/1/1.
8.   CLP Spain (November 1514).
9.   SLP Henry VIII. (December 1514).
10. Pratt, Dolores, *Childbirth Prayers in Medieval and Modern England*', unpublished (McGill University, Canada).
11. Sarum Missal, volume 2, 161.
12. Sierra, G., 'Recipes for Health: Magical, Religious and Pharmacological Remedies for Female Ailments in Medieval England', *Colombia Undergraduate Journal of History* (online, 2008).

13. Weston, 'Women's Medicine', *Modern Philology*, 92 (1995) 279–293.
14. Bentley, Thomas, *The Monument of Matrons* (1582).
15. Guillemeau, Jacques, *The Happie Deliverie of Women* (London: Hatfield, 1612).
16. Ibid.
17. Pelling, Margaret and White, Frances, *Database of Physicians and Irregular Medical Practitioners in London 1550–1640* (Institute of Historical Research, 2004).
18. MS in author's possession.
19. SLP Henry VIII. (January 1516).
20. Ibid. (October 1518).

5. Elizabeth Blount & Mary Boleyn, 1518–1526: Illegitimate Royals

1. Song rumoured to have been written by Bessie Blount to Henry VIII.
2. SLP Henry VIII (July 1517).
3. Norton, Elizabeth, *Bessie Blount, Mistress to Henry VIII* (Stroud: Amberley, 2011).
4. Cotton Mss Caligula.
5. St Hildegarde of Bingen, *Scivius*.
6. Brown, Petrina, *Eve: Sex, Childbirth and Motherhood Through the Ages* (Summersdale, 2004).
7. SLP Henry VIII (October 1518).
8. Daybell, James. *Women Letter-Writers in Tudor England* (Oxford University Press, 2006).
9. Ibid.
10. Ibid.
11. Bodl. MS Rawlinson B. 381, fos 5v-10.
12. Mendelson, Sara and Crawford, Patricia, *Women in Early Modern England* (Oxford: Clarendon Press, 1998).
13. Ibid.
14. SLP Henry VIII (November 1537).
15. Talbot, C. H., Fanous, S., Leyser, H., *The Life of Christina of Markygate* (Oxford World's Classics, 2008).
16. City of Chester Assembly records. ZA/B/1/70v.
17. ERO Q/SR 104/59a.
18. ERO Q/SR 80/53.
19. SLP Henry VIII (May 1519).
20. Murphy, Beverley A., *Bastard Prince: Henry VIII's Lost Son* (History Press, 2001).
21. Weir, Alison, *Mary Boleyn: the Great and Infamous Whore* (Jonathan Cape, 2011).
22. SLP Henry VIII (July 1520).
23. ERO Q/SR107/44.
24. ERO Q/SR 80/53.

25. ERO Q/SR 82/44.
26. ERO Q/SR 124/57–58.
27. ERO Q/SR 109/62a.
28. ERO – Based on analysis of seven parish registers: Little Clacton, Chelmsford, Colchester, Burnham, White Notley, South Ockenden and Good Easter.

6. Anne Boleyn & Elizabeth, 1526–1536: Miscarriage & Misogyny

1. Firth, C. H., *The Ballad History of the reigns of King Henry VII and Henry VIII* (Spottiswoode, 1908).
2. Hall, E., *Chronicle*, and SLP Henry VIII (June 1533).
3. Warnicke, Retha, M., *The Rise and Fall of Anne Boleyn* (Cambridge University Press, 1999).
4. SLP Henry VIII (Sept 1537).
5. SLP Henry VIII (June 1533).
6. Ibid. (July).
7. Ibid. (August).
8. Froude, A. J., *The Divorce of Catherine of Aragon* (London: 1891).
9. SLP Henry VIII (June 1533).
10. Warnicke, R., *Rise and Fall of Anne Boleyn*.
11. SLP Henry VII (June 1533).
12. Starkey, David, *Elizabeth* (Vintage, 2001).
13. Thurley, S., *The Royal Palaces of Tudor England*.
14. Fox, Julia, *Jane Boleyn: The Infamous Lady Rochford* (Phoenix, 2007).
15. ERO D/DBa T3/10.
16. SLP Henry VIII (Sept 1520).
17. ERO Q/SR 87/109.
18. ERO T/A 418/48/51.
19. MS in author's possession.
20. ERO D/P 57/1/1.
21. ERO Q/SR 129/34.
22. ERO Q/SR 54/5.
23. ERO D/P 139/1/0.
24. ERO Q/SR 74/23.
25. ERO Q/SR 156/2, 3.
26. Dee, John and Halliwell, James (ed.), *The Private Diary of John Dee* (Orchard: Camden Society, 1842).
27. Warnicke, R., *Rise and Fall of Anne Boleyn*.
28. SLP Henry VIII (April 1534).
29. Warnicke, R., *Rise and Fall of Anne Boleyn*.
30. Chapman, Hester W., *Anne Boleyn* (Jonathan Cape, 1974).

31. Dewhurst, Sir J. 'The alleged miscarriages of Catherine of Aragon and Anne Boleyn', *Medical History*, 1984, 28(1). 49–56.

32. Ibid.
33. SLP Henry VIII (Feb 1536).
34. Clifford, Henry, *The Life of Jane Dormer, Duchess of Feria* (London: Burns & Oates, 1887).
35. Ives, Eric, *The Life and Death of Anne Boleyn: The Most Happy* (Blackwell, 2005 ed.).
36. Duffy, E., *The Voices of Morebath: Reformation and Rebellion in an English Village*. (Yale University Press, 2003).
37. *The Diary of Henry Machyn, Citizen and Merchant-Taylor of London* (London: Camden Society, 1848).
38. EBBA 20210 Pepys 1.44–45.
39. Ibid.
40. Starkey, David, *Elizabeth* (Vintage, 2001).

7. Jane Seymour & Edward, 1536–1537: A Son at Last

1. Mary of Hungary to Ferdinand, King of the Romans, SLP Henry VIII (May 1536).
2. Ibid.
3. Ibid.
4. Ibid.
5. Starkey, David, *Six Wives: The Queens of Henry VIII* (Vintage, 2004).
6. SLP Henry VIII (May 1536).
7. Ibid. (June).
8. Skidmore, Chris, *Edward VI: Lost King of England* (Phoenix, 2008).
9. SLP Henry VIII (October 1536).
10. Skidmore, Chris, *Edward VI: Lost King of England* (Phoenix, 2008).
11. Ibid.
12. Ibid.
13. Ibid.
14. SLP Henry VIII (November 1536).
15. Ibid.
16. Ibid. (October).

8. Anne of Cleves & Catherine Howard, 1537–1542: The Rules of Attraction

1. Motto on Anne of Cleves' wedding ring; motto chosen by Catherine Howard.
2. SLP Henry VIII (December 1537).
3. Starkey, David, *Six Wives: The Queens of Henry VIII* (Vintage, 2004).
4. SLP Henry VIII (September 1539).
5. Ibid.
6. SLP Henry VIII (Jan 1540).
7. Thurley, S., *The Royal Palaces of Tudor England*.

8. SLP Henry VIII (July 1540).
9. Brown, Petrina, *Eve: Sex, Childbirth and Motherhood Through the Ages* (Summersdale, 2003).
10. McLean, Teresa, *Medieval English Gardens* (London: Barrie & Jenkins, 1989).
11. SLP Henry VIII (July 1540).
12. ERO T/A 418/13/30.
13. ERO Q/SR 104/29.
14. ERO Q/SR 148/139.
15. Sierra, G., 'Recipes for Health: Magical, Religious and Pharmacological Remedies for Female Ailments in Medieval England', *Colombia Undergraduate Journal of History* (online, 2008).
16. Ibid.
17. ERO D/P 80/1/1.
18. Sierra, G., 'Recipes for Health: Magical, Religious and Pharmacological Remedies for Female Ailments in Medieval England', *Colombia Undergraduate Journal of History* (online, 2008).
19. Cited by Jorge H. Castelli on 'Tudor Place' website. (www.tudorplace. com.ar/Documents/prostitution.htm)

9. Catherine Parr, 1543–1548: The Virtuous Wife

1. Parr, C., 'Lamentations of a Sinner', in *Writings of Edward VI, William Hugh, Queen Catherine Parr, Anne Askew and Lady Jane Grey* (London: Hamilton and Balnaves, 1831).
2. Douie, D. and Farmer, D. (ed.), *Magna Vita Sancti Hugonis: The Life of St Hugh of Lincoln* (Oxford University Press, 1961).
3. Sim, Alison, *The Tudor Housewife* (Sutton, 1996).
4. Porter, L., *Catherine the Queen: the Remarkable Life of Catherine Parr* (Pan, 2011).
5. Ibid.
6. SLP Henry VIII July 1543.
7. Borde, Andrew and Furnivall, F. J. (ed.), *The Fyrst Boke of the Introduction of knowledge* (London: Early English Text Society, N.T. Trubner, 1870).
8. Ibid.
9. Frere. Catherine (ed.), *Propre Boke of New Cokerye* (1545, reprinted 1913).
10. Norton, Elizabeth, *Catherine Parr* (Stroud: Amberley, 2011).
11. Ibid.
12. Brown, Petrina, *Eve: Sex, Childbirth and Motherhood Through the Ages* (Summersdale, 2003).
13. Ibid.

10. Henry's Legacy, 1534–1553: Reform in the Birth Chamber

1. 'In the Wreck of Walsingham', Philip Howard, 1578? in Gillett, H. M., *Walsingham: The History of a Famous Shrine* (Burns, Oates & Washbourne, 1946).
2. SLP Henry VIII (January 1540).
3. Vail, Anne, *The Shrines of Our Lady in England* (Gracewing, 2004).
4. Waller, Gary, *The Virgin Mary in Late Medieval and Early Modern English Literature and Popular Culture* (Cambridge University Press, 2011).
5. Duffy, Eamon, *Stripping of the Altars* (Yale University Press, 1992).
6. Raine, James, 'Fabric Rolls of York Minster' quoted in Rowland, B. (ed.) *Medieval Women's Guide to Health* (University of Kent, 1981).
7. Brown, Petrina, *Eve: Sex, Childbirth and Motherhood Through the Ages* (Summersdale, 2003).
8. McLean, Teresa, *Medieval English Gardens* (London: Barrie & Jenkins, 1989).
9. ERO Q/SR 96/47.
10. ERO Q/SR 83/16.
11. ERO Q/SR 123/40.
12. Thomas.

11. Mary & Elizabeth, 1553–1603: A Dwindling Dynasty

1. 'Nowe singe, now springe, our care is exil'd; Oure virtuous Quene is quickened with childe.' Printed in London, by William Riddell at the sign of the eagle, 1555. Reprinted in Rollins, Hyder, E., *Old English Ballads 1553–1625* (Cambridge: 1920).
2. Forrest, William, 'A new ballade of the Marigolde', Ibid.
3. Stopes, Leonard, 'An Ave Maria in Commemoration of Our Most Vertuous Quene', Ibid.
4. Dekker, Thomas and Webster, John, *The Famous History of Sir Thomas Wyatt, With the Coronation of Queen Mary and the coming in of King Philip* (London: 1607).
5. Elder, John, *Copie of a Letter Sent Into Scotland* (London: John Waylande, 1555).
6. Davis, James C., *Pursuit of Power: Venetian Ambassadors' reports on Turkey, Spain and France in the age of Philip II 1560–1600* (New York: Harper & Rowe, 1970).
7. Wriothesley, Charles, *A Chronicle of England during the Reigns of the Tudors* (London: Camden Society, 1877).
8. Ibid.
9. Porter, Linda, *Mary Tudor: the First Queen* (Portrait, 2007).
10. Kamen. H., *Philip of Spain* (Yale University Press, 1998).
11. *The Diary of Henry Machyn, Citizen and Merchant-Taylor of London* (London: Camden Society, 1848).
12. Particularly J. A. Froude.

13. Porter, L., *Catherine the Queen: the Remarkable Life of Catherine Parr* (Pan, 2011).
14. Ibid.
15. Ibid.
16. Ibid.
17. R Bakan, *Elizabeth I: A Case of Testicular Feminization?* (Canada: Simon Foster University, 1985).

Bibliography

Primary and contemporary sources

Agrippa, Heinrich Cornelius, 'De nobilitate et praecellentia feminei sexus' (Germany, 1534), trans. Clapham, D., *A Treatise of the Nobilitie and Excellencye of Woman Kynde* (1534 and 1542).

Bacon, Francis, *History of the Reign of King Henry VIII* (1622) (Cambridge University Press, 1901).

Bentley, Thomas, *The Monument of Matrons* (1582) (Henry E. Huntington, 1894).

Borde, Andrew and Furnivall, F. J. (ed.), *The Fyrst Boke of the Introduction of knowledge* (London: Early English Text Society, N. T. Trubner, 1870).

Calendar of Assize Records, Kent Indictments, Elizabeth I (HMSO, 1979).

Calendar of Close Rolls, of the Reign of Henry VII, ed. K. H. Ledward, 1955.

Calendar of State Papers, Domestic: Edward, Mary and Elizabeth. ed. Robert Lemon, 1856.

Calendar of State Papers, Foreign, ed. William. B. Turnball, 1861.

Calendar of State Papers, Spanish, ed. G. A. Bergenroth, 1862.

Calendar of State Papers, Venetian, ed. Rawdon Brown, 1864.

City of Westminster Archives.

Davis, James C., *Pursuit of Power: Venetian Ambassadors' reports on Turkey, Spain and France in the age of Philip II 1560–1600* (New York: Harper & Rowe, 1970).

Dee, John and Halliwell, James (ed.), *The Private Diary of John Dee* (Orchard: Camden Society, 1842).

Dekker, Thomas and Webster, John, *The Famous History of Sir Thomas Wyatt, With the Coronation of Queen Mary and the coming in of King Philip* (London: 1607).

Elizabethan Receipt book in possession of the author's family.

English Broadside Ballad Archive, University of California (http:/ebba.english.ucsb.edu/).

Erasmus, Desiderius, *Pilgrimages to St Mary of Walsingham and St Thomas of Canterbury* (1512) (Westminster: J. B. Nichols, 1848).

Essex Records Office, parish registers and Assize Court Records.

Firth, C. H., *The Ballad History of the reigns of King Henry VII and Henry VIII* (Spottiswoode, 1908).

Flete, John, *The History of Westminster Abbey* (*c.* 1450).

Frere, Catherine (ed.), *Propre Boke of New Cokerye* (1545, reprinted 1913).

Guillemeau, Jacques, *The Happie Deliverie of Women* (London: Hatfield, 1612).

Hall, Edward, *Chronicle; containing the History of England, during the reign of Henry the fourth and the succeeding monarchs, to the end of the reign of Henry VIII, in which are particularly described the manners and customs of those periods (Collated with the editions of 1548 and 1550)* (London: J. Johnson, 1809).

Harrison, W., 'Elizabethan England' in Withrington, L. (ed.), *Holinshed's Chronicle* (London: Walter Scott, 1876).

Holinshed, Raphael, *Chronicles of England, Scotland and Ireland* (London: J. Johnson, 1807).

Kent County Council Archives.

Nicolas, N. (ed), *Privy Purse Expenses of Elizabeth of York: Wardrobe Expenses of Edward IV* (London: Pickering, 1830).

Rollins, Hyder E., *Old English Ballads 1553–1625* (Cambridge: 1920).

Spencer, W. G. (trans.) *Celsus de Medicina* (1476) (Massachusetts: Heninemann, 1935).

State Letters and Papers, Foreign and Domestic of the Reign of Henry VIII 1509–1547 eds. J. S. Brewer, (1864, 1865, 1867, 1920) J. Gairdner (1880, 1882, 1883, 1885–8, 1890–6, 1898, 1901–3, 1905, 1907–8, 1910) R. H. Brodie (1894–6, 1898, 1901–3, 1905, 1907–8, 1910).

Stowe, John, 'Historical Memoranda of John Stowe: The Baptism of Prince Arthur, Son of Henry VII' in Gairdner, J. (ed.), *Three Fifteenth Century Chronicles* (1880). 104–105.

The Diary of Henry Machyn, Citizen and Merchant-Taylor of London (London: Camden Society, 1848).

The National Archives.

Wriothesley, Charles, *A Chronicle of England during the Reigns of the Tudors* (London: Camden Society, 1877).

Writings of Edward VI, William Hugh, Queen Catherine Parr, Anne Askew and Lady Jane Grey (London: Hamilton & Balnaves, 1831).

Secondary sources

Baird, Ian Forbes, *Poems Concerning the Stanley Family (Earls of Derby) 1485–1520*, PhD thesis (University of Birmingham, 1989).

Borman, Tracy, *Elizabeth's Women: the Hidden Story of the Virgin Queen* (Vintage, 2010).

Brown, Petrina, *Eve: Sex, Childbirth and Motherhood Through the Ages* (Summersdale, 2004).

Burton, R., *The Anatomy of Melancholy* (Oxford: 1621).

Butler, Derek, *The Quest for Becket's Bones* (Yale University Press, 1995).

Bibliography

Bynum, Caroline Walker, *Holy Feast and Holy Fast: The Religious Significance of Food to Medieval Women* (University of California Press, 1992).

Capp, Bernard, *When Gossips Meet: Women, Family and Neighbourhood in Early Modern England* (Oxford University Press, 2003).

Chapman, Hester W., *Anne Boleyn* (Jonathan Cape, 1974).

Clifford, Henry, *The Life of Jane Dormer, Duchess of Feria* (London: Burns & Oates, 1887).

Colquhoun, Kate, *Taste: The Story of Britain Through its Cooking* (Bloomsbury, 2007).

Cressy, David, *Agnes Bowker's Cat: Travesties and Transgression in Tudor and Stuart England* (Oxford University Press, 2000).

Cressy, David, Birth, *Marriage and Death: Ritual, Religion and the Life-Cycle in Tudor and Stuart England* (Oxford University Press, 1999).

Cressy, David, *Literacy and the Social Order: Reading and Writing in Tudor and Stuart England* (Cambridge, 1980).

Crow, John L., 'Miracle or Magic: the Problematic Status of Christian Amulets' in Braak, J. and Malone, D. (eds.) *Van Discussie tot Beleving: Religiestudies aan de Uva* (Ars Notoria: University of Amsterdam. 2009) 97–112.

Daybell, James, *Women Letter-Writers in Tudor England* (Oxford University Press, 2006).

Denny, Joanna, *Anne Boleyn: A New Life of England's Tragic Queen* (London: Portrait, 2005).

Denny, Joanna, *Catherine Howard: A Tudor Conspiracy* (London: Portrait, 2005).

Dewhurst, Sir J., 'The Alleged Miscarriages of Catherine of Aragon and Anne Boleyn' in *Medical History*, 1984, 28(1). 49–56.

Donnison, Jean, *Midwives and Medical Men: A History of the Struggle for the Control of Childbirth* (Heinemann, 1988).

Douie, D. and Farmer, D. (eds.), *Magna Vita Sancti Hugonis: The Life of St Hugh of Lincoln* (Oxford University Press, 1961).

Duby, Georges and Aries, Phillipe, *A History of Private Life* (Harvard University Press: 1998).

Duffy, Eamon, *Stripping of the Altars* (Yale University Press, 1992).

Duffy, E., *The Voices of Morebath: Reformation and Rebellion in an English Village* (Yale University Press, 2001).

Dunn, P. M., 'Jacob Rueff (1500–1558) of Zurich and The Expert Midwife' in *British Medical Journal*, 85, Issue 3.

Fox, Julia, *Jane Boleyn: The Infamous Lady Rochford* (Phoenix, 2007).

Fox, Julia, *Sister Queens: Katherine of Aragon and Juana, Queen of Castile* (London: Wiedenfeld & Nicolson, 2011).

Froude, J. A., *The Divorce of Catherine of Aragon* (London: 1891).

Grandsen, K. W., *Tudor Verse Satire* (Athlone Press, University of London, 1970).

Gristwood, Sarah, *Arbella, England's Lost Queen* (Bantam, 2008).

Gristwood, Sarah, *Elizabeth and Leicester* (Bantam, 2004).

Guenther, Megan, 'To all grave and modest matrons: Practical midwifery and chiurgery in De conceptu et generatione hominis (1580)' in *Anatomy of Gender* (2005).

Gunn, Stephen and Monckton, Linda (eds.) *Arthur Tudor, Prince of Wales: Life, Death and Commemoration* (Boydell, 2009).

Hart, Kelly, *The Other Tudors: Henry VIII's mistresses and bastards* (London: New Holland, 2009).

Harvey, Nancy Lenz, *Elizabeth of York, Tudor Queen* (New York: Macmillan, 1973).

Haynes, Alan, *Sex in Elizabethan England* (Sutton, 1997).

Hopper, Sarah, *To be a Pilgrim: the Medieval Pilgrimage Experience* (Sutton, 2002).

Hutchinson, Robert, *Young Henry: The Rise of Henry VIII* (Weidenfeld & Nicolson, 2011).

Hutton, Ronald, *The Rise and Fall of Merry England: the ritual year 1400–1700* (Oxford: 1994).

Ives, Eric, *The Life and Death of Anne Boleyn; The Most Happy* (Blackwell, 2005).

Jerdan, William (ed.), *Rutland Papers. Original documents, illustrative of the courts and times of Henry VII and Henry VIII* (London: Camden Society, 1842).

Kamen. H., *Philip of Spain* (Yale University Press, 1998).

Lee, Becky, R. 'The Purification of Women after Childbirth: A Window onto Medieval Perceptions of Women', in *Florilegium*, 14 (1995–6).

Lemnius, L., *The Secret Miracles of Nature in Four Books* (1658).

Loades, David M., *The Tudor Queens of England* (Hambledon Continuum, 2009).

Loxton, Howard, *Pilgrimage to Canterbury* (David & Charles, 1978).

McLean, Teresa, *Medieval English Gardens* (London: Barrie & Jenkins, 1989).

Mendelson, Sara and Crawford, Patricia, *Women in Early Modern England. 1550–1720* (Oxford: Clarendon, 1998).

Millet, B. and Wogan-Browne, J., *Medieval English Prose for Women* (Clarendon, 1992).

Murphy, Beverley A., *Bastard Prince: Henry VIII's Lost Son* (History Press, 2001).

Norton, Elizabeth, *Anne Boleyn in her Own Words* (Stroud: Amberley, 2011).

Norton, Elizabeth, *Ann of Cleves: Henry's Discarded Bride* (Stroud: Amberley, 2010).

Norton, Elizabeth, *Bessie Blount: Mistress to Henry VIII* (Stroud: Amberley, 2011).

Norton, Elizabeth, *Catherine Parr* (Stroud: Amberley, 2011).

Norton, Elizabeth, *England's Queens: The Biography* (Stroud: Amberley, 2011).

Norton, Elizabeth, *Margaret Beaufort: Mother of the Tudor Dynasty* (Stroud: Amberley, 2010).

O'Day, Rosemary, *The Routledge Companion to The Tudor Age* (Routledge, 2010).

Okerlund, Arlene Naylor, *Elizabeth of York* (Palgrave Macmillan, 2009).

Paden, William D. and Paden, Frances Freeman, 'Swollen Woman, Shifting Canon: A Midwife's charm and the Birth of Secular Romance Lyric.', *PMLA*, 125, 2 (March 2010) 306–321.

Bibliography

Pelikan, Jaroslav, *Mary Through the Centuries: Her Place in our Culture* (Yale University Press: 1998).

Pelling, Margaret, *The Common Lot: Sickness, Medical Occupations and the Urban Poor in Early Modern England* (Longman, 1998).

Pelling, Margaret and White, Frances, *Database of Physicians and Irregular Medical Practitioners in London 1550–1640* (Institute of Historical Research: 2004).

Penn, Thomas, *Winter King: the Dawn of Tudor England* (Allen Lane, 2011).

Perry, Maria, *Sisters to the King* (Andre Deutsch, 2007).

Plowden, Alison, *Marriage with my Kingdom: The Courtships of Queen Elizabeth I* (Macmillan, 1977).

Porter, L., *Katherine the Queen; the Remarkable Life of Katherine Parr* (Pan, 2011).

Porter, L., *Mary Tudor; the First Queen* (Portrait, 2007).

Pratt, Dolores, *Childbirth Prayers in Medieval and Modern England*, unpublished (McGill University, Canada).

Prescott, H. F. M., *Mary Tudor* (Eyre and Spottiswoode, 1940).

Raine, James, 'Fabric Rolls of York Minster' quoted in Rowland, B. (ed.) *Medieval Women's Guide to Health* (University of Kent, 1981).

Rollins, Hyder, E., *Old English Ballads 1553–1625* (Cambridge: 1920).

Scarisbrick, J. J., *The Reformation and the English People* (Blackwell: 1984).

Schofield, Roger, 'Did the mothers really die?' in *The World we have Lost* (Cambridge Papers, 1993).

Shorter, Edward, *A History of Women's Bodies* (Allen Lane, 1983).

Sierra, G., 'Recipes for Health: Magical, Religious and Pharmacological Remedies for Female Ailments in Medieval England', *Colombia Undergraduate Journal of History* (online, 2008).

Sim, Alison, *The Tudor Housewife* (Sutton, 1996).

Skidmore, Chris, *Edward VI: The Lost King of England* (Phoenix, 2008).

Skidmore, Chris, *Death and the Virgin: Elizabeth, Dudley and the Mysterious fate of Amy Robsart* (Phoenix, 2011).

Souden, David, with Worsley, Lucy and Dolman, Brett, *The Royal Palaces of London* (London: Merrell, 2008).

Starkey, D., *Elizabeth* (Vintage Edition, 2001).

Starkey, D., *Henry: Virtuous Prince* (London: HarperPress, 2008).

Starkey, D., *Six Wives: The Queens of Henry VIII* (Vintage, 2004).

Stone, Laurence, *The Family, Sex and Marriage in England 1500–1800* (Penguin, 1990).

Thomas, Keith, *Religion and the Decline of Magic* (Weidenfeld & Nicolson, 1971).

Tremlett, Giles, *Catherine of Aragon, England's Spanish Queen* (Faber & Faber, 2010).

Thurley, Simon, *The Royal Palaces of Tudor England* (Yale University Press, 1993).

Vail, Anne, *Shrines of Our Lady in England* (Leominster: Gracewing, 2004).

Walker, Damian and Walker, Godfrey, 'Forgotten But Not Gone: The Continual Scourge of Congenital Syphilis', *The Lancet Infectious Diseases*, 2, Issue 7 (July 2002).

Waller, Gary, *The Virgin Mary in Late Medieval and Early Modern English Literature and Popular Culture* (Cambridge University Press: 2011).

Walsh, James, J., *Medieval Medicine* (A. C. Black, 1920).

Warner, Maria, *All Alone of Her Sex: the Myth and Cult of the Virgin Mary* (Littlehampton, 1976).

Warnicke, Retha, M., *The Rise and Fall of Anne Boleyn* (Cambridge University Press, 1999).

Weir, Alison, *Children of England: the Heirs of Henry VIII, 1547–1558* (Jonathan Cape, 1996).

Weir, Alison, *Mary Boleyn: the Great and Infamous Whore* (Jonathan Cape, 2011).

Weir, Alison, *The Lady in the Tower; the Fall of Anne Boleyn* (Jonathan Cape, 2009).

Weisner-Hanks, Merry, *Women and Gender in Early Modern Europe* (Cambridge University Press, 2008).

Whittock, Martyn, *A Brief History of Life in the Middle Ages* (London: Robinson, 2009).

Worsley, Lucy, *If Walls Could Talk: An Intimate History of the Home* (Faber & Faber, 2011).

List of Illustrations

1. © Amy Licence
2. © Ripon Cathedral
3. © Ripon Cathedral
4. © Elizabeth Norton & Amberley Archive
5. © Amy Licence
6. © Amberley Archive
7. © Ripon Cathedral
8. © Jonathan Reeve JR982b20p83715001600
9. © Josephine Wilkinson
10. © David Baldwin
11. © Amy Licence
12. © Amberley Archive
13. © Ripon Cathedral
14. © Amy Licence
15. © Amy Licence
16. © Amy Licence
17. © Elizabeth Norton & Amberley Archive
18. © Elizabeth Norton & Amberley Archive
19. © Amberley Archive
20. © Amy Licence
21. © Jonathan Reeve JRCD3b20p102515501600
22. © Amberley Archive
23. © Elizabeth Norton & Amberley Archive
24. © Elizabeth Norton
25. © Amy Licence
26. © Elizabeth Norton & Amberley Archive
27. © National Gallery of Art
28. © Ripon Cathedral
29. © Jonathan Reeve JR1168b4fp74715001600
30. © Jonathan Reeve JR996b66fp6815001600
31. © Elizabeth Norton

Index

More Tudor History from Amberley Publishing

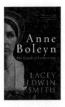

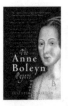

ANNE BOLEYN
Lacey Baldwin Smith

'The perfect introduction'
SUZANNAH LIPSCOMBE

£20.00   978-1-4456-1023-8   240 pages HB 60 illus, 40 col

INSIDE THE TUDOR COURT
Lauren MacKay

'Superb... highly recommended'
ALISON WEIR

Feb 2014 £20.00   978-1-4456-0957-7   240 pages HB

THE ANNE BOLEYN PAPERS
Elizabeth Norton

'A very useful compilation of source material on Anne'
ALISON WEIR

£12.99   978-1-4456-1288-1   384 pages PB

IN THE FOOTSTEPS OF ANNE BOLEYN
Sarah Morris & Natalie Grueninger

£20.00   978-1-4456-0782-5   288 pages HB 100 illus, 70 col

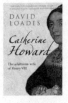

KATHARINE OF ARAGON
Patrick Williams

£25.00   978-1-84868-325-9   512 pages HB 70 col illus

THOMAS CROMWELL
J. Patrick Coby

£20.00   978-1-4456-0775-7   292 pages HB 30 illus, 10 col

ELIZABETH OF YORK
Amy Licence

£20.00   978-1-4456-0961-4   272 pages HB 40 illus, 10 col

CATHERINE HOWARD
David Loades

£20.00   978-1-4456-0768-9   240 pages HB 27 illus, 19 col

JANE SEYMOUR
David Loades

£20.00   978-1-4456-1157-0
192 pages HB   40 illus, 20 col

THE BOLEYN WOMEN
Elizabeth Norton

£20.00   978-1-84868-988-6
304 pages HB   40 illus, 20 col

Available from all good bookshops or to order direct
Please call **01453-847-800 www.amberleybooks.com**

Also by Amy Licence

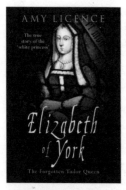

Elizabeth of York

£20.00   978-1-4456-0961-4   272 pages HB   40 illus, 10 col

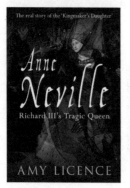

Anne Neville

£20.00   978-1-4456-1153-2   256 pages HB   30 illus, 10 col

Royal Babies

£16.99   978-1-4456-1762-6   208 pages HB   25 illus